Lord Snowdon

Lord Snowdon

HELEN CATHCART

 W. H. ALLEN *London 1968*

© Helen Cathcart, 1968
Printed and bound in Great Britain by
The Garden City Press Limited
Letchworth, Hertfordshire
for the publishers
W. H. ALLEN & CO. LTD.
Essex Street, London WC2

491 00381 1

Contents

Illustrations

For the interest, among others,
of Viscount Linley on his
coming-of-age, November 3rd, 1982—
this story of how it all happened . . .
and what happened then.

H.C.

Author's Note

This book was suggested by the Investiture of the Prince of Wales in 1969 and the role of the Earl of Snowdon as Constable of Caernarvon Castle. The need of an interim biography had become apparent, not least to dispel the popular illusions and misapprehensions that I felt had gathered around Lord Snowdon, and I am most grateful to all the busy men and women who gave me assistance by providing information and ensuring accuracy on many specific points.

In particular, my special thanks are due to members of the Armstrong-Jones family for their help in checking early family history, and to the Countess of Rosse for permission to quote from her Nymans memoirs. I acknowledge my debt to the Nymans papers of the late H. Clifford Smith and to Mr. Harold A. Albert, who first brought to my notice the remarkable link between the Messels and Mountbattens.

Mr. D. C. Howes, Headmaster of Sandroyd School, and Mr. A. Chenevix-Trench, Headmaster of Eton College, furthered my enquiries into Lord Snowdon's schooldays, under permission, and I acknowledge quotation from the *Sandroydian* and the *Eton College Chronicle*. The helpfulness of the librarians of the Royal Society, the archivists of the City of Westminster and the staff of the Probate and Divorce Registry should not pass without mention; and indeed I also owe much to the staff of the Central Office of Information and the American Embassy in London and to good friends with *Look*, *Life* and *Vogue* in New York.

My thanks and appreciation for information, correction, quotation or reference must also be expressed to: Mr. D. A. Gwyer-Gibbs of

Baron Studios Ltd.; Mr. S. J. Sharpless of Kodak Ltd.; Loelia, Duchess of Westminster; Christabel, Lady Aberconway; Mr. Cecil Beaton; Mr. John Betjeman; Sir Paul Channon; Mr. John Barber; Mr. David Sim; Mr. Keith Croft; Mr. Andrew Grima; Mr. Geoffrey Turk; Major D. Neville-Willing; Miss Heather Dean of B. T. Batsford Ltd. for details concerning *Malta* by Sacheverell Sitwell and Lord Snowdon; Miss Jeanne Soloman of the Columbia Broadcasting Service; Mr. Bryan Robertson and Mr. John Russell, co-authors of *Private View*; Mr. Jocelyn Stevens, Sir Paul Reilly, Mr. Michael Tree and members of the staff of the Council of Industrial Design; Mr. Mark Boxer, Mr. David Holden and other members of the staff of the *Sunday Times,* and Mr. Alexander Liberman.

I also most gratefully acknowledge brief incidental quotation from *Tony's Room* by William Glenton, published in the United States by Bernard Geiss Associates; from *Photographer Royal* by A. V. Swaebe, published by Leslie Frewin; from the reminiscences of Carol Coombe, published by Beaverbrook Newspapers Ltd.; from *Once Upon a Time* by Robert Glenton and Stella King, published by Anthony Blond and from *Roy Thomson of Fleet Street* by Russell Braddon published by Collins.

HELEN CATHCART

1 *The Genes in Their Courses*

I

In the days when Princess Margaret's great-great-great-great-grandfather was King George III of England—and in the very year when the Boston colonists dunked their tea-chests rather than pay the royal dues—a beautiful eighteen-year-old singer named Elizabeth Linley sang before the King and his Queen Charlotte at Buckingham House. Three days later, on April 13th, 1773, just as the news of her command performance had crept into the public news-sheets, the lovely Miss Linley was married at Marylebone Church to Richard Brinsley Sheridan, the rising young poet and playwright.

The town rang with the affair, for the match sealed the gossip of a highly romantic attachment and, indeed, of a secret wedding staged at a village near Calais the previous year. Discovering that the celebrated Miss Linley was pestered by rival admirers, the audacious twenty-year-old Sheridan had whisked her away by night from her father's house in Bath, with all the glamorous accessories of an elopement: a sedan chair to carry her through the streets and a post-chaise awaiting the lovers in the shadows on the London road. Historians differ on details: some say that Sheridan provided a maid-servant as chaperone, that he was a chivalrous and irreproachable escort and that he went through a form of marriage "without departing from honour". Within a few weeks, however, the fugitives had returned to England, and Elizabeth Linley fulfilled a string of professional singing engagements in Bath, Chester, Oxford and Cambridge without a hint that she was already a wife. Yet there were whispers of love-letters and secret meetings and under-currents of gossip sufficient to set the magazines and newspapers aglow.

In the space of four months Sheridan fought two duels for his lady's honour. In the second he is said to have received twenty sword wounds, but presumably this was counting the scratches, for the *Bath Chronicle* pronounced him out of danger within the following week. On both sides, the two fathers insisted that the sweethearts should be separated and sternly forbade them to see one another again. It was all a love-story of such appealing sentiment and enchantment that Linley descendants and kinsfolk have proudly flourished their romantic family tradition ever since, right to the heraldic culmination in the winter of 1961 when Princess Margaret and the Earl of Snowdon selected the title of Viscount Linley for their first-born son.

The Linleys of Bath were in any event a good-looking and gifted family. Elizabeth's father, Thomas Linley, was a versatile professional musician, still remembered for his score to the operetta *The Duenna*. His handsome son, Tom, began as a child violinist but composed violin concertos, anthems and songs, with sprightly facility and sang in public as readily and charmingly as his sisters, Elizabeth, Mary and Jane. In fact, the whole family were as happy in their world of concerts and music, in the mêlée of the Bath Assembly Rooms, as swans on a lake. Gainsborough drummed up business by painting their portraits, as attractive a group of sitters as he could desire, and Fanny Burney has given us her pen picture of Elizabeth Linley, her "fine, luxurious, easy-sitting hair, a charming forehead, pretty mouth and most bewitching eyes". King George III also was so delighted with the family concert that he presented Thomas *père* with a £100 note. After a furore so gay and pleasant, it seems a pity to tarnish the legend by mentioning that the last descendants of this pleasing family died out before Queen Victoria came to the throne. Nevertheless, a memorial tablet in the Church of St. Paul's, Covent Garden, firmly testifies that the final survivor was William Linley, novelist and composer, "the last of a family endowed with genius".

Lord Snowdon graced his little son—and enhanced the viscounty— with no more than the Christian name of his Uncle Linley, his mother's elder brother. Happily, researchists can show that the endowment of talent, and what Fanny Burney called "a strong desire of pleasing", came down through more than one branch of the family. Genealogists, of course, know that desirable forebears can be found in any line, given both patience and luck in the course of enquiries. A certain "Richard, son of Baldwin de Lintlega" is named in an ancient charter within one hundred years of the Conquest; Sir Thomas Lyndeley, knight, fought at Agincourt, and with him "Nicholas and John Lyndeley, lances". But perhaps we need not stray so far from the Assembly Rooms, for the true family trends can be traced through close cousins.

With all his talent, Thomas Linley was in reality the son of a carpenter named William Linley who was born in the Derbyshire parish of Norton. This William later moved to Badminton, where Thomas was born, and subsequently gained reasonable prosperity in Bath as a builder. We discover a background closer to solid yeoman stock and more down-to-earth than the artistic bohemian concert-hall Linleys lead us at first to suppose. There are Linleys in Derbyshire who manufactured clay churchwarden pipes, and one Samuel Linley who stamped his trade-mark on the early scythe blades that furthered the world-wide reputation of Sheffield steel. While Thomas Linley and his family were basking in celebrity at Bath, the Linleys of Norton were still living in their old family home, an ancient stone-built house named Bole Hill.

The cousinhood gives us the clue. It seems likely that the Linley spark came unpredictably from carpenter William's mother and she no doubt had other sons and grand-children to carry down the family gifts. As the eighteenth century drew to its close, at least three Linleys still remained in Norton, three brothers perhaps, Peter, Samuel and John, all of whom, according to the parish registers, married between 1796 and 1803. One of this Linley trio had a daughter, Frances Linley, who was born—probably a younger child of her family—at Bole Hill. And now suddenly our search shows a glint of treasure, for she was Lord Snowdon's great-great-grandmama, his equivalent of Princess Margaret's Queen Victoria, a figure so close to our own time that her son, Lord Snowdon's great-grandfather, made a sentimental pilgrimage to Bole Hill and photographed her birthplace within the present century.

Her destiny lay elsewhere, however. The family lived for a time in one of the charming houses of Paradise Square, Sheffield, where Elizabeth Linley's brother, Charles, seems to have visited them, and then the scene shifts to London. In the ever-changing square-dance of the genes, the future of Frances Linley hinged on another of Lord Snowdon's interesting great-great-grandparents, a young

American named Edward Mott Sambourne. This not too remote ancestor was, at least, an American by birth, having first seen the light of day in 1802 in Easton, Pennsylvania, where his English father had settled after becoming a naturalised United States citizen. But as so often happens Edward Mott returned to the land of his fathers to seek new opportunities, and soon established himself in London as a fur importer, with a warehouse in the shadow of St. Paul's Cathedral. Then he met and married Frances Linley and they set up house together in a pleasant little villa in the then green suburb of Islington, 15 Lloyd Square, where their son, Edward Linley Sambourne, was born in 1844.

II

As a seven-year-old, Edward Linley Sambourne—Lord Snowdon's great-grandfather—was no doubt taken to the Great Exhibition in Hyde Park to stare entranced with all the other small boys at the whirring masses of "moving machinery". This is all we may deduce of his childhood, but at sixteen he was so enthralled by the maiden voyage of the passenger liner *Great Eastern* that his parents apprenticed him to a marine engine works at Greenwich, under the mistaken impression that his talent for drawing evinced promise as an engineer's draughtsman. As it happened, the Linley artistic strain could not be so readily fettered. Edward Linley worked out his interminable seven-year indentures but he was for ever throwing off sketches and caricatures, one of which struck his fellow apprentice, Alfred Reed, as so funny and yet so well-drawn that he took it home to show to his father, German Reed. Fully agreeing with his son's opinion, Reed passed it on to his friend, Mark Lemon, the editor of *Punch*, and the young artist was overjoyed to learn that his sketch could be published.

A milestone from which Sambourne never looked back, it appeared in the issue of *Punch* of April 27th, 1867. Four years later, when only twenty-five, he was invited to join the editorial board of the magazine and for the next forty years he contributed to nearly every issue. Poking fun in every direction, he designed the characteristic initials and headings (used until 1949) and it was a national event when he succeeded Sir John Tenniel as chief political cartoonist in 1901, a post he held until his death in 1910.

Though describing himself modestly in the early editions of *Who's Who* as "a journalistic draughtsman and designer", Edward

Linley Sambourne ranked in fact as one of the ablest black-and-white artists of the day. Phil May once said, "All that I know as an artist I learned from Sambourne", and we can well believe it. One opens the old magazine volumes to find as distinctive a world of the imagination as the creations of Cruickshank or "Phiz", from the cherubic figure of John Bull in his white pantaloons to the flag-draped imperious Britannia, from the Spirit of War with her Balkan dogs to the militant wax-moustached Kaiser Wilhelm. Sambourne was so conscientious that rather than draw a distorted impression of the British lion, he once kept watch at the London Zoo for a week or more to see a lion yawn, intent on the difference in appearance between a yawn and a roar. Yet above all—and here we discover an enthusiasm inherited by Lord Snowdon—his sketches were prepared with the aid of an astonishing collection of props and photographs, and he built up an extraordinary library of 12,000 photographs, many from his own camera.

"Photography," Sambourne once said, "is a most useful servant but an impossible master. People are wrong to sneer at the mention of photographs." He is known to have drawn on the photographs of four beautiful women for the characteristic attributes required for his Britannia, and no topical event could ever catch him out on points of detail, whether he needed the shape of a German forage cap or a Japanese sailor's uniform. He was a thickset rubicund man, not unlike his own John Bull, but with "an expression capable of extreme vivacity, his eyes quick and bright", as E. V. Lucas once described him. He worked hard and played with equal vigour, on one occasion listing "hunting, yachting, shooting, golfing, cycling and motoring" all alike among his recreations, an inkling, surely, of Lord Snowdon's versatility. This remarkable forebear claimed also that he had never received any professional artistic training, except perhaps a fortnight at the School of Art at South Kensington. And during this brief encounter with the student world, it may be that he first met his wife, Mary Anne Herapath, who came of a family of scientists, her father a Fellow of the Royal Society, a woman of emancipated intelligence who might have stepped from the pages of H. G. Wells.

Linley Sambourne brought his bride home to a then newly-built mansion in Kensington, 18 Stafford Terrace, which is still owned by his grand-daughter, Lord Snowdon's mother. With Morris wallpapers, plush curtains, stained glass and masses of Japanese porcelain balanced above the picture rails, it is also much as the

15

Sambournes furnished it, complete to an astronomical clock designed by Mary Anne's grandfather, John Herapath, the mathematician, and man of science who no doubt supplies an infusion of practical-minded genes in our ancestral biology. The personality of the Sambournes' daughter, Maud Frances Sambourne, was similarly to shape true to Linley form, for she herself contributed drawings to *Punch* before she was sixteen, perhaps with her Papa's influence, and at twenty-three she staged a remarkably effective marriage with the one man with whom she felt she had everything in common, a quiet and discriminating young stockbroker not three years her senior, a connoisseur of the arts with an intriguing touch of German blood in his veins.

The tradition lingers that Maud first took the young man home to her parents with the words, "This is Leonard Messel—he's a friend of Max Beerbohm!" With the progress of their friendship probably hastened by the free seats that Max used to give his friends to see his elder brother, Beerbohm Tree, at Her Majesty's Theatre, their courtship was a speedy one, and Leonard Messel and Maud Sambourne were married in 1898. Both will always be firmly planted in Lord Snowdon's affectionate family memories, for they were of course his maternal grand-parents. Their only daughter, Anne Messel, Lord Snowdon's mother, is the present Countess of Rosse.

III

In all the tangled complex of royalty, one can surely find no stranger coincidence than the tracer element in the veins of Lord Snowdon and Prince Philip alike that places the origins of the two royal husbands in the little German Rhineland town of Darmstadt. Devoted as he was to calculations of solar and sidereal time, the mathematician among Snowdon's forefathers, John Herapath, F.R.S., would have been hard tried to estimate the chances of ancestry, springing from the same small speck of the earth's surface, that within four generations would unexpectedly give the husbands of both the Queen and her only sister, Princess Margaret, such common ground.

The astonishing link between the Mountbattens and the Messels belongs, moreover, to the same era. The forebears of Prince Philip and Lord Snowdon knew the same streets and squares, attended the same Court functions and may indeed have been on terms of strong friendship in that narrow Germanic social fabric of one hundred and twenty years ago.

The Mountbattens, as is well known, took their original name of Battenberg from a village adjoining the hunting preserves of the grand duchy of Hesse. The Messels owed their name to a hamlet in the self-same region. Yet there is another interesting early link in turn between the Messels and the Rothschilds. In 1810, when the five sons of old Meyer Rothschild were settling down to family life as well as finance in Frankfurt, Aaron Messel married the daughter of Jakob Stern, a banker of the same city. Three years later Meyer Rothschild summoned his five sons to his death-bed to counsel them to carry on the family business in London, Vienna, Paris, Naples and Frankfurt itself, and in three years more Aaron Messel founded his own banking business in Darmstadt, only fifteen miles to the south.

The moment could hardly have been more opportune. With the coming of peace after the long Napoleonic wars, the Grand Duke (Prince) Louis I of Hesse and his son, later Louis II, were laying out Darmstadt as a new city of broad avenues and tasteful gardens; and a banker with Rothschild funds was needed to subsidise the builders and painters and commerce of reconstruction. Aaron Messel, moreover, profited from old Rothschild's example in extending family connections. In 1846, when Louis II reigned in Hesse, Aaron's son, Simon Benjamin, married Emilie Lindheim, whose father was none other than the Grand Duke's Private Secretary and Counsellor.

The whole princely family assuredly attended the wedding reception in the old *Residenzschloss*. The bridegroom was in his thirtieth year, and among the guests we may notice the tall, soldierly figure of the Grand Duke's youngest son, twenty-three-year-old Prince Alexander, resplendent in the dress uniform of the Household Cavalry of the Czar of Russia. Alexander's sister had married the Czar's eldest son some years earlier, and the Imperial Russian Army was therefore shaping Alexander's military career, with as fast a string of promotions as anyone could expect. Unluckily for Imperial hopes, Prince Alexander had not long returned to St. Petersburg from the Messel wedding when he seriously blotted his copybook by falling in love with orphaned Julie Hauke, his sister's lady in waiting.

The Czar had a more august match in mind, a marriage to his own niece, the Grand Duchess Catherine. Declining to consider this honour, Alexander eloped with Julie, speeding across the Russian

17

border, to a hasty marriage in Breslau and then home to Darmstadt. The rules of the House of Hesse could regard the alliance only as a morganatic marriage, but the rash young man's only brother was now the reigning Grand Duke Louis III and he obligingly created the bride Countess of Battenberg. The couple settled into a rococo mansion on the Luisenplatz, and funds for their endowment may well have been organised by the banking house of Messel. When Alexander—Prince Philip's great-grandfather—and his Julie were raising their own five children, Simon and Emilie Messel were arranging the future for their own three sons. Ludwig—Lord Snowdon's great-grandfather—who was born in 1846, should one day follow in Rothschild's profitable footsteps, they agreed, by perhaps launching the family banking business in London. Alfred was clearly cut out to be an architect, and what better profession could he follow when every city in Germany was growing ever-larger? The third son, Rudolph, was a dreamy boy of scientific bent, ardently intent upon the new worlds to be conquered in the widening sphere of chemistry.

The plans for the three boys were cut-and-dried, except for the one event that Simon Messel had not foreseen, his own early death in the prime of life. His eldest son, Ludwig, was then only twelve, and we know from Rudolph's own account of their early circumstances that it was soon essential for the boys to earn their own living. Rudolph at first assisted his schoolmaster, Philip Reis, in inventive work—including the invention of the first telephone no less than seventeen years before Graham Bell. Ludwig was probably apprenticed to a firm that salvaged the Messel banking fortune. Both Ludwig and "Rudi" were still in their teens when they first visited England and the two permanently settled in London shortly after the Franco-Prussian war, in which they had both served as stretcher-bearers. The splendour of the Prussian victory created an insatiable need for Alfred Messel's drawing-board in Berlin: baroque banks and opulent residential palaces, whole streets of mansions and business buildings, the Messelstrasse and Messelplatz, were all to spring from his inventive and artistic brain. Meanwhile, in 1871, Ludwig married Anne Cussans, the daughter of an Indian Army officer. On leave from the Madras Artillery, Captain Cussans' hobby was genealogical research and, proudly boasting his own descent from Charlemagne through a dynasty of the kings of France, he probably looked askance at a German son-in-law just at that juncture.

18

In finance and chemistry, however, Ludwig and Rudolph respectively prospered in their adopted country, the former never more assured than in 1890 when he bought the Sussex estate of Nymans—which some say was once called No Man's—and so could face middle-age with the comfortable background of an English family home. "This will surely always be remote, unspoiled, unbuilt over", he said with satisfaction, as he viewed the countryside around his domain; and from the back of the house, towards the north-east, the spreading green bastion of St. Leonard's Forest seemed to afford a firm guarantee against change, as it does to this day.

Although reputed to have been built upon Elizabethan foundations, Nymans was an early Victorian house, guarded by cedars and the inevitable monkey-puzzle tree, and edged by a decrepit orchard. With the adaptability, imagination and persistence that so strongly marks the Messels, Ludwig saw the possibility of creating an earthly paradise. Falling under the spell of William Robinson and Gertrude Jekyll, those exponents of the free-planted and natural garden, he visualised a garden that should be "enchanting and full of surprises", to use his grand-daughter's words, and no effort or money was spared in making the dream come true.

A friendly neighbour, Sir Edmund Loder, who was two years ahead of him in planning and planting the nearby garden of Leonardslee, gave Ludwig the benefit of his experience; and as he became more practised, and gifts poured in from his friends, the perfections surpassed his early ideas. Few difficulties could stand in his way. He commissioned plants from China and Tibet and had exotic shrubs freighted by the Trans-Siberian Railway, but achieved his effects equally well with more homely and yet original plantings. Ludwig Messel laid out one of the first heather gardens seen in England, and his wife accompanied him in his interest by creating a garden of her own of sweet-scented old roses.

At the same time, they had brought up a family and their eldest son, Leonard, was an undergraduate at Merton College, Oxford, when he established his friendship with Max Beerbohm. It might have disconcerted Ludwig could he have known that the two young men were initially drawn together by the discovery that they each had immigrant German fathers. "Quiet and gentlemanly", Max reported his impressions to his older confidante, Reggie Turner, when Leonard Messel first visited his rooms and turned an attentive eye on his collection of framed caricatures. They canoed on the Char together, and Messel probably showed himself a good listener as Max discoursed of William Rothenstein, Aubrey Beardsley and other friends, talk fascinating to the banker's son with his own inherent aesthetic interests. Messel was in fact selected to make the fourth on an evening in 1893 when Oscar Wilde and Lord Alfred Douglas dined in Max's blue-painted rooms, "the visit quite a success", as Max reported. At Merton also, Leonard Charles Messel stroked the College eight, thus foreshadowing the role of his grandson and part name-sake, Antony Charles Robert Armstrong-Jones, as cox to the Cambridge crew over half-a-century later.

Five years after leaving Oxford, Leonard Messel married the *Punch* artist's daughter, Maud Sambourne, and on an autumn day in the closing year of the nineteenth century, the young couple showed agreement at the christening of their first-born son that they, too, considered there could be no nicer name than "Linley".

IV

The young Messels lived in town in a dignified colony of cream stucco houses north of the park. They began by leasing No. 27 Gloucester Terrace, where their only daughter, Anne, was born early in 1902 "in good time for the Coronation". In the optimistic atmosphere of the new reign of Edward VII, the advent must have seemed propitious to Ludwig Messel, urbane and middle-aged, walking round to see the baby from his own nearby house in Westbourne Terrace. His business friend and former neighbour, Sir Ernest Cassel, had been similarly blessed with a grand-daughter only shortly before Christmas and, mingling shrewdness and sentiment, Ludwig would not have failed to commiserate with him on this patriarchal pleasure. Delighted to visualise their progeny growing up in the twentieth century, the two men could not know that both the babies would one day each hold the rank and style of countess. Nor could they recognise the embroidery inexplicably worked in the Darmstadt tapestry by their friendship, for they never knew that Cassel's grandchild, Edwina Annette, was destined to become the Countess Mountbatten of Burma.

Not that Cassel would have been surprised by the firmest links with the Royal Family. He was already a close friend and financial adviser of the new King, and plashlets of inspired investment cascaded sufficiently far down the social pyramid to benefit even the junior partners of the firm of Messel. In 1904, Leonard and Maud Messel were blessed with a third child, Oliver, as a brother to Linley and Anne, and the proud parents were readily able to afford a much larger house, 104 Lancaster Gate, a tall and narrow, balconied and cream-painted mansion, facing pleasantly across the Bayswater Road towards Kensington Gardens.

Now a department of the Bulgarian Embassy, its formerly opulent entrance hall gloomily illumined by only a single naked electric-light bulb, No. 104 has survived into its own unimaginable future, austere and bleak, yet its halcyon Messel heyday might have suggested a house in the *Forsyte Saga*. It, too, had a close resemblance to "other houses with the same high aspirations . . . the door knocker of individual design, windows altered to open outwards, hanging flower boxes filled with fuchsias . . ." In the interior of Soames Forsyte's house "were countless nooks resembling birds' nests, and little things of silver were deposited like eggs". In the more fastidious Leonard Messel's house were fragile treasures of rare Venetian glass and romantic iridescent early goblets from Bohemia, an enthusiasm his wife endeavoured to match by collecting eighteenth-century fans. Soames' first household lacked a nursery; but the three Messel children had their own calm domain on the third floor with their Nanna.

Little Anne Messel especially liked to sit at the window and gaze down from this eyrie at the carriages in the then-placid Bayswater Road and, when the trees dropped their cloak of leaves, she could just see the chimneys and cupolas of Kensington Palace gleaming in the westering sun. It was her mother's tranquil custom to visit the nursery after tea-time and lift her on her knee to tell her a fairy-tale. But surely no tale ever told, no story either read or made up, could be stranger than the untold true story that lay unguessed in the future?

"Once upon a time there was a little girl who lived at the top of a very tall house from which she would sometimes watch the rose and gold of the sunset over a royal palace that stood not far away. Then one day she left the house to get married and presently had a son. And when he grew up he married the highest and most beautiful princess in the land and went to live there in the palace happily ever after . . ."

V

On an only slightly diminished scale, the Messels enjoyed the same affluent ease of life at Lancaster Gate which the Strathmores, the present Queen Mother's parents, knew in St. James's Square. In both households the same quiet, almost stealthy current of servants flowed up and down the artery of the staircase: the steward, the housekeeper, the maids and nursemaids. In both homes were held similar luncheon-parties and receptions, and both houses knew the same seasonal migrations. Her life similar to that of little Elizabeth Bowes-Lyon (the Queen Mother), dark-eyed Anne Messel (the present Countess of Rosse) knew the same golden summers of Edwardian childhood; and both the Bowes-Lyon country home at St. Paul's Walden Bury and the Messel country home at Nymans were social phenomena of an identical pattern.

To be sure, Leonard and Maud Messel at first had a country house of their own, Balcombe House, on the farther side of St. Leonard's Forest, a jaunt of only a few minutes from Ludwig's home, through the winding lanes in the rasping dog-cart, and the two houses merge in the earliest family memories. Nymans was even farther from London than the Waldens, and as deeply tranquil. "Little else than farm carts, dog carts and the carriages of the local gentry disturbed the quiet lane . . ." Lady Rosse recollects. "The Weald and woodlands belonged to themselves and to the neighbourhood, to live in peacefully, to farm in, and to enjoy. Sundays were kept as Sundays should be, then, and farmers tossed their hay on summer evenings in linen smocks."

The Queen Mother recalls the childhood wood "where the sun seemed always to be shining . . . the carpets of primroses and anemones . . ." The Countess of Rosse remembers a walled garden, with a spring bulb border "tightly packed with hyacinths, tulips, daffodils and anemones of all colours". And in one of the sharp-lit vignettes of remembered childhood, Anne Messel stands beside her grandfather's gardener, old Mr. Elwes, child and man both held captive to the spectacle of a golden mass of wild daffodils on the sloping fields. Then the man drags himself away and says gruffly, "No time to waste on Nature", a bewildering statement to the small girl who knows he has spent his entire morning poring over rhododendron seedlings, a remark fathomed only years later when she had learned to understand the dry humour of gardeners.

Her Sambourne grandpapa, also, was a man of many curious and long-remembered sayings, "It was so still you could pick up a pin", "He hadn't a rag to stand upon", "It was a white elephant around his neck", metaphors delivered with such solemnity that his closest friends could not tell whether or not he were serious or revelling in his own comic invention. He had a fund of stories to tell of his encounters with the reputed warrior who kept the grocer's shop in the village, "General Stores" and could gravely enumerate the varied posts, from mere penny sticks to twelve-foot poles, kept at the post office. It was an early grief to Anne when this grandfather Linley Sambourne died in 1910, and Nanna perhaps had to explain why birthday cards—always addressed in two inks, red and black—ceased to come from him in Heaven. For consolation, her mother might stress that no other little girl had story-books to treasure, *The Water Babies* and *Hans Andersen's Fairy Tales*, for which Grandpapa had done the illustrations. To preserve these special volumes, they gradually became "Sunday only" books and it created a nursery scandal when Anne's younger brother, Oliver, boldly pencilled a drawing of his own within one of the covers.

Like all middle children, Anne had her own special equilibrium, poised between her desire to emulate her elder brother and the need to protect the younger. Linley occasionally devised games of hide-and-seek in the laurels, culminating in shrieks of mingled glee and mock terror, and his sister stopped play when the ambushes beneath the glossy leaves all but caused little Oliver to burst into tears. If grown-ups complained that the children were never still, all three at all events remained still long enough to sit to Glyn Philpot for a portrait, spellbound by the promise of the fun after he had finished working, when he scraped the paint from his pallet on to paper which he would then fold and tear to create flocks of butterflies of every brilliant hue.

The Queen Mother's girlhood was diversified by the home-comings of innumerable elder brothers and sisters. Through Anne Messel's childhood there equally moved an extraordinary assortment of aunts and uncles and cousins in a constant procession of visits to Nymans and Balcombe. Leonard Messel's younger brother, Harold, had married Laura Putnam from Philadelphia, giving the children the sense of wider horizons always achieved by an American aunt. Leonard's eldest sister, Ottilie, married a Captain Loring, afterwards a Vice-Admiral and A.D.C. to the King, thus bringing to Nymans an uncle who was full of tales of the sea and, not least exciting, the stories he told on his very rare visits during the war when he had served as a naval transport officer at Gallipoli. Another of Leonard's sisters, the children's Aunt Ruth, had married

Eric Parker, the author and magazine editor, ultimately editor of
The Field, a journalist uncle who taught the children to watch birds
with gentle stillness until the wild became nearly tame. "Down to
Nymans; met by Ruth and children. Nightingale in evening," runs
one entry in his journals. "Next morning took children on the lake.
In afternoon caught one fish. Looked at duck and pheasants with
Owen. Went round flowering trees with Mr. Messel."

During another visit he records a shooting day at Nymans—with
the children's Uncle Arthur, Major Arthur Gibbes—"52 pheasants,
69 duck, 5 hares, 2 rabbits", and hints of futurity emerge in a visit
of Gibbes and Parkers and Messels to Scotland when the grouse-
shooting adjoined the Ogilvy moors at Cortachy. Then there were
summers when Leonard Messel rented a house on the River Lee in
County Cork for the salmon-fishing, and little Anne Messel (Lady
Rosse) was only seven years old when the first of these visits propa-
gated the seeds of her attachment to Ireland.

At the outbreak of the first world war she was too young and
sheltered to understand the distress of her grandfather and her old
"Uncle Rudi", the two Darmstadt brothers who had to endure in
the eventide of their lives the agony of the division and fighting
between their adopted countrymen and their own blood cousins.
Ludwig Messel died in 1915. It appeared that he had discussed with
his sons his wish to leave half-a-million pounds, apart from a large
family trust fund that he and Rudolph had devised with great financial skill, and his affairs were in such meticulous order that Ludwig
actually left £589,706. Rudi survived him by five years, suffering the
disillusionment of an idealist who had contributed his progressive
ideas to industry only to see them misspent in war and ruin. Hon-
oured as a President of the Society of Chemical Industry and a
Fellow of the Royal Society, his was the brain behind the chemical
works of Spencer, Chapman and Messel at Silvertown. He had
improved a process for manufacturing sulphuric anhydride—in
plainer terms, a process used in dyes, glucose, sugar refining, cellu-
loid and explosives—and wealth had accumulated effortlessly
around his dreams as a scientist. In his will, Rudi bequeathed the
bulk of his fortune of £174,000 to the Royal Society "having left my
family provided for". He had never married and the phrase thus no
doubt discloses his own contribution to the trust that has always
protected the Messels from financial stringency and in turn can one
day be expected equally to benefit Lord Snowdon.

VI

In worldly terms, the Jones and Armstrongs have never attained the riches of the Messels, nor displayed the ingrained artistic traits of the Linleys and Sambournes. Their assets lie instead in Celtic romanticism balanced by adventurous pugnacity and Welsh religious strength, enriched by a purposeful yeoman strain from Cumberland. In seeking to prove that the shepherd-boy is really a prince, the genealogists have traced Lord Snowdon's paternal line back to Llewelyn the Great, the native Prince of North Wales, with an alternative line attaching to his twelfth-century contemporary, Rhys ap Gruffydd, the Prince of South Wales. One could hardly wish a better lineage but, for full measure, a genealogical table at Clarence House shows that Lord Snowdon and Princess Margaret both descend from Dafydd ap Einion, leader of the men of Harlech against the Yorkists, and accordingly are twelfth cousins twice removed.

Precarious as it may appear to all save the well-versed antiquary, Lord Snowdon's descent has also been traced from Edward I through that stern monarch's daughter, Princess Elizabeth, and a subsequent score of generations. There are ancestral links with the Stanleys and Fitzalans, and with the Mostyns, from whom the Queen Mother also descends. But no oral tradition of this pedigree survived within the Armstrong-Jones family, although Lord Snowdon's father, it seems, would sometimes tell with twinkling eyes of reputed ancestral links with Collwyn ap Tangno, founder of the fifth noble tribe of Wales, a noble man who held his lands before the first Normans ever landed. Yet this royal and ancient blood was well watered down, at best, and perhaps closer family roots may suffice us.

In the days, then, when the musical and good-looking Linleys were enchanting the rank and fashion of Bath, a farmer named John Richard Jones ploughed a rough and stony Merioneth hillside never dreaming that in the times of his remote posterity some traces of his personality and that of his king, George III, would unite. In every sense, it would have seemed inconceivable that within five generations any descendant of his would marry the sister of the reigning Queen. One may suppose that John Jones—Lord Snowdon's great-great-great-grandfather—was not an imaginative man. Every day of his life, save perhaps the Sabbath, he toiled on the same stony slopes, unaware that the view from his land embraced the whole

25

story of his family line. Past and future were there, from the distant prospect of Harlech Castle in the south to the mountain glimpse of Snowdon to the north.

The house where John Jones and his wife, Ann, reared nine children still stands, overlooking the sweep of the Lleyn peninsula. Ty Newydd, "the new house", was in all probability a gift from his parents-in-law, a small slate-roofed homestead built of the local rubble, its rooms partitioned by matching. The meagre evidence indicates that Jones was a dour, pious and hard-working man, and a stern father. Two of his sons, Robert and Thomas, ran away to sea at an early age and were taken prisoner from the brig *Fame* in some affray of the Napoleonic wars. Held in a prison in Rouen until the Peace of Amiens in 1805, they returned home to find that their widowed father had taken a young wife, and had looked no farther for his bride than the next farmhouse.

The two brothers prospered, however, in the seafaring life, and by 1820 had some interest in no fewer than three brigs, *Providence*, *Brothers* and *Dryades*. Clues to their careers lurk in the very names of these vessels. Robert died when still a young man, but Thomas found his own dryad in the parish of Ynyscynhaiarn, Caernarvon, a girl of some gentle refinement named Elizabeth Thomas, whom he married on May 5th, 1820.

Although Thomas Jones is described as a mariner in the baptismal record of his first son, Richard (who emigrated to Australia) he evidently left the sea shortly afterwards and moved with his wife into the somewhat splendid Queen Anne house of his widowed mother-in-law, and we find him classed as a gentleman at the baptism of his second son four years later. While the Messels were infiltrating into the court life of Darmstadt, indeed, Thomas Jones drew an assured income from ownership of the brig *Esther* of Pwllheli, and had time to devote to the management of parish affairs. He held the post of overseer of the poor, was a churchwarden and in 1830 he busied himself in raising local funds to build a road to the parish church.

His youngest son, Thomas Jones—Lord Snowdon's great-grandfather—was born in 1826. In this same rural Welsh parish with the name (so difficult to Englishmen) of Ynyscynhaiarn, a tiny Nonconformist chapel was built in the very year of Thomas Jones II's birth, and young Thomas grew up not only to become a chapel convert but also to lose his heart to a farmer's daughter of Eisteddfa, near Criccieth, whose family had owned and farmed their land for generations. Thomas married Jane Elizabeth Jones in 1855, and since she was an only child he took over and farmed the lands of Eisteddfa after the death of her father four years later. Jane was descended on her mother's side from one of the more important county families and may have owned other property in her own right. Her only differences with her husband however were narrowly religious rather than financial. She staunchly brought up all her children as members of the Church of England while her husband became a Congregationalist minister and built the little chapel of Tabor, as well as several other Nonconformist chapels elsewhere in Caernarvonshire.

Jane and Thomas increased the always bewildering array of Jones by five sons and three daughters. A group family photograph still survives, taken nearly a hundred years ago, and there sits Jane, in apron and crinoline, blonde or greying—a secret the fading print does not tell—with her youngest girl perched upon her knee. The picture provides ample evidence that Jane had the means to ensure that all her children were respectably turned out, the eldest son, Robert, affecting a smart and even modern air in his grey double-breasted jacket. The boys in particular bear a marked resemblance to the Earl of Snowdon, all alike with the strong chin, direct look and quiffed hairline that we now know so well.

VII

The time came when Robert Jones—Lord Snowdon's grand-father—attained the rare distinction of being a Fellow of both the Royal College of Surgeons and the Royal College of Physicians and could claim nearly a column in *Who's Who*, mentioning that he was born in 1857 "eldest son of Rev. Thomas Jones, Eisteddfa, Criccieth, North Wales" and listing his life's work as a specialist in mental disease. The stubborn enduring strain that we have seen in the Messels, on Lord Snowdon's mother's side, is equally exemplified in his paternal line. Deciding early that he wished to be a doctor, Robert Jones fought his way doggedly from the grammar school at Portmadoc and through the University of Wales to medical studies in London. He was a student at Bart's, and in 1888 he had cause to take a special professional interest in the Jack the Ripper murders, for this was the very year when he was appointed the first Medical Superintendent of the new L.C.C. asylum at

Claybury, Essex, and the anonymous and undetected Jack may well have become one of his patients.

The Ripper murders at all events whetted Dr. Jones' all-absorbing interest in insanity. While other men went on fishing trips, Robert Jones spent his holidays abroad, visiting asylums. With the enquiring zeal of a reformer and a connoisseur's enthusiasm, he inspected mental hospitals diverse or distant as those of Norway and Italy, Poland, Switzerland, Austria and France. He once travelled far into Central Russia to see the advanced therapeutic workshops and tiled hygienic corridors of a model institution at Nijni-Novgorod, and one is tempted to picture the young Welsh doctor perhaps returning on the same Trans-Siberian Express which chanced to carry in its freight some of the rare Asiatic shrubs consigned to Ludwig Messel at Nymans. Yet the Jones and the Messels had already a trivial and yet curious link.

On one of his rare holidays at home in Caernarvonshire, Dr. Jones renewed acquaintance with Margaret Elizabeth Roberts, the daughter of a neighbour and old family friend, Sir Owen Roberts, of Plas Dinas. Destined to become our Lord Snowdon's paternal grandmama, Margaret was a woman of exceptional intelligence and her father was in fact a pioneer in women's higher education. A barrister by profession, he had been knighted by Queen Victoria not long before for "services to technical education" and was one of the founders of Somerville College, Oxford. As it happened, Sir Owen Roberts lived in town at No. 48 Westbourne Terrace and Ludwig Messel lived at No. 8 in a house of identical stucco and opulent columned portico, twenty doors nearer the park. So it came about that Lord Snowdon's great-grandfather on his father's side and his great-grandfather on his mother's side lived on the same side of the same street although, like most London neighbours, the two men probably never met and remained total strangers.

Margaret Elizabeth's history, too, was tragic as the heroine of any Victorian novel. Her mother had died when she was less than a year old and she remained with her father, in the care of a nursemaid, until Sir Owen remarried, and this new young stepmother died in turn, presumably in childbirth, when Margaret Elizabeth was still barely eleven years old. Owen Roberts then took a third wife, as though establishing the family pattern that was to be threaded through the divorce courts by his grandson, Ronald Armstrong-Jones. This third marriage proved a long and happy one.

Such was the strange, somewhat melancholy story of the young lady whom Dr. Robert Jones met when in his mid-thirties, and whose clear intelligence, charm and sympathy, he so deeply admired that he developed a familiar emotional obsession of mankind and fell in love.

The worlds of medicine and the law, religion, teaching and finance mingled at their wedding. Sir Owen Roberts was clerk to the ancient Clothworkers Company and may have hoped that his daughter would have found her husband within the prosperous social fabric of the City guilds, but the romantic atmosphere of Wales had proved the stronger. All the Jones were frequent visitors both at Plas Dinas and Sir Owen's Surrey estate of Henley Park, between Guildford and Farnham. Dr. Robert Jones, however, took his wife to live among his lunatics or as close to them as one could get in one of the Claybury staff houses. The new Mrs. Jones ordered his life in such a calm and methodic manner that he found time to write a treatise on the mouths of Mongolian idiots and a study of the psychological benefits of electric light at Colney Hatch. In 1899, when his son, Ronald Owen Lloyd, was about to be born, he busied himself by preparing a paper on "emotional states and grey hair" only hours before the happy event.

Sir Owen Roberts gazed proudly at his eldest grandson and may have influenced the Jones in their decision that the boy's name should be put down for Eton. By the turn of the century, Dr. Jones was himself winning considerable professional prestige, and in 1903 he headed the psychological medicine section of the British Medical Association. In 1907, when Sir Owen was appointed High Sheriff of Caernarvonshire, Dr. Jones was already an eminent specialist. The good doctor had his weak spots, notably his annoyance at the constant confusion of his work with another Robert Jones who was a distinguished surgeon of the day. In 1913 the difficulty was resolved by changing his name by deed-poll to Armstrong-Jones. The first name had been the maiden name of his wife's mother, who had been born Jane Armstrong in the Northumberland village of Haltwhistle, and is thus perpetuated today in the name of Princess Margaret's daughter, little Lady Sarah Armstrong-Jones.

The double-barrelled name was also promulgated in time to confer its suggestion of pedigree upon young Ronald Armstrong-Jones as he commenced his career at Eton. Old Sir Owen Roberts was no doubt delighted, especially as he had transferred the 800-acre Plas Dinas property to his daughter, Mrs. Armstrong-Jones, as a family home. Sir Owen Roberts died in 1915 at the age of eighty and so, alas, did not survive to know of his son-in-law's knighthood the following year. The doctor was knighted in recognition of his outstanding services at Claybury, but he had also been responsible for the treatment of hundreds of British and American shell-shock cases among Army casualties brought home from France, and his grateful patients felt the honour rightly accorded when King George V had cause to say, "Rise, Sir Robert Armstrong-Jones".

2 *A Marriage*

As her eldest son, Lord Snowdon, was to do a generation later, Anne Messel entered her teenage years amid the disruption, comparative deprivations and deep-running hysteria of a world at war. Her parents observed the social convention that required a schoolroom and a governess, and there was no question of her going away to school or she might otherwise have faced the antagonisms and phobias, especially in a school atmosphere, that lay in wait for a girl named Messel.

These were the days when the owners of dachshunds were hissed in Hyde Park, and hundreds of shops with German-sounding nameboards were sacked in wild anti-German riots in London and the provinces. Prince Louis of Battenberg had been compelled to resign his office of First Sea Lord of the Admiralty by the "fanatical and malignant outcry" against his Darmstadt parentage and birth as a Rhineland prince, and the hatred of everything German was as agonising to London-born Leonard Messel as it was cruel and unjust to his father and uncle, the Darmstadt brothers, Ludwig and Rudi. Solid sensible Sussex was not as rife with anti-German rumour as other parts of the country; but it has been noted that the shock and stress of it all contributed to Ludwig Messel's death in 1915, although other family fears proved unfounded. The loyalty of young Linley, Leonard Messel's eldest son, was unquestioned when he joined the Eton O.T.C. and subsequently served in France. Leonard Messel's local prestige was never diminished and he rose to a lieutenant-colonelcy in the home service of the Territorial Army, a distinction later as impressive to some as the hyphen of the Armstrong-Jones.

Anne's younger brother, Oliver, who was not strong as a child, was deeply unhappy at both his prep schools; and when at home he shared Anne's wartime education with successive governesses, English and Belgian. One lady, it would seem, won popularity from her readiness to relinquish lessons at any time and work in the garden, while another evidently found favour by extending the drawing-lesson half the day through. In London, later on, the children's French teacher, Mlle. Jacquenot, found that they showed the usual resistance to grammar but eagerly assimilated fresh words and phrases from the titles of French Impressionist paintings.

Mrs. Messel, glancing at the dark young rounded heads bent over their drawing-pads, would call them her "two young artists", delighted that they showed the Sambourne flair. The steadfast bonds between brother and sister slackened a little soon after the war, when Oliver went to Eton, but drawing remained the family pastime. This was strengthened when Colonel Messel and his wife began making sketches and designs for his long-cherished dream of rebuilding Nymans into the perfect semblance of a large Tudor manor-house. Leonard Messel now had money enough to indulge his whims and his new home was intended to form a perfect setting for his splendid collection of fifteenth and sixteenth century furniture. The furnishing decided the house: friends said that if Lennie had collected eighteenth-century pieces, he would have built himself another Chatsworth.

Yet the joke was amiable. No ethical problems of architectural forgery were ever posed, and Colonel Messel could not know that fire and ruin would add their own dreadful hallmark of authenticity to his home within his life-time. The nineteen-twenties saw architectural reproduction enjoying a new heyday, guided by Sir Lawrence Weaver's eclectic rejoicing that "sleeping traditions have been renewed . . . in the spirit of the old work" and so father, mother and daughter immersed themselves in "Tudor domestic Gothic", in the details of mullions and ribwork, bargeboards and oriels, chimneys and plaster. The new Nymans was to be both beautiful and completely "authentic" in texture and style. At the same time, one of the foremost architects known to City men, Sir Walter Tapper, was called in to ensure that, among other essentials, the medieval manor had a damp course.

Mr. Ian Nairn has called Nymans "an amazingly deceptive evocation" and it must be said that Colonel Messel's meticulous artistry was implemented by both historical fact and astonishing luck. Old

Ludwig Messel, in purchasing the nineteenth-century house, had heard of an earlier house on the site which was declared "in ruins and defective state" in 1509. The ugly eastern face of his home was speedily hidden behind a new garden entrance hall with an inviting Tudor hearth and a plaster ceiling of careful Tudor detail, but when the Victorian brickwork of the southern façade was pulled down at Colonel Messel's bidding, he and his wife received the wonderful news that the original old fourteenth-century walls still existed behind it, and were almost intact to first-floor level.

Their children and grand-children recall charmingly that "Colonel and Mrs. Messel *always* did everything together" and husband and wife supervised the uncovering and restoration of the walls with infinite care. In the anxious quest for perfection, a fine Tudor fireplace was moved from Gloucester and installed in Mrs. Messel's bedroom, completely preserved to the last inch of old carving and the earlier coats of whitewash. Where Ludwig's guests had once flicked their billiard cues, a splendid library apartment arose to house a great collection of botanical books. The quintessence of every fine manor-house lingered in the great hall, with its musician's gallery, where bluff Linley Sambourne would have been astonished to find the coat-of-arms of the Sambourne family imposed with Cussans heraldry upon the rich fireplace. Leonard Messel indulged his taste for the ancient without stint and the firelight glimmered on oak polished by the centuries, on rich tapestries and old weapons, pictures and porcelain and fine furnishing. The pride of the house was a great Velasquez *A Man Reading* which hung in the library; and when young Oliver brought friends home from Eton the owner of Nymans had reason to reflect contentedly that no family home, no matter how stately or decked in tradition, could possess a finer painting nor more perfect suits of medieval Flemish armour.

II

It was Colonel Messel's pleasant custom to make a gift to Staplefield parish church in private commemoration of family events. His gift of a sanctuary lamp in 1913 had appropriately marked the fifty years of the Messels in England, and no doubt the presentation of a private Communion set in 1922 signified the successful conclusion of the Nymans transformation scene. On the occasion of his daughter's wedding in 1925, the gift of a copy of a Titian painting of the

Holy Family was to seem less in keeping, and the suggestion of the spurious perhaps troubled the donor, for he implemented it two years later with a magnificent set of six seventeenth-century Italian altar candlesticks for the birth of his first grandchild, Susan Anne Armstrong-Jones.

Yet we have glanced ahead a little. The milestones of human life are more often in uncommemorated events, even in incidents which prove persuasive in the lives of others only long afterwards. Seven years before Lord Snowdon was born, for instance, it was a moment of significance to his future when Oliver Messel summoned up courage one day to tell his father that he did not wish to go on to Cambridge but longed to study art at the Slade. He approached the matter with trepidation, only to find that he had no need to marshal arguments, no need to mention that his mother and her father had been artists nor to stammer something at last of the unhappiness he had known at school. A little to his surprise, indeed, the prospect of resistance from his parents dissolved like magic. Mrs. Messel had proudly watched all the striking manifestations of Linley genius welling up in her younger son and found herself contentedly in agreement with her husband that the boy should take his time. "You must do everything three times to be successful," she insisted. And Oliver truly tried.

At the Slade, moreover, he gathered congenial friends around him with the dexterity of a jackdaw amassing twigs for its nest, and the Messel's London house in Lancaster Gate began to resound with youthful new voices. In the big drawing-room upstairs, anecdotes of Professor Tonks and his Slade teaching staff flew back and forth in an atmosphere of coffee and laughter. Gusty argument crackled on Nigel Playfair's latest stagecraft at the Lyric or the new exhibition of Epstein at the Leicester Galleries, on the Astaires, on "Back to Methuselah" and the latest German avant-garde films at the Poly. Rex Whistler, Stephen Tennant, Simon Elwes and many others are remembered joining in the banter and talk. It was all immensely stimulating to Anne Messel, although it had to be admitted that most of the young men were in their teens and she was now twenty-one.

She had "come out", as they said, the previous year. Not that this implied any part in the gossip-column vulgarity of "the deb of the year" but the phrase carried the social cachet of presentation at Court. It involved the fun of practising curtsies with one's friends and the gratifying éclat of dressing up with the regulation head-dress of "three small white ostrich feathers" and the train "not more than eighteen inches on the ground". All the servants were invited into the hall to watch her departure for the Palace, and then came the ordeal of waiting in one's car in the queue in the Mall while the passers-by of the fine June evening drifted up and down, inspecting the cars and the debs and enjoying the show. Anne was a beautiful debutante exciting the undisguised admiration of the crowds: that she was embarrassed and nervous had also been obvious to her experienced companion.

Under the rigorous etiquette prescribed by King George V and Queen Mary, the Lord Chamberlain ruled that a mother could not present her daughter unless she had herself been presented at Court, and Anne was accordingly sponsored by a Mrs. Cyril Potter. As Loelia Ponsonby was to note, "the actual ceremony was over in a flash". Reaching the head of the line in the Throne Room, one "handed one's invitation card to a splendid official" who "shouted aloud one's name and tossed the card into a rather common-looking little wastepaper basket. One advanced along the red carpet, stopped and made two curtsies to the King and Queen, who were sitting on a low dais surrounded by numerous relations . . ." How those relations would have whispered, watching the obeisance of the pretty brown-eyed Miss Messel, could they have known that her future son would one day seek refuge from world attention in the Palace itself. But the date of June 8th, 1922, was notable for another rapport in time and tradition, for nearly 150 years had passed since Elizabeth Linley had so charmed King George III with her bewitching eyes and sweet voice, and now a kinswoman of hers resumed the Linley story within the Palace walls.

On the Armstrong-Jones side, it was also just five years since Sir Robert Armstrong-Jones had knelt for the accolade of knighthood. Only a week earlier in that summer of 1922, his son, Ronald, also underwent an important personal ceremonial when he was called to the Bar of the Middle Temple, an inauguration which would have pleased no one more than young Ronald's barrister grandfather, Sir Owen Roberts, could he have lived to see it. As we have observed, Sir Owen had been married three times and had three daughters, the eldest of whom was now Lady Armstrong-Jones, Ronald's mother. As his eldest grandson, Ronald Owen Lloyd Armstrong-Jones had been the apple of Sir Owen's eye. The old man had hoped to see the boy following in his footsteps through Eton and Oxford, and so into the law, and Ronald had been in the process of gratifying this dream, midway through his career as an Eton schoolboy, when Sir Owen died. Only the Kaiser's war then caused an interruption in this programme. Straight from his Eton O.T.C., Ronald spent two years soldiering, first as a gunner and then as second-lieutenant in the Royal Artillery until, on being demobbed in 1919, he went up to Magdalen College and successfully took his pass degree in law. It is clear that the persistence we have watched in the careers of the Linleys and Sambournes and Messels flourished with equal pertinacity and strength in the Armstrong-Jones soil.

III

The church of St. Margaret's, Westminster, nestles beside Westminster Abbey, it has been said, like a lamb beside its mother. The parish church of Parliament and, indeed, the mother church of the city of Westminster itself, St. Margaret's has long been the scene of fashionable weddings, and romantic onlookers can be counted on to throng the pavement at the first glimpse of a satin-clad page in the purposeful grasp of his nanny.

On the summer morning of July 22nd, 1925, connoisseurs might have anticipated a Sussex bride from the arrival of a troupe of Handcross and Staplefield Girl Guides who were to form a guard of honour. The two attendant policemen found themselves giving salutes of startled recognition to Judge Tobin, of the Westminster County Court, among the arriving guests, followed soon by none other than Lord Justice Greer and his lady, and Lord Denman, then deputy Speaker of the House of Lords. The inevitable photographers appeared, in time to identify the Baroness Zouche, Lord and Lady Tweedmouth, and the former Prime Minister's daughter, Miss Megan Lloyd George. A wedding is a wedding, and if the waiting bridegroom, Ronald Armstrong-Jones, had opportunity to survey the crowded church, he may have complacently reflected that no one had let down his side of the aisle.

If he had not precisely landed the Lord Chief Justice of England, the wife of the same, Lady Hewart, was prominent in impeccable millinery. The groom's aunt—his mother's half-sister, Lady Davison—looked about brightly, and her husband, Sir William Davison, M.P. for South Kensington, reflected all the assurance of one of the safest seats in Parliament. Then there were Sir Jeremiah and Lady Colman, whom Ronald had met through Regate petty sessions and whom everyone knew were as much concerned with wealthy City insurance companies as with mustard and starch. There were Marjoribanks and Trustram Eves from the Middle Temple, Harley Street friends of his father's such as the Lockyers, and cousins and kinfolk like Sir Thomas and Lady Carey-Evans. We need not forbear to exchange glances and gossip as we wait for the bride until, suddenly, all anticipations are fulfilled and she walks up the aisle on Colonel Messel's arm, her gown and train of white satin shimmering with embroidered pearls. The garden of Nymans itself is evoked in the demure sweet procession, for the four senior bridesmaids carry bouquets of white roses, the three child brides-maids are unencumbered in cream chiffon and the heads of all seven are wreathed in green leaves. It is an effective touch, Oliver Messel's touch, evoking classic arcadian beauty for Herapath and Messel and Loring and Parker cousins, though none are more lovely this day than Anne Messel, the dark-eyed bride, herself.

The marriage ceremony was conducted by the Archbishop of Wales in the full glory of his cope and robes. "I, Ronald, take thee, Anne . . ." The old immemorial emotive formula, while some of the women dabbed their eyes and some perhaps wondered whether the bride had knowingly defied superstition by wearing pearls. And then the brief retirement, the final orison of the Wedding March, the pealing church bells, the Girl Guides with their banners and the smiles of friendly Londoners, craning and waving from every passing open-top bus as the bridal car drove out of sight . . . up Birdcage Walk, as it happened, past Buckingham Palace and through the park.

The wedding reception was held at 104 Lancaster Gate, and the tall sunny house had never been more crowded, more lively with laughter and conversation, amid the speeches, the toasts, the champagne. A Slade student recalled irreverently that "some of the choice fish of medicine and the law, of Parliament and Welsh local government, City business and Chelsea art, swam about happily for a time in a ferment of goodwill". Going up to her room and changing into her going-away frock, did the bride recollect for an instant, as if with a passing fragrance, the little girl who had sat at the window looking at Kensington Palace in its autumn glow?

In a final crescendo of confetti, the young couple left for their honeymoon in France and Italy, and *The Times* recorded that "the bride wore a white dress with a blue cape and hat". No one troubled equally to record the minor and fanciful circumstance that in all their journeys of the day, to Westminster and back to Lancaster Gate and then outward again to Victoria Station, the bride and groom had passed and repassed Buckingham Palace three or four times, like riders circling on a carousel.

IV

How did they first meet, the good-looking well-built Ronald Owen Lloyd Armstrong-Jones and the beautiful Anne Messel? Ronnie had befriended Anne's elder brother, Linley, at Eton, where both were new boys in the same term. All three were at a Loring family wedding in Sussex, it appears, in 1920, and the young barrister probably came more conclusively into the family picture late in 1922 during the complicated administration of the estate of old Uncle Rudi Messel. There were legal questions to settle in Chancery and hearings in Chambers, and indeed it was not until 1926 that the Royal Society received the last payments of their handsome legacy. Colonel Messel occasionally entertained solicitors and accountants and Counsel to lunch at Lancaster Gate, and while the seniors were deep in discussion, the apprentice barrister renewed his acquaintance with the attractive daughter of the house.

Anne had grown into an extremely beautiful woman . . . and that Ronnie was bowled over, as the saying goes, is beyond question. It was an attraction of opposites, of solidity and quicksilver, of practical strength and poetic imagination, of his trained self-assurance and her inward shy calm. They were "such a good-looking couple", as others recall. Besides Ronnie's good looks, women were captivated by the resolute, romantic Celtic streak in his temperament, a charm heightened by the dash of professional histrionics in his manner and by the slight occasional Welsh lilt in his superb speaking voice.

One remembers that he was eight parts in ten a Welshman, with the minor admixture of the Armstrongs of the Northumbrian border. His father's father had been a Welsh pastor, though no social match for his maternal grandfather, that opportunist barrister; and perhaps only his father, the eminent brain specialist, could fully assess the dour, possessive, pugnacious strain of generations of Welsh farmers that toughened his character. Anne Messel's very differently cultivated world and her sensitive, impetuous and artistic personality must have seemed a revelation. But Ronnie's senses were ravished anew when Linley took him down to Nymans, now so suggestive of wealth and ancestral tranquillity in its settled garden. The white doves fluttered and cooed around the great fifteenth-century dovecote, and the possibility that it was a mere reproduction piece never entered the visitor's head.

He was adept and genially extrovert, however, in catching every bubble of conversation. Mrs. Messel's sympathy was won by the contrast that while Anne was the middle child between two brothers, her visitor was the only son between two sisters. Discovering that Ronnie had been a "wet-bob", an oarsman, at Eton, Colonel Messel was drawn into talking of his rowing days, only to learn with enthusiasm that his young guest had been in the winning Grand Crew at Henley not three years earlier. Next, when their visitor suggested that Anne might care to dine at his parents' home in Bramham Gardens, it was Mrs. Messel's turn to be astonished. "I know it well. My own parents lived not far away, in Stafford Terrace . . ."

Ronald Armstrong-Jones would have made the most of that pleasant Kensington coincidence. The Messels themselves recognised the attraction between their daughter and this purposeful and determined young man. In the summer of 1924 Colonel Messel accepted an invitation to spend a month at a friend's house in Norway, trying a fishing beat on the Sundal River, and one may judge the implicit hope that the two young people might see more of one another, left more or less to themselves in England. The opportunity indeed enabled Mrs. Messel to pay a visit with Anne to Sir Robert and Lady Armstrong-Jones at Plas Dinas. They sat about on the long lawn or strolled under the shade of the beech-trees, and there were romantic drives into the Caernarvon countryside, including a visit to Bodnant, where the Messels knew the Aberconways. It would be pleasant to discover that Ronald proposed in that glorious garden, but the reality is that Anne remained irresolute, her happiness troubled by inklings of doubt.

Truth to tell, she had always felt more at home with Oliver and his younger ebullient age group, three years her junior, than with men companions three years older than herself, with the slightly stuffy elder constraint of some of Linley's friends. At the same time, with her warm, impulsive sympathies, she fully shared Ronnie's love of country pursuits. Her father had taught her to be a keen fisher, and she was also a good shot. These were topics that could occupy her father, her Uncle Eric and others, for hours on end and these were the very themes that found Ronnie most in his element.

One day he took her to see Henley Park, to the north of the

Hog's Back, near Guildford, where his Grandfather Roberts had lived. Sir Owen had in fact rented the estate for many years and Ronnie was full of jocular reminiscences of his boyhood: here was the lake where he had caught his first perch, here the spinneys where, when his sisters made him ill-tempered, he could work it out, shooting at pigeons. The local village of Pirbright was unspoiled at that time, and the woodsman's axe had not deprived the Henley Park drive of its fine old elms. Ronnie's nostalgic enthusiasm was exhilarating, and like a bird seeking a nesting-place, Anne divined perhaps for the first time not only the strength and security that Ronald Armstrong-Jones offered her but also the prospect of happiness as his wife.

V

Among his wedding gifts, Colonel Messel gave his daughter the long Grosvenor lease of No. 25 Eaton Terrace, with an endowment to clear the ground-rent and certain other outgoings for more than fifty years. This was no ordinary settlement. There is still no enclave of small town houses anywhere in the world more elegant or select than this southernmost region of the Belgravia estate which Cubitt and Basevi laid out for the first Marquis of Westminster on the former marshlands and pastures of Pimlico, and Eaton Terrace itself was firmly planned half as wide again as the average residential thoroughfare as if to enhance the quiet distinction of the orderly façades.

As one approaches from the aristocratic venue of Eaton Gate, little more than a hundred paces from Eaton Square, No. 25 is the first house on the eastern side, distinguished immediately by its exotic first-floor verandah, the only one of its order in the street. If this balcony instantly announces itself as rococo Nash-out-of-Messel, the shallow pagoda curve of its roof and intricate wrought ironwork nevertheless enhances the prim four-storey exterior with delectable charm. One suspects that the addition is more recent than the early autumn of 1925 when the new Mrs. Armstrong-Jones returned from her honeymoon as into a doll's house and plunged into the amusement of choosing the final decorative details and furnishing. That her new home was small was undeniable. The ground floor offered only the dining-room and a little morning-room at the rear opening into the garden. The space of the first floor was allotted to an L-shaped drawing-room, and the narrow staircase led up to one main bedroom and a spare room, a tentative nursery. Above this again were only three small bedrooms for the servants.

"Mrs. A. J.'s" youthful taste was inevitably influenced by the Syrie Maugham vogue for sheer white with strong touches of colour, balanced by the instinct for baroque which she shared with Oliver. Each of the three reception-rooms had a pretty chimney-piece demanding utmost precision in the selection of eighteenth-century brass or steel fenders, and each room flowered with wedding-gift pieces of furniture embellished by a dozen smaller decorative touches of distinctive splendour. It may well be that the new master of the house feared there would not be moving space for his bulky frame, and some of his wife's favourite ideas were sharply modified. But by the New Year the moving-in was complete and the newly-wed couple were truly embarked on the pattern of dinner-parties, theatre parties and the other sociabilities on which the ambitious young husband set considerable store.

Oliver, too, soon injected his own exhilarating atmosphere of the theatre into the domestic scene. After his Slade studies, he had apprenticed himself for some months to the stage design studio of John Wells, and the benefit of this practical experience was proved when his exhibition of theatrical masks at the Claridge Gallery gained the interest of C. B. Cochran, always alert for new stage ideas. The thrill of the applause for Oliver's settings at the first night of the Cochran revue of 1926 provided one of the early memorable occasions of the Armstrong-Jones' married life, like a curtain-raiser of innumerable pleasures to come. Through Oliver, personalities such as Tilly Losch, the dancer, Olga Lynn, the concert singer, Gladys Calthrop, the scenic designer, and Noel Coward came into the orbit of No. 25 as yeast to some of Ronnie's heavy-weight legal and business friends. After some years in the drudgery of county courts and the South-Eastern Assizes, Ronnie was beginning to specialise in accident and insurance cases, and his steady prosperity gave Anne a sense of fulfilment in three lives, the careers of her husband and younger brother and now her own. In 1927 she had hoped to attend the first night of Noel's costume play *The Marquise*, but this was an event she missed for the best of reasons, for her daughter, Susan,* was born only five days before.

---

* m. John Vesey, May 20th, 1950, who succeeded his uncle, 1958, as 6th Viscount de Vesci' and has had issue: Emma Frances, March 17th, 1951; Catherine Anne, May 19th, 1953: Thomas Eustace, October 8th, 1955.

Her husband did his best to conceal his chagrin that the anticipated son proved to be a girl. In an early phase of the pregnancy,
Lady Maud Warrender fluffily reported that "little Mrs. Armstrong-
Jones did wonders with just a cook-housekeeper, a houseman and a
maid". But when the baby arrived there were obvious limits to
wifely skill. Anne had enjoyed preparing for the newcomer, stitching and embroidering some of the layette, and contentedly sewing
absurd stuffed cotside toys. During placid weekends at Nymans,
those two old mentors, Lizzie Hart and Mrs. Noel, her parents'
nannas, fluttered around her like anxious hens. The head housemaid
at Nymans, Margaret Bell, mentioned the nursemaid of a neigh-
bouring family whose children were growing up, and so little Laura
Gunner came up from Sussex to take charge of the baby.

The young mother was then twenty-five and her husband twenty-
eight when, one evening, he rushed home, cock-a-hoop with the
news that his father had been nominated as High Sheriff of
Caernarvonshire. Until this very moment Ronnie had begun to fear
that the honour accorded his Grandfather Roberts might not be
repeated, and his tacit faith in knowing the right people had been
edged with misgivings. In buoyant mood, he proposed a celebra-
tion at Ciro's or the Embassy, and his joy and exhilaration would
have been unbounded could he have known that he would himself
be nominated as High Sheriff only seven years later.

The Armstrong-Jones were amused when the flash-bulbs popped
as they danced together. Ronnie was proud of his beautiful wife,
pleased again with her slim figure, and he liked her to be admired.
He felt flattered at a fancy dress ball when the Prince of Wales
sought her out as a dancing partner, and he liked to repeat the
compliment paid on another occasion by Prince George, the Duke
of Kent, "She's the best-looking girl in the room!"

A later acquaintance, Loelia, Duchess of Westminster, has told of
the passion for dressing-up that marked the social life of the 1920s.
There was particularly the craze for charity matinees at which beautiful and noted women paraded in gorgeous finery across the stage
of Drury Lane or His Majesty's in pageants such as *Lovers Through
the Ages* and *Old Mayfair Fayre*. Lady Diana Cooper, Lady Edwina
Mountbatten, Lady Oranmore and Browne, the Countess of Carlisle,
the Countess of Seafield, and similar socialites lent their names and
graces to these fund-raising amusements. Oliver designed some of
the costumes, his sister helped Lady Juliet Duff with the dress-
making and sewing, and it was but a step to persuading Anne to

take part in these affairs herself. She proved a notable recruit. In a glittering costume as the Queen of Snow and Ice at a charity ball she looked so beautiful that her arrival elicited a storm of applause.

At the *Pageant of Hyde Park* at Daly's Theatre, the young photographer, Cecil Beaton, appeared as Gainsborough and this was perhaps the occasion when Anne dressed in eighteenth-century picture hat and flowing skirts as Elizabeth Linley. Cecil Beaton was enraptured, snatching up pencil and pad to sketch this charming vision. "Mrs. Armstrong-Jones ... of exquisite carriage with sloping creamy shoulders and bright bird-like eyes", he hastily jotted down, and Cecil Beaton, Oliver Messel and his sister rapidly became firm friends.

In all these swirling incidents were set the seeds of a future royal marriage.

3 *Children of Divorce*

I

Antony Charles Robert Armstrong-Jones was born at 25 Eaton Terrace on the evening of Friday March 7th, 1930. Keyed up to face the slightly disappointing prospect of another daughter, Ronald Armstrong-Jones had remained at home all day. The three-year-old Susan had been taken to her grandmama at Lancaster Gate to be out of the way and had been brought back again at bedtime. When the gynaecologist, Mr. C. C. Barry, arrived, the anxious husband was nervously waiting with a friend in the morning-room. Presently an infant cry was heard from an upper floor, and one of the women servants saw the master of the house taking the stairs two at a time. A few minutes later he came down beaming and announced, "It's a boy!"

Frank Sheldrick, the butler, had brought champagne, and Mr. Armstrong-Jones and his domestic staff toasted the new arrival then and there: Sheldrick and Nanny Gunner; Mrs. Mortlock, the cook-housekeeper, Ethel Oliver, the maid, and a Miss Rudd, a temporary lady's maid. Next day, Ronnie saw that the birth announcement was top of the column in its alphabetical order in *The Times*, "Armstrong-Jones—On March 7th, 1930, at 25 Eaton Terrace, S.W.1, to Anne, wife of Ronald Armstrong-Jones, a son." He had taken trouble to ensure this immediate notice, and he put his son's name down for Eton within the month; but in the pleasant torrent of congratulations he overlooked the legal formalities, and the birth was not registered until the day of the christening on Saturday April 5th.

Even then, in his haste, he omitted to give all the baptismal names, for the baby was christened Antony Charles Robert Owen

44

Lloyd that same afternoon and only the first three appear on Lord Snowdon's birth certificate. The proud father had nevertheless energetically organised no fewer than seven sponsors and had gone to no little pains to ensure an unusual and exclusive setting for the christening of his son. As a member of the Middle Temple, Ronnie was entitled to the ministrations of the Temple Church, and so his infant son was named at the Purbeck marble font of what was then the largest of the only five ancient round churches of Norman style remaining in all England. The Master of the Temple, the Rev. Lewis Wilford, officiated, and the surroundings suggested to more than one of the seven godparents that they might be watching the baptism of a future Lord Chief Justice or at least of a child destined to play a leading part in the highest public ceremonies of the land.

As if to represent Wales, the sponsors included Sir Michael Duff, then only twenty-three, who gave the child a large silver christening mug and was by a happy chance to become Lord Lieutenant of Caernarvonshire in the same year as his godson, Antony's, marriage. For the family, there were cousins and friends, such as Colonel Wingfield Digby and Mr. Nigel Gibbes, and Ronnie's sister, Elaine Wauchope, side by side with Lady Forres, the sculptress, and Anne Armstrong-Jones' old friend, Lady North, the future Countess of Guilford. Both she and Colonel Digby gave the baby gold pins as symbol of a gleaming future. Yet the kindly fates, in choosing their portents, perhaps elected to throw their most fanciful garlands around the youngest of the four godmothers, the russet-haired Countess of Seafield. To the family, this rather shy young woman of twenty-three was merely Anne's close friend, Nina, who shared her zest for fancy-dress balls and parties and indeed, had once indulged in the great lark of playing a barrel-organ in the street with Oliver Messel, strictly for fun and for charity. To the world interested in such details, Nina Seafield was however that social rarity, a Countess in her own right and owner of 200 square miles of Scotland. Fortunate is the baby born with a silver spoon in his mouth, but what of the child whose silver spoon comes from one of the richest godmothers in Britain?

II

It has been said that a springtime baby has the vigour of the season, growing with the year. If so, the little Antony was an exemplar, strenuously kicking and stretching in the sunshine. A pleasant amenity of 25 Eaton Terrace lay in the curiously rural garden at the back, part paved, not too small, and complete even to its own towering and characteristic London plane tree. This garden in turn led out by a wooden door to the quiet cobbled cul-de-sac of Minera Mews, which had no doubt been Minerva Mews until a bygone sign-painter forgot the "V". Lady Armstrong-Jones, Ronnie's mother, would occasionally slip out that way, after perhaps spending part of a summer afternoon dandling her grandson in her lap. In his mid-seventies, her husband, too, liked sometimes to sit in the garden in the sun, watching the baby and day-dreaming, engaged in his favourite hobby—as he humorously listed it in *Who's Who*—of "retrospective contemplation". After his lifetime of inquiry into the human brain, Sir Robert Armstrong-Jones surely found it both diverting and at times oddly touching to watch the early conscious stirrings of individual personality in his descendant. On the other hand, as time went on, it dismayed the old man to note the obviously increasing dissonance between Ronnie and Anne.

As many people know, Lord Snowdon's parents were divorced in 1935. It is painful and perhaps unnecessary to probe the innumerable difficulties of a marriage in dissolution but it may be pertinent to our enquiry in studying the effect of the break-up on the children, and especially on the man who inevitably holds his place in history as the brother-in-law of the Queen.

Both parents were probably finding themselves in increasing, yet intelligent, disagreement before he was much more than a year old, though their friends could trace no single incident of disruption. Outwardly, nothing ruffled the surface in the summer of 1931 when, at Oliver's and Rex Whistler's suggestion, the Armstrong-Jones accepted Cecil Beaton's invitation to go down to Wiltshire one weekend to see Ashcombe, the Georgian house that he had discovered and renovated. The host has himself said that guests would arrive for the first time with a vague look in their eyes and Ronnie must have been bewildered, more than amused, by Cecil's "bizarre and eccentric" striving in decoration, by the "life-sized cupids, silver bird-cages, glass witch-balls, shell pictures and crumbling Italian console tables". The host affected a Tyrolean suit; the guests included elderly ladies in fancy-dress, giantesses like Viola Tree who strode the lawns barefoot, and neighbours from Wilton who arrived in the full spirit of carnival, cloaked and masked.

The long weekend, and the search for the perfect country retreat, were very much enthusiasms of the time. The preoccupations of a successful barrister did not however always match Anne's eager enjoyment of social pleasures with her friends, and the seventh year of marriage brought their insistent clash of personalities increasingly to the fore.

In 1932 Oliver Messel was furiously busy designing the entire décor and costumes for two notable Cochran productions, the stylised classic Grecian setting of *Helen* and the medieval pageantry of *The Miracle*. In all the turmoil and frustrations of this creative work, he often took his troubles to Anne. So did other friends, for she had the necessary intuition of the artistic temperament and could sympathise with problems that to Ronnie's firm and logical mind must scarcely have seemed to justify over-wrought discussion. Wearied by a difficult day in court or eager perhaps for a peaceable evening in which to get up his next day's case, he would arrive home to find the house in an unexpected pandemonium of artistic friends and kinsfolk, and the impassive barrister may often have felt heavy and even resentful, "an apple pudding", as one averred, "set in a soufflé". Ronnie could be urbane, jovial, hospitable, a delightful companion, but some of Anne's friends made him shrink into taciturnity and sit scowling: a photograph by his son was subsequently to capture just that scowl, the Counsel withering an opponent.

A legal friend has said that Armstrong-Jones was a solitary romantic at heart, and that he was not cut out for the Bar with its strong sense of fraternity. His favourite hobbies of fishing and wildfowling were at all events both expressions of his solitary mood. His professional life moreover required rigid punctuality and patient routine: the very antithesis of the heady social distractions in which his young wife was caught up. The Armstrong-Jones, however, celebrated their seventh wedding anniversary happily together and seemed to have composed their differences. In private, Ronnie may have expressed his exasperation with Celtic fire, and the thought of what was best for the children was ever present for them both.

The Armstrong-Jones thus spent part of the Long Vacation with Susan and Antony at Plas Dinas where, one day, Ronnie planted his son on a horse. Though only two at the time, Lord Snowdon was to remember that moment ever afterwards, the first conscious memory indeed of his life: his father's strong hands lifting him into the immensity of the saddle, the sound of hooves crunching on the

47

gravel, the long mane before him, the choking excitement of moving forward through a green sunlit world.

III

The irrevocable breakdown of Ronnie and Anne's marriage came in 1933. The attraction of opposites had proved to be the antagonism of opposite camps, both defenders irreconcilably besieged within the barriers of their own quite different natures. As the close yet powerless witness of their unhappiness, Oliver Messel made himself ill with worry and overwork. He had suggested to Cochran that a wonderful musical for Gertrude Lawrence could be made of his friend James Laver's novel *Nymph Errant* and yet his enthusiasm sank under the dismal load of private concerns, and Doris Zinkeisen had to take over the décor and costumes of the show. (As a good friend, Mr. Laver tried to distract Oliver by steering him through the publication of a book of his own, Oliver's, stage designs, but that is another story.) It was all the more ironic to Anne and Oliver that Linley, their elder brother, became engaged to a girl named Anne, a Miss Anne Alexander, that summer and against the bustle of preparations for the wedding the Armstrong-Jones finally decided that they should have a trial separation.

Linley and Anne Alexander were married in October at the church of Holy Trinity, Sloane Street, and little Tony made his first ceremonial public appearance on this occasion in his role as a page. In token of Colonel Messel's old regiment, his mother and Nanny had made him a miniature replica of the uniform of a mid-Victorian officer of the Middlesex Yeomanry, and he trotted behind the bride in a blue plumed helmet, a tight deep blue jacket with gold buttons and epaulettes, and white pantaloons strapped to the instep. An amusing picture shows us the plump fair-headed child, tightly holding his sister's hand, for Susan made an enchanting bridesmaid in white lace. He complained vociferously of a tight chin-strap but otherwise "behaved perfectly". Nanny Gunner moreover kept a close watch on her charges, for this was the one occasion when the disassociation of their parents would have been most evident.

In agreeing to separate, Anne and Ronnie had decided to have alternate care of the children, sharing Nanny Gunner as the one constant companion, a solution which seemed better for them than the constant domestic undertow of troubled emotion. From the start Laura Gunner was like a buoyant raft on the troubled seas so that, smoothly transferring with her from one household to another, neither Antony nor Susan were aware of the growing estrangement. An early photograph of Antony shows him clinging unhappily to his beautiful mother, while her arms are about him comfortingly, and yet the mood of tragedy is chiefly in the eyes of the beholder.

Ronnie hoped that the separation would not be permanent. Early in the winter of 1933–34 he had assumed the lease of a house in Trevor Square, No. 6 on the eastern side "between Harrods and the park" and, according to the electoral rolls, he was soon installed there with Nanny Gunner and the children, with the Sheldricks as cook-housekeeper and steward and with a maid-servant. Little Antony's adaptability to this new menage can be readily judged, for, within a month or two, Marcus Adams, that Paderewski of child photographers, found him a charmingly sturdy and independent little fellow, a trifle puzzled at being asked to throw flowers on the floor—the identical trick to capture a mischievous expression that Adams similarly tried with Princess Margaret that same year—but eagerly donning jersey and riding cap to pose forcefully with his riding-crop, feet well apart.

Yet this was evidently the very winter when Ronnie, chivalrous, compassionate and perhaps still hoping for a change of heart, supplied his wife with the necessary hotel evidence for a divorce, going through the cruel charade on which A. P. Herbert turned his scathing pen in *Unholy Deadlock*. He emerged from that winter as if awaking from a hideous dream. To welcome him home to Trevor Square, when the children were at Nymans, he enjoyed the society of a white bulldog and occasionally exercised this mournful animal in the Square. And it was there one misty Saturday afternoon in early March that a decisive turning point in his life was reached when his dog ran off the lead and chanced to follow a black cocker spaniel through the railings and down the basement steps of No. 24.

When the dog failed to reappear, Ronnie had no alternative but to follow. He rang the doorbell of No. 24 and raised his hat to the petite young blonde who answered. "I'm so sorry, but could I have my bulldog back, please?" After that, Ronnie was quite equal to asking his man Sheldrick to discover the identity of the young lady at 24, a Miss Carol Coombe, who was living there with her sister and mother, Lady "Allie" Coombe from Australia. Ronnie at this time was thirty-five years of age to Carol Coombe's twenty-two,

49

and on the Monday morning he walked into Harrods before going to the Temple and ordered a box of white tulips to be sent, "For the black cocker spaniel from the white bulldog, with apologies for my monstrous gate-crashing". As he may have hoped, when he returned from the office a message of thanks was awaiting him, "I enjoyed your gate-crashing and hope you will do it again" with the alleged signature of the black cocker spaniel.

The bulldog's master, indeed, wasted no time. Miss Coombe had a key to the gardens of the Square where she liked to walk up and down the paths while memorising her lines for a play. The dogs again served as an excuse for an encounter, and Ronnie could enquire what she was reading so assiduously. Carol Coombe explained that she was an actress and opening the very next night in a play at the Savoy. "I shall come and see you," Ronnie promised. Then and there he took a taxi to the Savoy to study the photographs outside the theatre. The play was called *Finished Abroad*. Carol had made her début in the London theatre only six months earlier in the stern drama of *Madchen in Uniform*, and the new piece, in contrast, was a lightweight comedy "concerned with the night escapades of schoolgirls", as Ronnie discovered on reading the reviews, and *The Times* added that Carol Coombe brought to her part "ingenuousness with a wide-eyed liveliness".

Despite the efforts of Ellen Pollock, Leontine Sagan, Carol and others in the cast, the production was suddenly withdrawn in its seventh week. But by this time, Carol and Ronnie had established firmer bonds of friendship. Ronald had diffidently felt it proper to explain that he was separated from his wife. Lady Coombe, he discovered, was equally separated from her Australian husband, Sir Thomas Coombe, and Carol was the youngest of a family of six. Through the summer months the neighbourly acquaintance between 6 and 24 Trevor Square deepened and meanwhile Anne Armstrong-Jones had also established new social textures in which her husband had no part. The legal delays had been endless and, as the timing of events sadly turned out, it was only ten days before Christmas when her solicitors filed a petition for divorce on the grounds of her husband's adultery.

The suit was not defended. The "other woman" was not named and, since the parents were in agreement on the protection of the children, the judge was required to make no order for their custody or care. The decree nisi, the status of conditional divorce, was granted on February 22nd, 1935.

Dining with her parents that night, Anne immediately had to grasp a nettle of courageous decision. The constant contrasts of human life are a strange phenomenon. Her wedding at St. Margaret's nearly ten years earlier was irretrievably at an end and yet an invitation to another wedding at the self-same church now gleamed on her mantelshelf. It was that of Antony's godfather, Sir Michael Duff, to Joan Marjoribanks on March 7th. "But of course you must go," Mrs. Messel no doubt urged in her forthright way. "I shall come with you. All your friends will be there." Some such persuasions were used.

And so it was again St. Margaret's, and another bridal procession to take tribute of her emotions, this time with little Laura and William Smith, Viscount Hambleden's children, in the roles of diminutive bridesmaid and page. And presently, with the church hushed, another bridegroom's responses, "I, Michael, take thee . . ."

Were there echoes? At the reception there were so many people whom Anne knew: Sir Robert and Lady Armstrong-Jones, Ronnie's parents, Lady Juliet Duff, the bridegroom's mother, Lord Charles Cavendish, who had been at Eton with Oliver, David Herbert, whom she had met at Ashcombe, and his elder brother, Lord Herbert, equerry to the newly-married Duke of Kent,* Lady Diana Cooper and Sir Henry "Chips" Channon, bubbling with impressions of Mrs. Simpson. There were the Earl and Countess of Jersey, Viscount and Viscountess Weymouth, Lord and Lady Airlie—parents of Angus Ogilvy, then seven years old—and Heber-Percys and Pagets, Montagu-Douglas-Scotts and Lygons and Hornbys. The discerning reader may recognise many family names of those who were to congratulate Princess Margaret on her engagement to Antony Armstrong-Jones precisely a quarter of a century later.

IV

For his fifth birthday, at Plas Dinas, on the same day as the Duff-Majoribanks wedding, Tony received a pony of his own, named Ladybird. The grown-ups in their wisdom had seen that a pony to brush and to cherish would carry him through the more difficult months ahead, and both the children were as pony-mad as those other two horse fanatics, the then Princess Elizabeth and Princess Margaret. Perhaps one would not see so much of Papa when one began lessons. Tony and Susan spent most of that summer

* Father of the present Duke

51

at Nymans, and a Miss Madeleine Martin came on the scene as a governess, a mentor who was "charming and excellent and was with us for years," as a member of the household has told me. This capable lady taught both the children until they went away to school, for at Nymans there was always room for "Marty", as they nicknamed the governess and Nanna and the children, and to spare. The house was so big that Mrs. Hart, Mrs. Messel's old nanny, is said to have lived there for three years without Colonel Messel really being aware of it. The nursery wing caught all the morning sun, for the two night nurseries, the day nursery and even the children's bathroom all faced east.

The decree absolute of the divorce case was pronounced by Mr. Justice Hilbery sitting in a Vacation Court on August 28th, and there must have been days in the Nymans summer when the children took it for granted that a fair-haired military young man whom they called Michael was more in the picture. They had, in fact, always known him from earliest memory and Michael was no stranger to Nymans. Oliver had first brought him home as a fourteen-year-old Eton schoolboy, and Michael was at the family wedding in Sussex, when Mary Loring married Colonel Charles Vesey, as early as 1920, years before Anne and Ronnie were married. He still preferred, in those days, to call himself Michael Parsons but in tragic reality his father had been killed in action in Flanders in 1918, only two years earlier, and as a boy of twelve he had succeeded as the sixth Earl of Rosse, owner of some 26,500 acres in Ireland and Yorkshire.

The Messels may subsequently have thought it a pity that Anne had not married him in the first place, but events had to take their course. When she was going to dances here and there, Michael was a romantic eighteen-year-old worshipping her from afar, though remembered by friends nevertheless for dancing a Charleston so vigorously that he shook the fabric of the house. The gulf of four years difference in age cannot be bridged when a woman is twenty-two, and Michael at eighteen still seemed a schoolboy. Yet he had never married and now he had come into her life again, nearly in his thirties to her thirty-three, still devoted to her and a staunch friend and counsellor. They seemed to have everything in common, their interest in art and the theatre, gardens, architecture, in country life and every heritage of the past. By degrees, through the anxious months, they had seen one another with the truth of maturity. "They are both in their thirties," Lady Maud Warrender was able to write to a friend, while the Earl of Rosse and his Countess were on honeymoon.

His birthday was, in fact, on September 26th, and he and Anne were married on the morning of September 19th, 1935 at St. Ethelburga the Virgin, Bishopsgate. The little church afforded room only for their immediate families and closest friends. The children were not present and there were to be no bridesmaids, but Sir Richard Sykes as best man watched Lord Rosse becoming unexpectedly nervous, for the bride was late. It happened, curiously, that the Royal Marines had been ceremoniously marching through the City of London to take up guard duty at Buckingham Palace for the first time. The traffic was diverted and so, in the fabric of fate, this touch of royal pageantry delayed the bridal car.

Sacheverell Sitwell and Cecil Beaton, among the guests, could agree that the bride had been worth waiting for, beautiful as she was in a Grecian gown of pale Wedgwood blue. Close to their side, the unfailing eye of Chips Channon would have noted Gerald Chichester, who had just become Queen Mary's secretary, among the Beauchamps and Lisburnes, Sutros and Cadogans, Arbuthnots and Ogilvie-Grants. We mention these names as merely indicative of the social ambience in which Antony Armstrong-Jones grew up. The new Lady Rosse had scarcely returned from her honeymoon, moreover, when she had occasion to attend a royal wedding in Westminster Abbey, for one of her closest friends (Lady Alice Montagu-Douglas-Scott) was marrying the Duke of Gloucester.

Amid these weddings and what might be called counter-weddings, one other ceremony perhaps holds our interest, for on April 22nd, 1936, *The Times* announced the engagement of "Ronald. only son of Sir Robert and Lady Armstrong-Jones of Plas Dinas, Caernarvonshire, North Wales, and Carol, youngest daughter of Sir Thomas Coombe, of Perth, Western Australia, and Lady Coombe, of 1 Cheyne Court, London, S.W." And it was at about this time that Tony, on being taken by Nanny Gunner to his father's house in Trevor Square, first met his future step-mother. Running as usual into the drawing-room, he was astonished to find a fair-haired lady standing there alone, in what he thought would be an empty room, and after the first look of blank surprise he ran back to Mrs. Gunner. "There's a lady there—"

"Then introduce yourself," Nanny advised him.

He was back in an instant. "I'm Tony," he announced, solemnly, putting out a hand. "Who are you?"

"I'm Carol," she said.

"How do you do? And this is Susan," he explained, as his sister came running in.

Carol had been prepared by Ronnie's enthusiastic description for a real boy, with fair hair and big blue eyes. She saw, as she wrote afterwards, "brown hair with a glint of red . . . a funny little monkey face, with its button of an upturned nose".

Ronnie and Carol were married at the Westminster Register Office on June 18th, 1936, with Carol's mother and Ronnie's clerk, Harold Standring, as witnesses. From that moment, the two parents shared the children equally, so far as possible, until they came of age. The grandparents were astonished, no doubt, to note how naturally Tony and Susan accepted the situation, adapting themselves readily and quite quickly to the contrasts of environment. Indeed, they were always to be very fond of Carol. Their nannie and governess also for a time provided an element of continuity. The brother and sister were always together and rather pleased, indeed, at the novelty of having parents in two different homes.

V

Birr Castle first came into the changing scene in 1936 when the children went there for part of the summer. Lord Snowdon will never forget the thrilling adventure of the voyage to Ireland, and of the green Irish landscape, full of donkeys and horses and cattle, the novelty made an indelible imprint on his mind. Arriving at Birr, he had been promised a real castle, with battlements and turrets, like the fort in his toy cupboard and so it proved to be . . . "larger and richer than Nymans", it has been said "and twice as real". The reality is relative: like Arundel Castle, Birr is largely a romantic nineteenth-century setpiece, built on the groundwork of earlier buildings. The Gothic remodelling had, however, fortunately not impaired the eighteenth-century splendours of the interior, and the new Countess of Rosse had the pleasure each night of climbing a yew staircase that had borne the soft footsteps of the successive ladies of Birr Castle for nearly three hundred years, and has been described as the "fairest staircase in Ireland".

Not that the children were aware of the aesthetic charm of atmosphere that gave their mother such tranquil happiness and contentment. Tony wrinkled his little nose at the smell of fresh paint and quickly discovered the fun of scuffing the sawdust in the estate carpenter's shop. An old cabinet-maker was making "a bookcase for her Ladyship" without causing the small boy to wonder whom her Ladyship might be. On that first visit, Susan was very much the leader in the exploration, leading her brother up the winding stairways to the fantastic heights of the battlements forty feet above the lawns or onto the exciting suspension bridge that crossed the River Camcor as it foamed and tumbled through the gardens.

She persuaded Michael to take them rowing on the lake, introduced herself to the kitchen and discovered that an Irish cook was as ready with new-baked cakes as anyone at Nymans. One day she cajoled Mr. Levy, the butler, into showing her the harmless basements that were sometimes styled "the Castle dungeons". Their stepfather, too, the children found, could tell them thrilling new stories, stories that *really happened*. One tale was about the wise Sir Laurence Parsons, the Englishman who built the castle in 1620 and carefully planted trees for the King, doing everything so well that when the sturdily-built fortress came under attack in his grandson's time it withstood a siege for five days. The castle would moreover have lasted out longer still but for the long memory of a mason who had helped to build it and knew best where to plant a mine close to its western wall.

And that the mighty stones might have withstood even this device was proved by another true story that Michael liked to read with every possible vocal sound effect: great guns that "never ceased but continued like a continued thunder . . . only now and then scolding would happen from our men, bidding the enemy go home and dig their potatoes . . ." This was the siege of 1690, when the castle stood for King William III, and in the end the garrison had to "cut and melt a leaden cistern" to make their own bullets, until the besieging army withdrew and slipped away in a night.

All this was exciting enough to a small boy, in a castle where piles of cannon balls still proved the reality of ancient times, and one suspects that Carol Coombe found it difficult to keep up with the wonderments that Tony at first incautiously carried back to her in London. Meanwhile, Ronnie chanced to pay a visit to Henley Park, which had been relinquished on the death of his grandmother ten years earlier. Although time had brought many changes to the environment of his old family home, one of the old cottages which had escaped attention still stood in the woods, neglected and inviting. This was the old estate laundry of his grandfather's time, forgotten and all but sinking into an overgrown wilderness just at the junction of two bubbling streams. Carol was delighted with the low and sagging tiled roof, the long line of casement windows and the placid sound of the nearby waters, and Ronnie viewed the cottage with a practised eye and saw the possibilities of conversion. And so 6 Trevor Square was presently relinquished, and the second Mrs. Armstrong-Jones became the chatelaine of Stream House, as they freshly named the old place.

The final decoration was entirely in Carol's hands and the alterations created space for a butler, cook and housemaid, as well as extra bedrooms for Nanny Gunner and for the governess, Miss Martin. Carol rather liked the effect of the schoolroom, painted in clear yellow and decorated with Peter Pan pictures, and to please her adventure-loving stepson she equipped his room as a ship's cabin, complete with bunks and a little red step-ladder by which he could climb into bed. Once in his bunk, he was supposed to use a ship's canvas bucket, attached to a pulley, to lower his juvenile comic papers to the floor before going to sleep. But young Tony had a far better idea and the bucket was invariably a convenient store for chocolates and sweets close to his pillow.

For their first Christmas, the children went with Carol to see *Peter Pan*, and Tony re-enacted the play for weeks afterwards, leaping off chairs, sofas and tables with abandon, as if he really could fly. This gave Carol one of her far-fetched but characteristic ideas. Why not produce the flying scene for the house-warming party she was giving? A rope and pulley fixed to a thick oak beam in the drawing-room might launch Tony into space in the role of Peter; she could be Mrs. Darling to Susan's Wendy, and the Labrador dog, Harvey, made a suitable Nana. Though too young to read his lines, Tony could memorise and mimic wonderfully when the text of the play was read aloud.

The first experiment, utilising Ronnie's strongest belt for harness, was a dismal failure. Little Tony hung gasping in the air, and the belt left his waist bruised and red with weals. Yet Carol persisted, hiring harnesses and flying wires from Joseph Kirby, the "flying ballet" specialist who supplied the actual equipment for *Peter Pan* in London. Tony gamely tried again, taking off from the window-sill to a piece of furniture nearby, and after a little practice with the springy wire he was able to take off and fly across the room as gracefully as any professional performer.

"A boy who can fly at six can do anything," said his father, blushing with pleasure. With an improvised stage and footlights fitted up at one end of the long room, the flying-scene at the party was an inevitable success. At rehearsals there were however times when Carol drove her young actors hard and one evening she was almost too severe. Although Tony said nothing at the time, Ronnie afterwards found him in bed in tears. "I'm not crying because Carol was cross," he sobbed. "I'm crying because she didn't think I was good tonight."

VI

Pursuing the separate courses of their own lives, both the Countess of Rosse and Mr. Armstrong-Jones received a jolt of adjustment every few months in attempting to follow the children's ever-changing interests and temperaments, especially Tony's. The *Peter Pan* affair led to a fever for dressing-up, and for his seventh birthday he was given a small boys' pearl-buttoned Mexican suit and sombrero. Told that a Cisco kid was more likely to be a "lazybones sleeping in the sun", he slouched down, sitting against the wall, eyes half-closed: a child, Carol Coombe found, who lived half in a world of make-believe, although remarkably adaptable and responsive to everyone he met in the constant changes of each new environment.

He discovered the miracles of Carol's old make-up box, how the Leichner No. 8 would change him into an Indian prince, how No. 5 would sallow him into a sick old man, and his stepmother showed him the secrets of white highlights to deepen the lines of age. Then a glimpse of some of his Uncle Oliver's miniature stage sets gave him a passion for making paper models, and when he next went to Birr Lord and Lady Rosse could scarcely keep pace with his incessant demands for paper and paste.

The arrangement that the children would spend half their holidays with their mother, half with their father, was so strictly observed that if they began one holiday with one parent, their next holiday would begin with the other. In concluding the New Year holiday of Birr in 1937, they saw their new baby half-brother, William (Lord Oxmantown), and were at the baptismal ceremony in the protestant church of St. Brendan's in Birr town on January 11th, when the eleven-weeks-old infant was sonorously christened William Clere Leonard Brendan Wilmer. The Parsons family pew was hung with the old traditional scarlet drapery in his honour; and Tony, white-gloved and scarved, was an elegant small figure in beige cap and overcoat.

This may be marked down as the occasion when, with distinct puzzlement, he first consciously faced the lens and antics of newspaper cameramen. Birr had long been known as Parsonstown, from the family name of the Earl of Rosse, and the naming of its heir was a news event of local importance, as was the similar ceremony held in 1938 for Tony's second half-brother, Desmond Oliver Martin Parsons. At the christening tea-parties we conveniently meet others of the family, such as Lady Rosse's sister-in-law, Bridget Parsons, and her mother-in-law, who had been the widowed fifth Countess of Rosse and had remarried to become the fifth Viscountess de Vesci. Nanny Gunner had also now largely transferred her attentions to the Rosse family group, and when Tony and Susan returned to Stream House, their father often mockingly complained that Tony was "putting on his castle airs". His stepmother may have been more accurate in saying that this was Tony's chameleon quality: the boy was always trying to fit in.

For botany lessons, their governess asked the children to bring in samples of leaves, and nothing would suit Tony but to set ladders against trees to secure the finest examples of foliage for his "Marty". From this evolved the tree-climbing craze which so alarmed Lady Rosse at Womersley Park, where every stunted oak, forked beech or mulberry tree of her husband's Yorkshire estate challenged Tony to attempt new heights. These excitements were followed by a succession of new interests, culminating in a flair for making model cars and ships with match-boxes, cardboard, matchsticks and bits of wire. Tony would sit for hours, with intense absorption, cutting and painting until he produced perfect miniatures of the real thing. The finished models would be proudly unveiled at lunchtime or centred as table decorations. A psychologist need not look far for the symptoms of a child who perhaps unconsciously—and, of course, quite falsely—felt himself rejected and who had found a way of gaining approval and admiration.

Susan was always more forthright, and Tony perhaps a shade wily and astute in discovering that stories of his adventures at Birr were not particularly welcome under his father's roof. At an early age he thus gained a strange facility in dividing his boyhood experiences into separate watertight compartments. He said nothing to Michael about his sailing and swimming with his father in Wales, and his father at Stream House was never receptive to anecdotes about the "bamboo jungles" of Birr. He learned to live each life separately. In the autumn of 1938 he and Susan were given ponies at Stream House: Susan's was a dappled piebald called Silver and Tony's an unpredictable steed named Clinker who had the trick of biting whenever he could catch Tony unawares. Rather than admit that he was a little afraid of Clinker, Tony was quite willing to pose as a complete innocent who had rarely ridden a pony before, and so adept was he at dividing his two worlds that the slate was washed clean of his earlier riding exploits and his step-mother was successfully persuaded that Clinker was indeed the first pony he had ever owned.

One might add that riding faults were more sharply noted at Birr than in Surrey. A routine of tuition was arranged at the castle under which he and Susan took lessons with a French governess every morning and then Tony had riding lessons with one of the farm overseers, Ger McGilty, who through the years trained him effectively in both riding and jumping.

Carol probably considered that the obvious improvement was due to a riding instructress at his local riding school, on whom, she claimed, Tony had a crush. For a time, at least, he was always attempting to draw this adored one's picture, filling page upon page of his sketch-pad. "I'll just do one more," he would say. One suspects that, in emulation of his Uncle Oliver, he had promised to draw her portrait and found the task a little beyond him, but he characteristically kept on trying.

4 *The Wartime Schoolboy*

Antony Armstrong-Jones went to Sandroyd prep school for the autumn term of 1938, when he was eight and a half years old, and for the next four years the then headmaster and his wife, Mr. and Mrs. Hugh Ozanne, were to be decisively included among the formative influences of his boyhood. In the pine-and-heather Surrey countryside between Esher and Cobham—not twenty miles from Stream House—Sandroyd was that rarity, a prep school specially built and equipped for its purpose. It had been Ronald Armstrong-Jones' old school and, revisiting it as a parent, he could note the changes of twenty-five years as he inspected the swimming pool, gymnasium, library, chapel, carpenter's shop and laundry: "All under one roof now, with the sanatorium quite separate," Mrs. Ozanne explained with pride. Within the forty-acre grounds, the school also boasted private riding and the ultimate refinement of a nine-hole golf-course. Two-thirds of the ninety boys went on to Eton or Harrow, Winchester or the Royal Navy; a teaching staff of twelve maintained the standards and, at sixty-five guineas a term, Mr. Armstrong-Jones must have felt that the school still gave good value.

Sandroyd had featured briefly in world affairs four years earlier, at the time of the assassination of King Alexander of Yugoslavia in Marseilles, when the Ozannes had the task of arousing the eleven-year-old Prince Peter to prepare him for the news that he was king. On his first arrival at the school, Peter had learned with boyish indignation that he was to take a bath, his second that day, and Tony underwent a similar initiation. The crowds of boys swarming in the shower rooms and jostling at the banks of wash-basins, the scuffle of dormitory life and the daily shock of the sumptuous but ice-cold swimming pool were all innovations to which the astonished eight-year-old instantly had to adjust, straight from the placid regime of his governess "Marty".

The Ozannes, now in retirement in the New Forest, remember a freckled, slightly auburn-haired boy, of average mischief but more than average charm, loquacious and often in trouble for talking in the corridors, inquisitive, anxious to create a good impression but often tiring too soon of a subject, "not particularly brilliant . . . too small to be much good on the playing fields . . ." In the school magazine, he nevertheless won popular mention as one of three football players who "showed particular promise and, whatever the conditions, played their hardest" and, as an eleven-year-old school featherweight boxing champion, he was equally one of the boys who showed a "good amount of pluck in taking punishment and in coming up again smiling". Among his school-fellows, too, Tony quickly discovered the currency of making friends with a technique acquired from old Mr. William Eade, the clerk of the works at Birr Castle, who had taught him the craft of making small boats that could float and sail in style, whittled or carved from any scrap of wood. Many a battleship or windjammer was launched in a Sandroyd puddle, and before long every junior boy was carrying a three-inch ship of the Armstrong-Jones fleet in his pocket.

Old Sandroydians also remember Tony's jackdaw proclivity for building in trees, creating illicit hides so firm and yet well camouflaged that two or three boys could thrillingly crouch in their nests, unseen by masters or senior boys stalking below. Some of these arboreal cronies were to become lifelong friends, notably the Sainsbury brothers, of the grocery family. A story is told of a tree-house which Tony built at Womersley and how he one day flung open his bower to a group of children whom he met in the park. They climbed up, inspected, clambered down and stood marvelling, while Tony remained aloft. Then a temptation that had frequently swept him at Sandroyd proved irresistible. Inside his lair, his store of provisions included a can of water and, gazing down on the sightseers, he solemnly emptied it over their heads.

Most of it drenched a little girl, and her contrite assailant instantly descended, risking revenge from the other boys, and hurried her to the kitchen. While she quickly dried off near the stove, Tony raided the pantry and filled her hat with cakes. It was more than making amends. Tony said afterwards that he had fallen in love, and the illusion outlasted the holiday. On his next stay at Womersley, he caused the subject of his passion to be invited to a party where, between the jelly and sugar-cake, he passed her a little note declaring that she was his sweetheart. The young lady's attitude however was wholly correct: she bitterly told him not to be soppy.

"Tony has settled down at school", Mrs. Messel explained to a Sussex friend, shortly before he appeared in a school production of *A Midsummer Night's Dream*. Mr. Armstrong-Jones meanwhile noted with less optimism that his son was uniformly near the bottom of the class in Latin, English, French and mathematics. Perhaps the trouble lay in Tony's ever-changing environment. He had indeed no sooner settled down at Sandroyd than, within the year, the outbreak of war in 1939 made it desirable to move the school to a more remote locality, safer from air-raids and the risk of invasion. The Ozannes found a large old house near Tollard Royal, on the Wiltshire–Dorset borders, an incongruous choice, as it ultimately turned out. The region was later to become a springboard for the Allied invasion of Europe, and the peaceful valleys became populated by shock troops whose gunfire and mock explosions usually aroused the neighbourhood at dawn.

Yet a boy's view of the war was not that of the adult world. The freezing first winter was a glorious opportunity for toboggan slides. The disappearance of household staff into the Services or wartime industry was an excuse for a ten- or eleven-year-old at Plas Dinas to dress up as "a new parlour-maid" one night and provide exemplary service to his father and grandfather as they sat at the big mahogany dining-table. Evidently his father failed to penetrate the disguise. Sir Robert Armstrong-Jones waited until the end of the meal before revealing with a portentous wink that he had not been fooled.

Again, it was recorded at Sandroyd that the boys had "little to learn in the making of beds and washing-up". The school was wrapped every night within a pall of black-out curtains, and enemy bombers droned overhead in the dark on their way to Bristol or Birmingham. One aircraft jettisoned a heavy bomb and destroyed a nearby keeper's cottage though the school itself was unscathed. As a patrol leader with the Boy Scouts, Tony led his Eagles Troop in combing farmyards and spinneys for rusting iron for scrap or collecting firewood for the local Home Guard. The rationed diet was enlivened sometimes with venison or pigeon-pie, and Tony and other Scouts—including King Peter's younger brothers, Prince

62

Andrew and Prince Tomislav—were occasionally pressed into service as beaters for a deer shoot.

King Peter revisited the school to see his brothers one weekend, giving Tony an impressive object lesson in the status of royalty. Normally the school might have trudged three miles to church in the village and back. On this day of days, King Peter spent part of his time "in taking large parties of clambering boys for short hurls" in his fast two-seater sports car, discipline all but abandoned and petrol rationing ignored. The following term, moreover, the King and his brothers presented a complete "new talkie cinema" to Sandroyd, and Tony's early awareness of filmic art was gleaned from *Owd Bob*, *Scrooge* and *The Lady Vanishes*.

Mimic warfare in tactical exercises with the Home Guard similarly enlivened his wartime schooling. Sandroyd had once been the home of General Pitt-Rivers, the Victorian archaeologist and rifle enthusiast, and the General's old .22 shooting range was brought back into use for wartime lessons in marksmanship. A surprising number of twelve-year-olds thus became proficient shots, an aptitude unknown to a somewhat derisive public nearly twenty years later when Tony Armstrong-Jones first joined a royal shooting party at Sandringham.

There were skills that young Tony was content to keep to himself, less from laziness than the satisfaction of suddenly springing a surprise. He learned to swim in the patio pool at Stream House but conveniently forgot this accomplishment on first arriving at Sandroyd, no doubt hoping to curtail his chilly early-morning plunge into the swimming-bath. Nor was this the only example of his schoolboy subtlety. When Stream House was requisitioned by the Services and Major Ronnie Armstrong-Jones was stationed near Reigate they moved to a little house on Batts Hill and rented a small adjoining meadow to keep a cow. One holiday, Susan and Carol took turns in milking her, without a move from Tony. "He wouldn't know how. He doesn't know one end of a cow from the other," said his sister. Then a crisis developed when the cow apparently fell sick and would allow no one near her. No vet was available; the textbooks stressed that she should be milked to relieve tenderness and in desperation, late at night, Tony was awakened and asked if he would try.

He displayed, according to Carol, "unusual alacrity" and did the milking beautifully, but Tony next day shrugged off any assumption that, after all, he knew more than he pretended. "I've just watched you and Susan," he insisted. "And, anyhow, if you've got to do something, you just make yourself do it."

His father, on being told the story, thought that this sounded like one of Grandmama Messel's maxims. But at Sandroyd the boys were encouraged to help local farmers by work on the land and it would be strange if the inquisitive Tony, then twelve years old, had missed the enticing opportunity of acquiring a little practice in the warm milking-sheds. Birr itself was left unvisited during the war, owing to the restrictions on travel to Eire, but Tony drove a tractor and helped with the haymaking at Womersley, and enjoyed impressing the Earl of Rosse with his marksmanship when his stepfather came home on leave from the Irish Guards.

The difficulties of wartime travel, too, meant that his Uncle Oliver seldom came to see him. In the summer before the war, Oliver Messel had occasionally driven over from nearby Ashcombe, when spending a weekend with Cecil Beaton, but he was now engrossed in camouflage duties. Ronnie Armstrong-Jones was posted with the King's Royal Rifles and, subsequently acting as a Judge Advocate at courts martial, was seldom home on leave. Flung all the more into the gregarious community of boyhood, the sociable Tony when on holiday occasionally experienced a loneliness which his sister could no longer alleviate. One summer, when staying with Carol's mother, Lady Coombe, at Petworth he joined the local Boy Scouts and quickly became sufficiently friendly to bring two or three of the boys home. Then an enemy bomb fell on the local school during classes one morning and Tony had to be told that all his new-found friends had been killed.

The adults broke the news as gently as possible and, for once, he appeared unresponsive. But silence with him was usually a distress signal and we may think it no coincidence that his school reports showed the improvement of sustained, steady work next term. Until then, the sight of a report envelope in his father's mail, would cause him to murmur, "I'm going out for the day." (In fact, the school records show that his fears were exaggerated.) Although a late starter, he put on a spurt at all events and successfully gained a pass in his Common Entrance exam for Eton.

II

Antony entered Mr. J. D. Upcott's house at Eton in the Michaelmas term of 1943 and, paying an early visit to his son, reviving his own Eton memories, Mr. Armstrong-Jones found him not only in his old house, in Keates Lane, but even in his own old room. This could have seemed a propitious omen that the boy might yet follow in his father's footsteps, except that Tony showed neither inclination nor the slightest aptitude for the Law. His tepid interest in the Army evaporated as soon as the Allies' desert victories gave promise that the war might be over within a year, and his future remained as perplexing a problem as ever. Old Colonel Messel cherished an affectionate belief that Tony shared the gift for architecture of his Berlin great-uncle, Alfred Messel. On the other side of the family, the death of Sir Robert Armstrong-Jones in January, 1943, kindled reminiscent hopes that his eldest grandson might yet find his star in medical research.

To this end, young Tony was given his grandfather's old microscope, a heavy brassbound old-fashioned instrument, almost a family heirloom. Through its lens, Sir Robert had once studied sections of Mongolian brain tissue and, that summer, Tony and his sister promisingly applied themselves by the hour, gazing at samples of milk and Stilton cheese, wasps' wings, blood and hair. This was a good beginning, and their father presently noted it with pleasure on Tony's "burry" or bookcase at Eton, polished and obviously well-kept.

But we may observe that in reality it was no more than a "prop", an accessory in Tony's first experiment in décor, sharing pride of place with two of his Uncle Oliver's stage-design sketches and one of his ships-in-a-bottle, with no deeper significance than his boot-box, the threadbare hearth-mat or the curtains concealing his bed. More subtle persuasions were, indeed, already winning the family tug-of-war of his future.

At about this time, probably on a Thursday half-holiday, Tony lunched in town with his grandmama Messel, and she afterwards took him to see his great-grandfather Sambourne's house, which had recently passed to her from her brother. The *Punch* cartoonist had lived for thirty-five years at No. 18 Stafford Terrace, on the leafy slopes above Kensington High Street, and scarcely a detail in the lofty mid-Victorian mansion had changed since the turn of the century.

Mrs. Messel could remember Tenniel, Phil May, Millais, Marcus Stone and Lord Leighton at the weekly dinners in the stylised Jacobean dining-room; and their original drawings still lined the walls, tier on tier, up to the picture-rail. Within ten years the

65

founders of the Victorian Society—John Betjeman, Lady Rosse, Professor Pevsner, Sir Kenneth Clark and others—were to meet in the drawing-room, in passionate agreement that the plush portière curtains, the silk-skirted electrolier, the pomegranate wallpapers and Eastlake furnishings were more precious than gold. A thirteen-year-old schoolboy could not however be expected to appreciate the unique flavour of the dark, over-crowded, rather sunless house, and Tony was more impressed by the erratic patches of disrepair where bomb blast had shattered some of the stained glass windows while curiously leaving others intact.

Yet Mrs. Messel believed in implanting enthusiasms in the young. She had inspiriting stories to tell of Bret Harte, Rider Haggard and other adventurous figures whom she still keenly remembered in the old days, and she drew stories from her father's collection of walking-sticks as if they were divining-rods of romance. (Her encouragement occasionally had unforeseen effects, and a Messel cousin of Tony's failed to work one boyish incentive out of his system until he had undertaken a journey to Patagonia, no less.) But for Tony the exploration of No. 18 proved truly memorable when his grandmother led him upstairs to the studio where she had worked as an artist, as she told him, "when I was not much older than you are now."

Ranged in cabinets and boxes around the walls was the remarkable collection of 13,000 photographs which Linley Sambourne had used for the detailed background accuracy of his *Punch* drawings, all the reflections of a past age stored like honey. Stored in a huge cupboard were all his grandfather's bulky cameras and photographic equipment, and Tony must have fingered them with astonishment. Many of the folders and albums had not been opened for forty years, revealing early photographs printed in vivid blue, and his boyish imagination was suddenly captured by this enthralling revelation of the latent power and permanence of the camera.

At Eton, shortly afterwards, he sought out another boy whom he knew had an unwanted box camera and swapped his grandfather's precious microscope in exchange. And henceforth his letters home were rarely without urgent entreaties to remember to buy film, for he could never find enough in the rationed shops of Eton and Windsor.

III

Eton is said to be synonymous **with the** network of the old school tie, but one searches the school lists in vain to distinguish any contacts that may have held the drawing strings of young Antony's future. Eton College is not merely a school but a complex community, with a lively population of more than a thousand schoolboys scattered among its twenty-five different houses. During his five years at Eton, Tony's interests at some point touched the lives of hundreds of his school-fellows in the continuous flux of new boys and leavers. Within this schoolboy populace, though in a senior age group, was Princess Alexandra's future husband, Angus Ogilvy; Angus's second cousin, Viscount Hambleden, whose mother was a close friend of the Queen (the present Queen Mother) and the young Marquess of Hertford, whose elder sister was lady in waiting to the then Princess Elizabeth. But all three were in different houses, no closer in social acquaintance than, say, Jack Worsley, whose deeds on the cricket field all warmly applauded and whose sister, Kate, was to become Duchess of Kent.

Tony's bewilderment as a new boy, however, was shared in Mr. Upcott's house with Douglas Montagu-Douglas-Scott, a nephew of the Duchess of Gloucester. Together they joined in the daze of lower boys hurrying through the smog to Early School at 7.30 a.m. Wildly they competed in the fagging rush in response to the senior boys' fearsome cry of "Boy!", their feet given wings by the Eton logic that the last to arrive does the job. His special Sandroyd friends, the Sainsbury brothers, also arrived at Eton shortly after to share the divisions and disciplines of the frantic school day. Far from acquiring a varnish of snobbery or the gloss of discovering who-was-who, indeed, we rapidly find Tony pummelling or deftly sidestepping his contemporaries.

By his third Half, in fact, the school was getting word of his boxing prowess and in March, 1945, he appeared as an "extra special weight" in the School Boxing Finals. "A very good fight with a great deal more skill shown by both boys than is customary in this midget weight," summed up the *Eton College Chronicle*. "A. C. R. Armstrong-Jones had the advantage in height and reach over T. Koch de Gooreynd and though at first he was slow to take advantage of them, in the last round he used them with decisive effect." The following winter Tony represented the school against Beaumont College. "Armstrong-Jones had the honour of fighting first for Eton and fought well," said the *Chronicle* of this losing battle. "All through the fight he watched his opponent with great skill and used his left to advantage. If he had forced the pace a little

more in the last round the verdict might have been reversed."
Then, the next term, when entered for the school against neigh-
bouring Bradfield, we find him "narrowly defeated by a heavier and
more aggressive opponent. He boxed well and his footwork was
good but he must fight and attack more if he wants to win."

Tony was shown to possess native caution, then, as well as courage, and both were to vindicate Mrs. Messel's edict that one must
try three times to be successful. Only a week later, when he again
represented Eton against Beaumont, he "fought with much more
confidence and aggressiveness. His opponent was also aggressive
but Armstrong-Jones was well able to compete with him and won
after a close fight." After that, there was no stopping the boy boxer.
In the next school finals, we find the *Eton Chronicle* could affirm that
he "had it more or less all his own way. His opponent boxed very
pluckily but could not avoid punishment from Armstrong-Jones's
left. The fight was stopped in the second round." One is not surprised that this copy of the school magazine was "left lying about
the house" at home, as Carol Coombe noted. Ronnie
Armstrong-Jones thumbed it through, and asked questions which
his son shrugged off with Etonian nonchalance.

It was of more moment that a new house tutor, Mr. D. C. Wilkinson, now considered Tony ready for some house responsibility,
and his fellows elected him to Debate, the lower group of the
two-tiered prefect system of Library and Debate, which accorded
him a new degree of leadership in the discipline and minor administration of the house. This implied a sober conversation between
Tony and the house-captain on the new standards expected of him,
and a session when his tutor stressed what was regarded as "the
most important lesson taught at Eton, that authority without a
sense of responsibility is vain and that privilege without service
corrupts". Behind his ebullient gaiety, Tony was gaining an under-
lying seriousness very different from the feckless adolescent of a
year or two earlier of whom one master had written scathingly in
his end-of-term report, "Maybe he is interested in some subject, but
it is not a subject we teach here."

His fun and mischief as a fourteen-year-old had been affirmed
when, isolated with measles in the "san", he arranged to pass mes-
sages and haul up chocolate bars with string and a jar, regardless of
any risks of an epidemic. Within two years, his elders could
however note a new steadiness. His photography, boxing and rowing were merely on the sidelines of his serious studies. On holiday

at Plas Dinas his father gave him a small motorbike on which he unleashed his nervous energy, going off for long spins on the mountain roads. His term reports were said to be showing consistent improvement. Then, when Tony was sixteen and all seemed to be going well, he was suddenly confronted with the greatest fight and the bitterest opponent of his career.

He had been out all day on his motorbike and returned to Plas Dinas complaining that he had possibly strained a muscle in his back. His stepmother rubbed him with embrocation but he still felt out of sorts, ate very little dinner and excused himself immediately afterwards to retire to bed. Carol thought it wise to take his temperature. It was 102 and Ronnie called the local doctor, who found it prudent to perform a lumbar puncture. The sample of fluid drawn from the spine proved to be cloudy when it should have been clear.

Next morning Tony's temperature had risen to 105 and he was gasping in terrible pain. Not knowing what to do for the best, Ronnie telephoned to Lady Rosse at Birr, urging that she should come at once, and she flew over on the next plane. A specialist on nervous diseases, Sir Gordon Holmes, was meanwhile on the way from London. The physicians suspected either tubercular meningitis or else poliomyelitis, and, in the summer sunshine, death paused as an unwanted intruder at the threshold of Plas Dinas.

IV

In 1946 Britain was on the eve of the worst epidemic of poliomyelitis ever recorded. The disease was less readily diagnosed then than now and, as Ronnie Armstrong-Jones understood the doctors, four days would have to elapse before they could tell whether his son had tubercular meningitis or polio. If the former, the boy would sink into a coma from which he could never awake, and nothing could be done, for the drug streptomycin was not then in general use. If the latter, then the other common name of the disease, infantile paralysis, disclosed the terrible hazards.

The agonised parents took turn with Carol and Susan to sit at the bedside: Susan especially spent long hours watching there with a calm youthful courage and loyalty of her own. Lady Rosse returned to her hotel room in Caernarvon every night to grapple with a mother's dreadful anxiety, and her brother, Oliver, hurried from London to be with her. "I could foresee nothing but a crippled life in front of him, even should he recover", Lady Rosse was to write, when the terrible need of resignation and courage had passed. Once Ronnie had taken the best advice in the land, and arranged for day and night nurses, her ex-husband felt helpless and passive. "We were simply spectators, watching and hoping and praying", wrote Carol, in recollecting their vigil.

When a crisis occurred in the small hours and the night nurse called Mr. Armstrong-Jones to the bedside he tried to telephone Lady Rosse at the hotel and could get no response. A groom was sent down from the house, only to ring the hotel bell and bang on the door without making anyone hear. Meanwhile, with the first light of dawn, the watchers in the sickroom noted that Tony's breathing strengthened. Not long after sunrise, he opened his eyes and murmured faintly that he could not move his leg. The four days of desperate tension were ended. This, at least, was not tubercular meningitis. "I would never have believed that I would find myself thanking God that my son has polio," Ronald Armstrong-Jones told his wife, with deep emotion.

With the wave of relief, however, the nurses were aware of elements of conflict. The Countess of Rosse was convinced that Tony should be moved to hospital. The senior physician of the Liverpool Royal Infirmary, Dr. Henry Cohen (now Lord Cohen) was consulted and agreed that the move would be advisable when the patient was stronger. Meanwhile, Tony could be boyishly encouraged with the news that police riders brought him fresh serum every day on their motor-cycles. An early sign of returning strength cheered the whole household when he asked to have a dressing-table mirror arranged near his bed, tilted so that he could see the reflection of the garden.

From the lawns a gardener sometimes caught the glint of light near the four-poster. From Birr came letters scrawled by his ten-year-old half-brother, William, and eight-year-old Martin, letters he still keeps with sentimental atachment and jealously guards from other eyes to this day. In September he kept up a fire of running comment with the Liverpool ambulance men and tried to make little jokes to comfort his mother, anxiously travelling with him on the ninety-mile ride to the hospital.

In later years—save for his public service as a Council member of the Polio Research Fund—Lord Snowdon would seldom speak of his six months in the Royal Infirmary except with reluctance. He did not realise at first how ill he had been. His initial confidence was buoyed by a rosy view that his recalcitrant neck, his back, his paralysed legs would respond to a few weeks' treatment. It is difficult to write of this period without tumbling into the clichés of courage and endurance. The disease had particularly affected only his back and left leg, not his chest, and Tony was never an iron-lung patient. Once he was allowed by gradual degrees to discover the truth, he was philosophic, co-operative and determined to make a complete recovery.

The benefit of group therapy lies partly in furthering the individual's confidence by watching the achievements of others more advanced in treatment. A wave of joy runs through a ward when someone can say, "Look, I walked today!" Lady Rosse has praised the "patient and persevering treatment added to determination" on the part of her son. Tony was absorbed, immersed, in the routine of exercises and manipulation, of baths and handle-bars. If he told his physio-therapist that he had once been Peter Pan and flown through the air, she may have thought it was make-believe. His sister made it her special task to provide every book and magazine he needed: it might be ranked as an oddity that, although Tony had seldom looked at a newspaper, he now read every word of the gossip about Princess Elizabeth's romance with Prince Philip of Greece.

His Uncle Oliver, who had been designing for Covent Garden and Glyndebourne, sent him copious and detailed instructions for model-making, and Tony amused other patients by raising whole stage sets on his coverlet. Discovering that one of his stepfather's ancestors had made some of the first cameras—a curious link with Sambourne—he took a camera completely apart and put it together again: a feat more than usually difficult when lying flat on one's back. And Tony progressed. The day came when he, too, at last walked a step, sliding a foot like a skater and when he learned to walk again, in irons, straps, plastic corset and with crutches. The reward of regained mobility was in the enjoyment of talking to every patient, intimately delving into a hundred unfamiliar and unexplored facets of other people's lives. Years later, when making an official tour of a Yorkshire carpet factory, Lord Snowdon came across a deaf and dumb craftswoman—and astonished everyone by talking to her in deaf-and-dumb language. The reporters plied him with questions but he merely shrugged . . . and chose not to explain that he had learned deaf-and-dumb from someone in Liverpool.

V

The New Year supplied a fresh incentive in Tony's stubborn

anxiety to be home for his seventeenth birthday on March 7th, and a letter to Nymans in mid-February was rosy with optimism. Colonel Messel was celebrating his own seventy-fifth anniversary on February 19th, shortly before he had to undergo an operation, and his grandson could cheerfully reassure him that hospital life was not too bad. But the postman had to deliver these birthday greetings under circumstances that had never been envisaged, amid the acrid smell of ashes and scorched stonework, picking his way across a welter of firemen's hoses, until he found Colonel Messel in one of the garage buildings, trying to supervise salvage operations from a bath-chair. Nymans, beautiful dreamlike Nymans, was no more.

During one of the coldest winter nights ever remembered, fires had been heaped on the hearths and the heat had evidently crept through the chimney parging into an attic where the timbers smouldered unobserved. At three a.m. Colonel Messel was awakened by the smell of smoke and burning. The garden flickered in a lurid glow; the Great Hall was well alight and flames already threatened the main staircase and library. Colonel Messel and his wife, with her companion, a nurse and five servants made good their escape by another route, but there was little they could do to prevent the fire spreading. Most of the valuable antiques, the paintings—including the precious Velasquez, *A Young Man Reading*—the tapestries and the collection of rare botanical books were all destroyed. Eighty firemen, including teams from as far away as Brighton, fought the flames and succeeded in saving the older south-east wing and the treasures it contained, but more than half the house was left a smoking ruin.

"Too many birthday candles," Colonel Messel bravely attempted to jest, as he faced the destruction of his life's work, and inspected the tragic end of so much of the beauty to which he had dedicated himself for so long. Happily, Colonel Messel lived to see beauty not effaced but enriched. "The tender plants were strangely unaffected by the fire," Lady Rosse noted, a few years later. "In fact, they seem to take advantage of the now windowless mullions to climb in and out at will. On the ruins of the Great Hall a *Magnolia grandiflora* makes chase with a double yellow Banksian rose for the topmost gable . . ." For present-day visitors to Nymans, indeed, the fire-ravaged walls enhance its loveliness, as the splendour of high noon is often outdone by the sunset.

As he had hoped, Tony celebrated his seventeenth birthday at home, at Womersley, although equipped to his disgust with a wheelchair as well as crutches. The chair was fitted with foot pedals to help strengthen his leg muscles, and he had also been measured for special boots, one of his legs now being slightly shorter than the other, but he had firmly made up his mind to dispense with "those ghastly boots" as soon as possible. Whether he wore them at all is doubtful in the calm and remarkable odyssey of his recovery. Whatever will-power could achieve, he would achieve. Rather than sleep in a room on the entrance floor, he half-walked, half-hauled himself upstairs to his old bedroom. Within a few months of convalescence, when he went to Birr, he had succeeded in discarding his crutches and began to walk with a stick. He took his young brothers rowing on the lake—a hand-painted screen in Lady Rosse's bedroom commemorates such a scene—and he was seen riding around Birr town on one of the Rosse milk-floats from the home farm and hobbling up and down the unfamiliar steps and paths to help serve the customers, though able to rest and ride again when he needed. He was encouraged with the thought of returning to Eton: the fire at Nymans had solidified his choice of a career into certainty. He wanted to be an architect, and when Lord and Lady Rosse gave him a camera as a birthday gift he found himself taking more photographs of buildings than people.

He was envious of all the photographs that Lord Rosse had taken of both Birr and Nymans and, some months later, when entries were solicited for the Eton photographic exhibition, he typically submitted a picture of the rebuilding of Upper School, then being restored after the 1940 bomb damage. No doubt it was equally characteristic that, when the picture was disapproved, Tony was not discouraged. "The picture might well have been made more exciting if there had been signs of human activity," said the report, chillingly, and the young photographer hoarded the comment among his papers until he had proved to all the world that he could do better.

His return to Eton was timed for the Summer Half, the term that divides the school into the 'dry-bobs' of cricket and the 'wet-bobs' of the river. He had been expected to follow family tradition as a wet-bob and permitted himself no excuses. On the Fourth of June, that red letter day of the Eton year, he was the cox for Wilkinson's House in the novice bumping races, but this was nothing to the culminating Daylight Procession of Boats. As each boat passes Fellows' Eyot, the crews led by each cox stand upright, wobbling, with their oars at salute. And there was Tony, in gold-braided uniform as coxswain of the *Alexandra*, standing erect with drawn sword, legs apart, shoulders back, in perfect balance, the boy who could not walk without crutches four months previously. Mr. Armstrong-Jones had true cause for pride that day.

Yet one suspects that, for Tony, the true highlight of his return to Eton occurred a few days later. More than two years earlier, in the very week in March, 1945, when Tony established his first school boxing championship, King George VI and his Queen, with Princess Elizabeth and Princess Margaret, had visited Eton College to attend Morning Chapel. After the service, the King had knighted Sir Henry Marten in the open air, a ceremony without precedent in Eton's history, and the scholars had lined the paths of School Yard as the Royal Family took their departure. This was the first time that the future Lord Snowdon ever saw his wife-to-be. It seems unlikely that Princess Margaret noticed him in the penguin flock of morning-coated schoolboys but Tony was impressed. He had celebrated his fifteenth birthday the previous day and, in a letter of thanks for a birthday cake, he had occasion, it seems, to mention the Princess's "beautiful large eyes".

A visit of the reigning monarch is a rare event at Eton through the centuries and yet, oddly enough, King George VI and his family paid a second visit on June 15th, 1947, this time to commemorate the visit in 1447 of Henry VI. After College Chapel the school assembled to watch the Royal Family walk through Weston's Yard, and this time Princess Margaret looked her prettiest, gay and summery in a flowered hat. Tony had stood there waiting to see her with the King and Queen before he had polio and now, by the turn of fate, he stood there, awaiting her again, almost completely cured. He did not dream that within thirteen years she would be his wife, but the double event in the Eton courtyards possessed its own quiet and mysterious affirmation.

5 *The Young Photographer*

Full-fledged, Tony Armstrong-Jones left Eton at the end of the summer term of 1948. In his last year he had the privilege of being elected to the Library as one of the four boys to watch over the activities and well-being of all his juniors in what was now Mr. Wilkinson's house and he had climbed the ladder of duty to a position second only to that of house captain. Among the advantages was the sociable use of a so-called library room furnished with comfortable though expendable chairs and decked wall to ceiling with cut-out pin-ups, mainly of the female form. What Tony thought of their poses and postures is not on record but he now had the satisfaction of seeing several of his own more orthodox photographs hung by the Eton Photographic Society.

This was a just reward for his pertinacity. Gone were the days when he took his films to Mr. Butler in Birr, or borrowed the chemist's dark-room to do his own developing: too slapdash and impatient, as Mr. Butler thought, and far too eager to take films from the solution when they were only half ready. Among Tony's Eton "acceptances" was a glamour-deb portrait in soft focus, with upswept hair and yearning eyes, in which his model had clearly received the full current *Vogue* treatment. She was, in fact, the chemist's assistant, Agnes Frawley, and she still treasures the print he sent her, solemnly inscribed on the back, "I am sorry the grain shows so much, but this is too big an enlargement from the negative, and I have had little time to touch it." Not every girl can boast a photograph from the hand that has also portrayed Marlene Dietrich, Leslie Caron, Lynn Fontanne . . . and Princess Margaret.

Yet Tony's enthusiasm was so compelling that Michael—as he

always called his stepfather—now provided him with a dark-room at Birr Castle, where every birthday or Christmas gift of equipment was bound to please. His own father similarly allowed him to arrange a dark-room at Combe Place, where he carpentered and fitted shelves with meticulous accuracy, painted and made good the plaster and cleaned up old junk furniture with a patience unusual for his eighteen years. Combe was the latest of the innumerable Armstrong-Jones homes, a rather fine eighteenth-century house at Offham, near Lewes, which Ronnie had been unable to resist buying not only for its name but because they all fell in love with it (and one must add that no real link with Carol's family was known). Tony faithfully photographed the exterior and interior, turned his camera on the garden and gardeners, snapped the whippet dogs and was saddened when his father sold the place in 1949. However, Ronnie then bought Tickeridge Mill, an old water-mill near Blackboys, where Vivien Leigh was subsequently to make her home and here Tony, undeterred, fixed up another dark-room, this time in an old brick-floored pantry.

At eighteen, Tony no longer winced when Carol fondly called him "Tone" and he could turn on the persuasive charm, which her sex were soon to find so beguiling. "What are you wearing tonight, Carol?" he would enquire artlessly, when they were going out. "But don't you think you would look nicer in the blue frock?" and Carol "invariably had to admit he was right", as she said, unaware of being tactfully handled. Eton had heightened Tony's good manners, his unsnobbish self-assurance and always quick-witted conversation. He had also acquired, as an accomplishment that was to serve him well in later life, the technique of secrecy. In his last year, he was coxswain to the Dreadnought eight and probably none of the oarsmen knew of the polio disability that sent him to a masseur twice a week.

Conscription for national service was still in force, and only Tony's closest intimates knew that the doctors had rejected him. He had always shared his father's zest for snipe-shooting and now the shooting parties at Plas Dinas involved the double challenge of walking and slithering across the bogs, up to his ankles in mud. When his leg muscles protested beyond endurance, he pretended to fall behind to take photographs and yet, as his stepmother ultimately testified, he "caught up gamely in the end and refused to admit either pain or defeat".

Tony passed his University Entrance examination and was

enrolled into Jesus College, Cambridge, on October 8th, 1949. There appear to have been last-minute family suggestions that he should study for a science degree but he was, after all, to read architecture. His composure was shaken, however, soon after he settled into his rooms in Chapel Court when he discovered that he and another friendly newcomer named David Bailey were the only freshmen reading architecture in all Jesus. The School of Architecture in Scroope Terrace proved, dismayingly, to be one of the smaller and less distinguished Cambridge buildings. Both undergrads joined the Society of Arts, but young Armstrong-Jones, was also an instant recruit for the Photographic Society, the Film Society and six or seven coffee-and-talk groups of more uncertain purpose. At Eton he had never been elected to "Pop", that bulwark of the flowered waistcoat trade, and at Cambridge he similarly never entered the socially exclusive Pitt Club—except later to take pictures—although he would have been highly eligible and welcome as an Old Etonian.

The Boat Club set its beguiling snares in his second term. Both he and David Bailey were rival lightweights for the Jesus first boat in the inter-college races but Armstrong-Jones was the Jesus cox in the Mays and at Henley. It has often been said that he joined the staff of the weekly undergraduate newspaper, *Varsity*, as a photographer, only to be "fired" after a few issues, but his name does not appear on the staff lists under the then editor, Trevor Philpott. He was not the Jones who secured such scoops as "Mrs. Harper taking part in the Pageant of Empire", nor was he the intrepid lensman who snapped Princess Margaret when she toured the Cambridge antique shops one January with the present Queen Mother. There is some indication that Tony began to think of himself as an architectural photographer, and his only traceable contribution to *Varsity* was in the October 22nd, 1949, issue with a photograph of some of the new buildings of Christ's College. By then, in his second year, his studies suffered the constant din of the building work outside the window of his lodgings in New Square, but Tony looked across at the cranes and scaffolding and readily took advantage of the easy, effective camera angle.

A new undergrad quarterly called *Panorama*, which first appeared in May, 1949, was also being edited by Daniel Farson, an American who had come to Cambridge under the G.I. Bill of Rights. Anthony West was co-editor, Anthony Blond figured on the "editorial board", Julian Slade contributed caricatures and Tony, though he has almost forgotten the magazine, seems to have contributed his stimulus in conversation.

Farson at all events shared his interest in photography and followed up an early lead to Cecil Beaton with transatlantic enthusiasm. When Tony first began day-dreaming of a photographic career, Uncle Oliver had always been responsive and encouraging but Tony found that Cecil Beaton, strangely enough, took an opposite view. To Dan Farson this seemed to have news value and a paragraph accordingly appeared in the first issue of *Panorama*, ". . . Beaton is probably best known for his photographs, especially those of the Royal Family, but ironically enough he has taken against photography. 'I am not as keen as I used to be,' he says 'and I don't recommend it as a career. It just takes you so far and no farther.' " If the fates have made Mr. Beaton appear wittily omniscient, the effect was curiously strengthened shortly afterward. Tony did not influence events but the next issue carried a full-page Cecil Beaton portrait of none other than Princess Margaret with "belated congratulations on her nineteenth birthday celebrated on August 21st. Her vivacity, a quality that is found all too seldom in the youth of today, has charmed Cambridge on her past visits."

Amid these diversions in the helter-skelter of Cambridge activities, Tony failed his first summer exams. He consoled himself that he could always pass next time, yet the siren call of the Cam was to prove irresistible. Early in 1950 he coxed the winning trial boat, and with his selection as cox to the Cambridge Boat Race crew, academic studies were irretrievably thrown to the wind. His twentieth birthday was keyed to the discipline of being up betimes to rouse the crew from their slumbers: no drinks and not as much as a visit to a cinema were permitted to curtail their training. Tony was both the youngest member of the boat and the only old Etonian. His weight at 120 pounds was two pounds heavier, it turned out, than his featherweight opposite on the Oxford side. At the boatyard, however, the little cox outshone them all with the initials A.C.R.O.L.A.J. for his full baptismal names and surname emblazoned across his sweater. A coxswain needs to assert himself; nerves tauten as the day of the race draws near and the oarsmen invariably vent their spleen on the ninth man.

The race the previous year had been rowed over the four miles 374 yards in a premature heatwave, and Cambridge had won by only a quarter of a length. The boat race of Lord Snowdon's year, the second to be televised, again saw the crews evenly matched, and the event aroused intense public interest. Oxford won the toss and chose the sheltered Surrey side and for more than two miles it was a neck-and-neck race, putting up the fastest timing known since the war. Then the increasing cross head-wind caused both craft to slow down until, nearing Chiswick Steps, a remarkable incident occurred. The oars of the rival crews touched for an instant, and bitter accents of vituperation were heard ringing across the water. Tony had found his craft being forced too near the bank. "I came out to shove him over a bit," he told a commentator afterwards. "We had a conversation." But after this hiatus Cambridge immediately drew ahead. Twenty minutes and fifteen seconds from the start, the crew heard Tony calling to them to "easy" and discovered they had won by three and a half lengths.

That evening, the crew celebrated at the Astor Club and took over the band as things warmed up, Tony on the cymbals. And then again, on returning to Cambridge, one faced the terrifying imminence of the exams, and the unpalatable discovery that a pass could not be gained without sufficient work. "Why don't you take a punt and work on the river?" Why not, indeed? Another preoccupation for Tony, moreover, lay in the marriage of his sister to John Vesey, the present sixth Viscount de Vesci. Not to distract her brother, Susan thoughtfully fixed her wedding-day for May 20th, a day or two after the strain of exams would be over.

This love-match was a union involving a tangle of family relationships which Tony enjoyed merrily propounding to his friends. His sister was marrying his mother's mother-in-law's nephew: was she thus marrying her uncle? The secret of the conundrum was that Lois, the Dowager Countess of Rosse, widow of the fifth Earl, had remarried in 1920, becoming the second wife of the fifth Viscount de Vesci when his nephew and ultimate heir, John Vesey, was only a year old ... and so Tony's step-grandmama is also his sister's aunt.

Tony was one of the Registrar's witnesses at the ceremony, and Ronald Armstrong-Jones gave his daughter away. The speeches at the wedding reception bubbled with jokes about "keeping it in the family" between the Rosse and de Vesci clans, and yet the wedding reception was in fact held at 104 Lancaster Gate, the last great family gathering at the town house that the Messels had known as their London home for nearly fifty years. In his seventy-ninth year, Tony's grandfather, old Colonel Messel, commiserated with him on the difficulties of exams, although the Cambridge results were mercifully still unknown. Perhaps grandmama Messel watched Tony flirting with Lady Barbara North, with whom he claimed to have been in love for years, daughter of the Lady North who had been his godmother. Barbara somewhat resembled Susan in her blonde good looks, but this was hardly a sufficient affinity and, in discerning old eyes, Tony was involved in a clear case of calf love. Sure enough, Barbara married Clive Bossom the following year, and Tony sealed his affection with a highly sentimental wedding photograph.

Tony's half-brothers were there, too, the eldest, Lord Oxmantown, being now in his first Half at Eton. Oliver Messel, also, came home for the wedding, bursting with theatrical news from Copenhagen and New York, where he had been working on the Pacific island scenes of *The Little Hut* and the French romantic décor of *Ring Around the Moon*. Uncle Oliver was the first to whom Tony entrusted the secret of his growing inclination not to be an architect but a photographer. "You must firmly make up your mind what you want to do," his uncle advised him, "and then do it with all your might."

II

Antony coxed the Cambridge Leander crew at Henley that summer and was considered for the future England crew at the Helsinki Olympic Games. He staged a summer holiday party at Tickeridge Mill for Leander, and was adding shelving to his dark-room in the old pantry when he learned that he had again failed his exams and would consequently be "sent down". Judging it wise to enlist his mother's support for his idea of becoming a photographer, he thought about it for days and then dispatched to Birr Castle one of the longest and most carefully worded letters of his life. Although Lord Snowdon does not consider that he materially followed the shining star of Cecil Beaton in shaping his future, I believe that he mentioned his photographic career to illustrate the summits of success that could be climbed. Apparently this all-important letter has long since disappeared but he has kept his mother's reply telegram ever since, "Do not agree suggestion changing career. Telephone this evening. Fondest love. Mummy."

The upshot of their conversation was that he should wait to discuss his future with Uncle Oliver and Michael (Lord Rosse) at Birr, but when Tony visited Ireland that August little progress was made. Though sympathetic, his mother's side of the family suggested that he would need to win his father's approval. Ronnie in turn was not at all sure that his son really knew what he wanted and there followed, according to Carol Coombe, "a terrible period of about three months when Tony didn't know what to do with himself and Ronnie didn't know what to do for him".

Mr. Armstrong-Jones sought out various friends—among them a wine merchant and the head of a tobacco firm—who might be able to offer a job in which a young man could start at the foot of the ladder. Enquiries were set afoot in a broker's office. Tony occasionally went to London for an interview, but rarely appeared a sufficiently eager candidate for a job to materialise. It might be mentioned that as a small sideline business venture at this time Ronnie and Carol had set up a small car-hire firm, Owen Lloyd (Hire Services) Ltd. which was carried on for several years, and in the registration documents Tony described himself as a salesman. But it was no more than a paper qualification and I know on good authority that he never went into the business.

Ronnie was content to give the boy his head, taking his time in choosing his career until, in one of their last discussions on the subject, he suggested he might be apprenticed to an architect's office. "You'll be wasting your money, Dad," Tony finally told him. "I don't want to work at something I'm not really interested in. I must be frank. I've been thinking all this time, and now I'm certain. I know this will be a shock to you, but all I want to be is a professional photographer." By this time, Ronnie had grown reconciled to the dismaying stubborn streak in his son, the reflection of his own qualities of concentration and determination. "We must see what we can do, then," he promised at last.

And from that moment—in November, 1950—he helped Tony in every way. The skies magically cleared and the difficulties dispersed. The Armstrong-Jones' then had what Ronnie liked to call "a set of chambers in Albany", that exclusive cloister off Piccadilly, and Ronnie cast an indulgent eye on his son's attempts to organise a dark-room in a cupboard of Flat E.5. Tony had the idea of taking and printing portrait photographs for people to use on their Christmas cards, but hardly knew where to begin. An actress friend of Carol's, Helena Pickard, first wife of Sir Cedric Hardwicke, came to tea one day and said charmingly that she thought his greeting cards a splendid suggestion. Better still, she gave him a sitting at her home, approved the result and ordered a hundred cards.

81

Tony made rapid calculations and pointed out that at three-and-sixpence each the cost would be more than £17. "Well," said Lady Hardwicke, comfortingly, "I shall need *at least* a hundred."

The delighted photographer was so raw and inexperienced that he bought all his materials retail and sat up all night, neatly pasting the prints into the white covers to deliver them on time to his client next day. Joan Morton, the actress, enquired if he could make *her cats* look Christmassy and then gave another, though smaller, order. The problem of finding a leading photographer who would be prepared to take Tony on as a pupil was also smoothly settled by the end of the year. The choice lay between Messel's close friend Beaton or the celebrated Baron. Tony knew little about the Royal Family, save his admitted admiration for Princess Margaret, but his prospects among the many eminent photographers who had not recently photographed royalty seem never to have entered his thoughts. Or was it that his father could think only of the two with whom he had some personal link? The difficulty with Beaton, who had known Tony from childhood, was that he had no orthodox studio. An Australian friend of Carol's knew Baron, on the other hand, and brought him along to Albany one evening for a drink.

An embarrassed and diffident Tony found himself displaying examples of his work, pictures that now looked all too amateurish in the master's hands, youthfully unaware that the charming Baron was assessing his personality and background with deep insight. Baron Nahum, to give his real name, mentioned that photography was a business one could enter without much capital and, given flair, without long training. He delicately alluded to his portraits of Prince Philip and his recent pictures of the christening of Princess Anne. (Little did anyone then realise that Antony Armstrong-Jones would privately take the christening pictures of the Queen's next child.) "When I began," said Baron, persuasively, "I couldn't find an outlet for creativeness because I lacked technical skill." Then he indicated gently that he had never before accepted a fee-paying student and would accept a premium of only five hundred guineas. Ronald Armstrong-Jones in turn could not know that money was never to be better spent.

The Baron studios were then in Brick Street, off Park Lane, almost facing the patch of shrubbery behind 145 Piccadilly where Princess Elizabeth and Princess Margaret had once played as children. They occupied a rambling red-brick former mews building, glamorised with blow-up portraits; the studio itself lush and pale-blue; with a hidden world of laboratory and development rooms, cluttered but efficient, beyond the pass-door. Any dream-pictures that Tony entertained of shortly entering Buckingham Palace as Baron's personal assistant were speedily dispelled in the routine of practical tuition. Tony found himself one of four young trainee assistants in an establishment of some thirty persons.

"You'll be trained in every studio duty," Mr. Newby, the production manager told him, "except typing and telephoning. You'll have to acquire a working knowledge of electrical equipment, as well as indexing and filing. You'll begin at the beginning, for one day you may have to cope with any emergency quite alone . . ." A photographer is a rugged individualist but Tony found himself a member of a team, with David Sim, Gerard Décaux and others. They were all inventive, irrepressible and yet dedicated. In the "spare studio" sessions, when the students took their own pictures, Tony is vividly remembered donning somebody else's too-small bowler hat, playing up quick poses till they became more and more comical. The boy who had once splashed water from his tree-house now helped another pupil to plunge a girl by surprise, fully clothed, into a tank of cold water to help the camera catch her outraged incredulity. Yet, despite the sky-larking, Mr. Newby and the studio director, Mr. Eyre, were good technicians and teachers and Tony learned everything he needed to know in the complex professional groundwork of the camera.

He gained, as Baron had promised, "a profound knowledge of film-loading, processing, mounting, trimming". He presently had his duty days in the studio when he was responsible for seeing that the equipment was in order, the lights in position and plugged in and everything in readiness, even to the flowers, before the arrival of the first sitter. Tony had blank spots when he would appear to go into a trance, a disability which overtook him one afternoon while cutting prints with a razor-edged knife in a guillotine frame when he nearly sliced off the top of a finger, and clinging frantically to his finger-tip, was rushed to St. George's Hospital, where six stitches in time happily averted permanent mutilation. At the wedding of Baron's own sister, all the photography was delegated to Tony, a critical illustration of Baron's own good opinion of him. As it happened, his pupil turned up twenty minutes late, loaded with cameras and equipment, but luckily the wedding was also delayed for other reasons and the pictures turned out well.

Probably he and Baron never realised that they shared some

coincidences of background. The Nahums emigrated to England and set up as cotton merchants in Manchester in the very year that the Messels first established themselves as bankers in London and, besides, like Ronnie Armstrong-Jones, Baron's own brother was a barrister. As a taskmaster Baron was temperamental but thorough, and generous in imparting trade secrets, although he could never really believe that his "young men" were future potential rivals. At the end of six months, however, he thought Tony sufficiently worth encouraging to be offered an extension of training, not as a fee-paying assistant but at a nominal salary.

Tony accepted on a part-time basis which left him free to under-take assignments of his own. He had studied Baron closely but, as his own master he at once faced the snubs and humiliation that so often come the way of the young. The Red Cross one evening gave him permission to cover a charity ball at Claridge's, where Tony knew that his father and stepmother would be seated at the top table with the principal guest, old Princess Marie Louise. "I think we both felt a little embarrassed at the sight of Tony moving around the hall in evening dress with his cameras slung from his neck," his stepmother related afterwards. But perhaps her most embarrassing moment was when Tony approached the top table and the head waiter intervened. "Young man," he said, "there are strict instructions that you are not on any account to photograph Her Royal Highness. She does not like it."

Under his father's sceptical eyes, Tony had no alternative but to accept the challenge. Disregarding the head waiter, he went directly to ask the Princess, turning on his charm. Ronnie saw her permissive smile, and Tony bowed and stepped back and clicked his camera, again and again, while the Princess beamed and nodded.

III

Tony celebrated his coming-of-age during his course with Baron, and his father observed the occasion by giving him a nominal flat of his own in Albany. In reality, this gift implied the tenancy of one of the guest suites or annexes available to Albany residents for occasional overnight hospitality, although this particular suite, on the mezzanine above the porter's lodge, had long since proved too cramped and awkward to offer the most uncritical guest. The commemorative plaques of Byron, Macaulay and earlier inhabitants endowed the broad stone approach staircase with a forbidding air and, opening off this, an enormous doorway gave on to an extremely small room, ill-lit by a semi-circular window at floor level.

Tony made the utmost of the cramped floor space by ingeniously arranging a folding bed in an alcove, and then busied himself with pots of paint, and installed a few pieces of junk furniture which the porters considered hardly worth carrying upstairs. He could never-theless now enjoy the sweets of bachelor freedom, taking a deb home to be photographed without first needing an okay from Carol. His stepmother noted that he was becoming "disturbingly attractive to women . . . such was his disarming charm that the most attractive girl at a party would invariably leave her escort and dance with him."

"He seemed to have an indescribably different style," said one partner, unaware that every dance triumphantly submerged the bit-ter memories of Liverpool. Many a young lady went on Tony's invitation to Albany "to be photographed", won over by his good manners, flattered by his grave interest, bewitched by his blue eyes and jutting lower lip, only to suffer disenchantment. The lights and cameras were always already set up, and romantic feminine hopes were dashed, for Tony really meant what he said: he really wanted only to take photographs.

He blacked out his small old-fashioned bathroom for use as a dark-room and faced the twice-daily chore of removing chemicals from the tub before he could take a bath. Glimpsing him, going out for the evening in the scarlet-lined cape he sometimes affected or escorting another young lovely up the stairs, the porters thought him "a one". As the youngest resident of the building, however, Tony satisfactorily passed the scrutiny of the oldest, the "squire of Albany", Mr. William Stone, who owned half the freeholds and took the stern moral view to be expected from his ninety-four years. Tony was very fond of the old man and listened to his advice on London restaurants without a quiver of the eye to suggest that some of the recommended establishments had closed their doors before the war.

It has been said that the low-level lighting effect of some of his earlier pictures was due to nothing more than the position of the floor-level window. This was a fault Tony turned into a virtue when he garbed one of Sir Douglas Fairbanks' daughters in a long white nightgown and gave her a lighted candle to hold, achieving a charming bedtime effect as she seemed to move from light into shadow. But the young photographer's spare-time clients were not numerous. Tony's extension with Baron had run for only a month or two when his fellow pupil, David Sim, also decided to set up business on his own. David was then in his mid-twenties, an equally camera-minded young man who, having begun a career in the Royal Navy, had battered in vain at the technical doors of the film industry and was one day to find his true metier when he married and developed a flair for designing and selling children's clothes. But now his enthusiasm was quickened by the discovery of a vacant basement which could be turned into a studio at 59 Shaftesbury Avenue, and Tony suggested they should join forces.

Tony's idea was a partnership on a basis which allotted Sim a percentage of Tony's future earnings, nebulous as they were, in return for use of the studio and materials, and in the late summer of 1951 the name-boards of David Sim and Antony Armstrong-Jones went up at the top of the steep basement stairs at 59, in the heart of London's theatreland, as David liked to claim.

It is a curiosity for sightseers that No. 59 still remains, an Edwardian office building halfway up the Soho side of Shaftesbury Avenue, and the photographic studio still occupies the basement. This was Tony's business H.Q. for nearly two years. The reception salon was under the pavement itself and he spent hours in a tiny converted coal cellar which he used as his dark-room. The motherly office char sometimes darned his socks, and in her shrewd London eyes, Mr. Armstrong-Jones was "one of the boys, always gentlemanly", a nice young man who did not have to work too hard, although she noticed that he faced difficulties at the end of the month when his allowance ran out and he had to make do. For her, in fact, the Armstrong-Jones saga reached its fairy-tale climax in 1966, when Andrew Grima, who had a workshop on the top floor, won the Queen's Award for his jewellery, and the news leaked out locally that the Earl of Snowdon would pay him a private visit. The bystanders gathered on the pavements of Shaftesbury Avenue. A policeman appeared and most of the office occupants of No. 59 mustered in the lobby, full of surmise about the royal limousine in which they expected Lord Snowdon to arrive. The char predicted to all and sundry that he would drive up in his nippy green Mini and she was right. To her delight, what was more, Lord Snowdon of course greeted her as a long-lost friend.

IV

Antony Armstrong-Jones' first acceptance in professional photographic journalism appeared in the *Tatler and Bystander* of September 19th, 1951, and the wildest joy assuredly swept young Tony's heart that Wednesday when he bought the magazine and found that he occupied the whole first page, with the credit "A. Armstrong-Jones" and the caption, "Cockle Hunting at Blakeney Point". The picture was totally untypical of the *Tatler*, a lone figure seen against a counterpoint of sand ripples left by the receding tide, but Baron had taught that one of the necessary ingredients of professional success was persistence and here was the triumphant proof. Baron had stressed, too, the vital need to study one's market, and Tony had obediently bought and studied a copy of the magazine a month earlier, only to find it splashed with photographs of Princess Margaret to commemorate her twenty-first birthday.

Sean Fielding, the editor, claimed to be particularly interested in "photographs of celebrities, taken in an unconventional way", and it was long Tony's favourite story that he first attempted to call in casually at the *Tatler* office only to be told by the commissionaire, "Run along, sonny, we don't buy snapshots here". David Sim, however, used his best line in sales talk to fix an appointment for Tony by phone, and Mr. Fielding soon discovered that an astonishing new star had arrived in his firmament, destined to enliven his pages for months to come. At that first interview he was to find Tony a spruce, engaging young man who produced a set of beautiful but wholly unsuitable photographs. As he did with all aspirants, the editor explained his requirements, his need of pictures of "interesting people doing interesting things" and his visitor surprisingly began chatting about his grandmother, who had just moved into her new home at Holmsted Manor. It suddenly dawned upon Fielding that this quick-talking youngster was Oliver Messel's nephew. "Well, if you could show me something ... perhaps concerned with Holmsted Manor and your uncle's latest work ... ? And meantime I will consider this Blakeney picture."

"Certainly," said Tony, suddenly right on his wave-length. "When would you like the photographs? By Monday ... ?"

And so Tony's first acceptance was followed only a week later by another Page One, this time of "Mrs. Messel photographed in her charming drawing-room ... looking at some pictures which her son, Oliver Messel, sent to her on her birthday recently." With its accessory tapestry and a gate-leg tea-table, the portrait more than fulfilled Fielding's highest hopes, and the following week even this was eclipsed by "The Countess of Rosse in the Gothic Saloon at

Birr Castle, looking at a photograph album with her son, Lord Oxmantown". No photographer had ever contributed a more graceful conversation piece. The same issue moreover carried a double-page spread of the "houseparty of young people at Birr", and here was "Lord Oxmantown trimming trees, David Tennant at cocktail time with Miss North, daughter of the Hon. John North" and so on, even to "the Countess of Rosse waving farewell to departing guests". It was a scoop enough, and only the most versed reader of society magazines could know that the credit line "A. Armstrong-Jones" was equally that of Mrs. Messel's grandson and of Lord Oxmantown's half-brother.

Having done her best to deter Tony when he first insisted on a photographic career, Lady Rosse was perfectly willing to press the launching button now that Tony's ship of destiny seemed ready to sail. Looking back, one cannot but admire her tact, dignity and restraint, for she agreed to help with the beginning but then, clearly, Tony was to be left to his own resources. With the next issue, of October 10th, the new *Tatler* contributor covered the party given by the Oliviers at Claridge's to welcome Jean-Louis Barrault, and his camera recorded the presence of Noel Coward, Terence Rattigan, Antony Asquith, Peter Brook, a beardless Peter Ustinov and Tony's own beaming Uncle Oliver, who had clearly tipped him off about the whole affair.

With the subsequent issue, the new young meteor had ascended to his own by-line, "by A. ARMSTRONG-JONES" in large letters and now, still learning fast, he was also contributing his own captions and script. "Four of us stayed with Lieut. General and Mrs. Percival for the weekend of the Puckeridge Hunt Ball. We arrived at Bullards—which used to be the old Bull Herd's House in the Middle Ages—on Friday evening in time to change, bath and have a cocktail . . ." And who should be in the foreground but Baron's own former publicity secretary, Mrs. Laurence Slingsby, in her prettiest Hartnell frock, "having a final cocktail with Miss Diana Crosland, Miss Dorinda Percival and Miss Delia Abel-Smith"? Fatuous as it may seem in retrospect, this was exactly what the editor of the *Tatler* wanted, and what Tony unerringly supplied, fully professional overnight. The same issue, indeed, carried two of his "photo stories". To turn the pages is irresistible, and here is a Wauchope cousin at Hugh Warrender's wedding, a "double-spread" already oddly vibrant with inklings of the future. For the best man is none other than Anthony Berry, of the *Sunday Times* family, and Tony's view-finder had turned also on an Eton friend, Dominic Elliot, son of the Earl of Minto, who already figured in "the Princess Margaret set".

Curiously, too, even before the momentous interview with Sean Fielding, one finds that Tony had himself appeared in the *Tatler*, now at a 21st birthday party, then at a wedding reception, photographed by the usual society cameramen. Tony's photograph of the Duke of Kent in 1956 is widely supposed to have been his first essay in royal portraiture, but in point of fact he rivalled Baron in the New Year of 1952 with a full-page portrait of Princess Georg of Denmark, the former Viscountess Anson, a Bowes-Lyon niece of the present Queen Mother, whose romantic marriage was then much in the news. Tony had submitted his "conversation piece" portrait of his mother by way of credentials, and Princess Georg gave him a sitting at her London home.

But by this time the fast-moving Tony was no longer in London to see this first royal study of his in print. His professional fortunes had improved so rapidly that he was enjoying a journalistic holiday at Funchal, photographing the celebrities at Reid's Hotel. From this lone holiday, he returned in time to photograph the members of the Cambridge University Food and Wine Club disporting in periwigs and eighteenth-century costume for their annual dinner at Trinity. Then, using Birr Castle as his base, he created a double-page on "Woodcock Shooting in Galway—by A. Armstrong-Jones, who also took the pictures . . . The sun had disappeared behind the mountains of Connemara on the Sunday I arrived at Castle McGarret for the famous Cong Woodcock Shoot which Lord Oranmore and Browne has recently syndicated. Next morning after an early breakfast we set out, and stayed out shooting until dusk . . ."

It scarcely mattered to the reader that Tony's shooting was chiefly by camera, although it mattered intensely to Tony that he was often off target. He found it particularly dismaying to face a constant flow of rejection slips from *Picture Post*. His hopes were particularly dashed with a set of photographs of the Cambridge boatrace crew, practising on the Cam, watching their weights, discussing the race, a photographic feature evidently refused by Hulton's although the *Tatler* still lapped it up. Tony attempted a colour picture of a swan for the cover of *Country Life* magazine, and still it was the *Tatler* that published, this time with a suspicious credit to "Armstrong Roberts".

89

V

If it becomes noticeable that young Armstrong-Jones turned his camera chiefly on his friends, this was only natural. It was easier to photograph his old Eton confrére, Anthony Tennant, at a first night than risk a rebuff from a total stranger. Anthony Tennant and blonde Camilla Grinling, daughter of Geoffrey Grinling, the Sussex artist, readily enjoyed a country spin, at Tony's suggestion, to be photographed at a Cambridgeshire point-to-point. In 1954, when Camilla married Jeremy Fry (who was subsequently invited to be Tony's best man) Tony was at their wedding as both photographer and guest; and Anthony Tennant, Dominic Elwes and other close friends needed no coercing to help create the resulting double-page spread.

Lord Herbert, an old family friend of Oliver Messel's generation as well as an intimate of the Duke of Kent's family, heard about Tony's budding career and helpfully suggested he should bring his camera to a weekend at Wilton. Oliver Messel asked Tony to photograph his Spanish costume party, and Cecil Beaton agreed to sit for a portrait. There were indeed some al fresco pictures in Beaton's London garden but they never came out. Lord Oranmore and Browne was so pleased with his "Woodcock" pictures that he asked Tony to photograph his daughter Pat's wedding to Anthony Cayzer. Tony produced a beautiful and thoroughly original set, from pictures of the bride trying on her wedding-gown to the departure of the happy couple in the bridegroom's private plane. Two years later, as a sequel, young Mrs. Cayzer wrote to Tony when she, too, wished to have portraits taken at her Cheshire home.

That was how it went. Tony's social photography was part of the very texture of his social background. He worked assiduously at the ever-flowing stream of commissions, chasing every butterfly idea until securely netted in his negatives, but he believed in playing hard, too. He was one of a group of young people who would sometimes dance out the night at Ciro's Club: young men with lush apartments in Eaton Square; married couples—such as Sir Hugo and Lady Deirdre Sebright—who were just setting up house in Belgravia mews cottages; girls like Camilla Grinling and Fleur Kirwan-Taylor, who shared a flat in Chelsea. There was "the other Tony", Viscount Furness; Sally Churchill, Sir Winston's great-niece; Davina Portman, Viscount Portman's niece; Viscount Pollington, heir of the Earl of Mexborough and thus a kinsman of the Brabournes, and David Hicks, who later married Lady Pamela Mountbatten. (May one detect that the fates were again already drawing the threads of Mountbattens and Messels closer together?)

They might have been called a way-in or swinging crowd, save that these terms had not been invented. Behind the outer skin of irresponsibility, they mostly had their daytime jobs or worked hard at their chosen careers. When they foregathered for relaxation none could tell what practical jokes or larks might ensue. There was the time when Tony was flung into a goldfish pool in white tie and tails. "I had no idea the pool was so muddy," cried his hostess, as he emerged, squelching slime. "Neither did I," said Tony, as he carelessly spattered mud upon the white shirt-fronts of his adversaries.

The manager of the Carousel, a club that insisted on formality, has related how Tony and a group of young men, dressed to shock in sports clothes with open-neck shirts, attempted to defy the dress regulations one night and stormed the club en masse. They successfully passed the first doorman but found the inner lobby manned by an ex-Guardsman and an ex-boxer, and were repulsed. At a mews party, where everyone was supposed to dress up as a Piccadilly character, one or two genuine street musicians and kerb vendors were imported for effect. Among these, was a hook-nosed old woman who made rather a nuisance of herself selling flowers to the guests . . . until her nose became dislodged, revealing Tony.

At Ciro's, another evening, Tony is said to have announced his engagement to Tanya Star-Busman, the redhead daughter of a Dutch diplomat, and was jubilantly carried shoulder-high round the room amid the cheering and singing throng. But it was no more than a make-believe prank, so light-hearted that Lord Snowdon can no longer recollect the incident, although he was very friendly with both the Star-Busman sisters and their parents, and in the summer of Coronation Year stayed with them in Vienna where Dr. Star-Busman was the Netherlands Ambassador.

In the early spate of newspaper "disclosures" about Lord Snowdon, an alleged intimate once attempted to list the girls he had dated: Anrobin Banks, who later worked in his studio; Sally Wilson, the tall blonde fashion model; Greta Watson, who understudied Vivien Leigh in *The Sleeping Princess* and so on. Carol Coombe noted that Tony in those days "had a turnover in new girl friends" of about two a month. "Don't you think she's pretty good? Isn't she fascinating?" he would say, occasionally bringing a new one home for inspection. His smile, however, was more often droll and mischievous, and he remained detached and heart-whole.

James Norbury recalls an evening in Chelsea when Tony talked enthusiastically of photography: the interest of getting character, mood, the essential person, on to a print. He was drifting away from the inanities of social photography to the more mature interest of portraying personalities of wider distinction and fame. "Whom would you like to photograph most of all?" his confidant chanced to ask.

Tony gravely considered the question for a moment. "Why, Princess Margaret, of course. I think she is the most vivacious person in the world!"

6 *Divertissement in Pimlico*

I

On Coronation Day in 1953 the Countess of Rosse sat among the peeresses in Westminster Abbey, never more beautiful than in her robe of crimson velvet, "bordered with the cream of ermine ... sprinkled with the sugar of diamonds", as Norman Hartnell said. The royal processions began: the Princess Royal, the Duchess of Gloucester, the then Duchess of Kent and Princess Alexandra, all of whom were personally known to the Countess. Then Princess Margaret slowly approached along the blue carpet, "like a snowdrop adrift from its stem", surrounded by the six Heralds of Somerset, Windsor, Richmond, York, Chester and Lancaster in their medieval costumes and, as they came nearer, a shaft of sunlight suddenly broke through the lofty stained glass windows and splashed the passing group in silvery light. Lady Rosse vividly remembered the moment, and never dreamed that within seven years her eldest son would walk down the same aisle, with Princess Margaret as his bride.

In piquant contrast, only a day or two earlier, Lady Rosse had driven round to her son's new studio at 20 Pimlico Road to be privately photographed in her own embroidered gown for what was to be one of her most treasured family portraits. It was a journey of scarcely a minute or two in the car from 25 Eaton Terrace, down to the bottom of that calm and self-assured thoroughfare, turning right into Ebury Street and right again past the little everyday provision shops to Tony's grey door and discreetly curtained windows ... but what a difference! The studio occupied a former ironmongery or hardware shop next door to the Sunlight Laundry ... and yet, stepping inside, the Countess of Rosse discovered that Tony had created his own atmosphere, with gilded lamps and framed prints of Audubon birds, a striped Regency wallpaper and a papered ceiling patterned with pale ivy, reminiscent of the first setting that her brother Oliver had created for himself nearly thirty years earlier.

Tony had tired of Soho within eighteen months, and the end of his beginner's phase coincides with a decline in his more trivial contributions to the *Tatler*. Impatient for the next step, he had dashed about in his little Fiat car, searching for new quarters, ceaselessly pursuing every wisp of rumour of anything remotely suitable, until his father finally came to the rescue with news of the disused ironmongery premises. Among his other interests, Ronald Armstrong-Jones had become a director of Greencoat Properties, a company controlling and proposing gradually to improve Coleshill Buildings, a group of weekly-rental flats in the Pimlico Road. No doubt the Buildings had originated in profit-making-Victorian philanthropy of the Peabody type, and the shops underneath were, in fact, still administered by the Improved Industrial Dwellings Co.

Once he had cleaned the years of grime from his back-window, Tony looked upon a courtyard and walk where the improved industrial dwellers occasionally exercised their cats; and the local inhabitants for their part observed with astonishment that the newcomer whitewashed the patch of wall of his small backyard and arranged potted plants and a stone Cupid behind a park bench.

At first, Tony occupied only the ground floor, where the old shop formed the studio, with a small dark-room and sitting-room at the rear. Possession of the basement was to come later, and he still lived in Albany. But No. 20 was entirely a place of his own, a demi-paradise. A Cambridge friend, Robert Erskine, painted a fashionable Beatonesque backcloth of Grecian columns for his portraiture, while Tony turned his own practical skill to designing and making the graceful semi-circular fanlight of the Georgian doorway, a contribution to the townscape which still enhances the Pimlico Road. In the sitting-room, too, he presently completed the main fitment which has been described all too often; the built-in wardrobe with bookshelves at one end that also served as steps by which one mounted to the bunk at the top. At Stream House, long ago, an alert small boy had hauled sweets to his sleeping bunk, and now Tony's ceiling-high bunk at No. 20 was equipped with the luxuries of a fitted radio and sun-ray lamps beneath which friends occasionally basked when Tony was busy elsewhere.

94

In those days, seven years before the Casa Pupo began an even greater transformation of a rival ironmongery establishment a few doors away, Tony was the first innovator in a district now cluttered with antique shops. Absorbed in his painting and carpentry, he forgot 59 Shaftesbury Avenue so completely that the powers-that-be became alarmed and seized his cameras there, locking them up in a cupboard, while magazine cheques waited uncashed in a drawer because Tony could not be bothered to pay them into his bank.

The young photographer was, indeed, so unbusinesslike that his father supervised the details of founding "Armstrong-Jones Ltd." as a company, with £750 as controlling share capital for Tony and £250-worth for himself. Tony's flair for total immersion in one interest at a time may explain the debacle of the Golden Cage ball at the Dorchester. Tony photographed the guests with their heads in a gilded cage, inviting his sitters to contribute whatever they wished to the evening's charity, and he thus collected a great deal of money and then tragically lost his reels of film. Frantic with remorse, he ransacked the Dorchester, searched his car inside and out, and repeatedly telephoned friends and even taxi-shelters, but the films were never found. "Fortunately everyone took it very well," Tony said, "and they never asked for their money back."

His father persuaded him that he could not possibly be in business single-handed but would need a full-time secretary. He took on a suitably "debby" girl who discovered that her first duties were to cook sausage-and-mash on his single gas-ring and drive his Fiat car. Although Tony explained he had sprained his ankle, one suspects that the fatigue of the renovations had not improved his lame leg. Hobbling about, temperamentally subject to alternating moods of elation and depression, as one assistant has said, "Tony would often get excited and say things he didn't mean", and one secretary succeeded another. At an early stage, however, he was joined by "Anrobin" Banks, daughter of a retired R.A.F. commodore, who served him devotedly for several years and succeeded in "systematising" him surprisingly well.

II

Though unfinished, the studio was inaugurated shortly before Christmas, 1952, with a dinner-party for twenty-two people, among them Clarissa Chaplin and Sally Churchill, David and Anthony Tennant, Gina North, Dominic Elwes, Davina Portman, Mary

Williamson and Robert Erskine. Instead of place cards Tony used photographs of his guests, pictures they had never seen before, a novel idea to set the ball rolling. A young man in Spanish costume strummed a guitar; the table was decorated with out-of-season lilac as if from the sunny south and, later on, a cabaret of Spanish players entertained the company with castanets and flamenco. Tony was deliberately courting good omens for, some six months earlier, his Uncle Oliver had held a genuine flamenco party with six imported dancers, and Tony had photographed it and at last entered the pages of *Picture Post*. At his own party, a guest recalls, the only hiatus occurred when the first course of melon was finished, the plates were collected and the twenty-two-year-old host unaccountably disappeared. Everyone enjoyed conversing by candle-light but the delay was prolonged. Camilla Grinling was roasting the turkey in her own Chelsea kitchen, and the bird and accompaniments had to be rushed through the streets.

The subsequent réclame of a more formal opening, with cocktails, brought in a dribble of clients though not the newspaper publicity for which Tony had hoped. In Coronation year he accomplished his move from Albany by gradually transferring his goods and chattels by Fiat, but friends knew he had truly moved into No. 20 when they noticed his most precious mascot, the polished rudder of the 1950 Cambridge boat, on the studio wall. Now he once again attempted to capture *Picture Post* with a set of candid camera photographs of the beginning of term at Eton. Instead, the *Tatler* published yet again, and the unforeseen sequel deeply dismayed him. The embarrassed farewells with parents, the nervousness of new lower boys, the departure of gleaming limousines and lugging of shabby baggage, were all recorded; and for the scene of a boy unpacking in his room Tony had penetrated the lair of his younger half-brother, Martin Parsons.

Unhappily, the Eton feature had no sooner appeared than it brought a rocket. The headmaster, Mr. Robert Birley, sternly pointed out that the photographs should not have been taken without permission. "I understand you are the photographer concerned," Mr. Birley wrote to the offender, "And as one of the pictures was of your half-brother, I take it that my information was correct . . . I think you should know that I am writing to the parents of the boys whose photographs appeared with their names to let them know that this was done without my knowledge."

Tony had innocently fallen into one of the pitfalls that ambush all

At six months, with his mother and sister, a study by Yevonde

Christmas at Birr, 1938, with his sister, Susan, his mother and young half-brother, Lord Oxmantown

Birr Castle

Father and son at Tickeridge Mill, 1949

Autographs and cameramen—the Boat Race, 1950

The Rotherhithe room, from the painting by Marian Mowka which hangs in Lord Snowdon's study

The studio in Pimlico Road

At the gala performance at Covent Garden Opera House, March, 1960—the first public appearance of the betrothed couple

On the balcony of Buckingham Palace on their wedding day

ASSOCIATED I

Top table, Brussels, 1967

Top table, New York, 1965

CENTRAL I

Appreciative guests of honour, Uganda, 1965

British Week celebrations in Copenhagen, 1964

British Week celebrations in Amsterdam, 1965

Hong Kong, 1966—visiting a housing estate in Kowloon

CAMERA I

With film and sound equipment, Lord Snowdon in his study in Kensington Palace, photographed by Cecil Beaton

With President and Mrs. Lyndon Johnson at the White House

Filming "Don't Count the Candles" with Derek Hart, 1968

Lord Snowdon and his family: Lady Sarah Armstrong-Jones, Princess Margaret and Viscount Linley

Fleet Street photographers but the rebuke depressed him for weeks. Painstaking and rarely content with his best, he sometimes embalmed letters that upset him in an album he still keeps at Kensington Palace. An indignant mother complained that her daughter's wedding pictures were "awful". Another mother expressed herself as "bitterly disappointed" in her daughter's portrait. "But you should have seen the girl—and the mother!" Tony once said, brightening as he told this cautionary tale.

An early problem at the studio was that he had to wait months for a telephone. Regardless of the difficulty of arranging appointments for sittings by letter or even the hazards of climbing into a friend's empty flat to use his 'phone, as Tony did on one occasion, the Post Office implacably observed fairness in its waiting-list of subscribers. When a line was at last connected, in the late summer of 1953, Tony decided to make a chaste announcement in the personal columns of *The Times*: "Mr. Antony Armstrong-Jones has just opened a new photographic studio at 20 Pimlico Road, S.W.1. Tel. SLO 5324". By happy chance, the advertisement coincided with the publication of two or three Armstrong-Jones portraits in the society magazines, and debutantes flocked to his elegant door.

Money was no object in the eagerness of these young things to achieve the social éclat of having their portraits published on a Page One. Tony never made promises, but his credit-line underneath a magazine photograph week by week was an unmistakable lure. Until this moment, his secretary had helped him cope with the endless processing chores in the dark-room but Tony now clearly needed a full-time assistant. Characteristically, instead of selecting one from the host of giggly young acquaintances who would have leapt at the opportunity of working with him, he rang up the local labour exhange and they sent along a lanky fifteen-year-old youngster straight from school who had registered as a would-be trainee-photographer.

"These are some photos I've taken," he said, shyly producing some family snapshots.

"They're not photos but photographs," Tony told him, by way of a first lesson. "Good! Can you start at ten o'clock tomorrow?"

Not long after Christmas, however, the boom of Coronation year collapsed. The young clientele made a mass exodus to winter sports and by mid-February Tony and his assistant, Keith Croft, found themselves with time on their hands. For the first time in his career Tony decided that he needed newspaper publicity, something that would make the gossip columns and bring in new clients. His twenty-fourth birthday provided the opportunity and whether by chance or on his Uncle Oliver's advice he hit on the idea of the notorious baby party of the 1920s when the Prince of Wales and the Duke of Kent had arrived dressed as little boys. Tony's guests were invited to come dressed as they would have been at his christening. Rather than duplicate the atmosphere of the Temple Church, the studio was festively decked as a French café, and the crowning moment came when the birthday boy, wearing baby white and blue, with bib and dummy, was wheeled in, in a pram, by none other than Nanny Gunner.

Tony's father strongly expressed his disapproval, but the publicity had its intended effect, and business flowed in again. The difficulty, as young Keith Croft noted, was that the deb clients were "all much of a type". Tony grew tired of his stereotyped sitter's chair, with its curving arm. He draped yards of cellophane or white tulle around sitters and background, utilised fishing-net and flowers and bamboo canes, trained his camera from the heights of a step-ladder and sometimes had Keith simultaneously puffing at three cigarettes to produce a mystical fog. These novelties, implemented by Oliver Messel's unceasing recommendation, produced a dribble of concert and theatrical clients: Eileen Joyce, the pianist, tall Cy Grant, the guitar singer, Joyce Grenfell, Anna Massey and Sir Alec Guinness.

Whenever business slackened, Uncle Oliver invariably seemed to have an uncanny knack of detecting the lull; and at these times he always urgently needed Tony to rush to Pelham Place to photograph his stage sets, his models for *The Barber of Seville* at Glyndebourne or his decorations for a gala performance for the King of Sweden at Covent Garden. Among his friends, Lord Snowdon has never ceased to acknowledge the immense debt he owes to his uncle's understanding, constant encouragement and practical help. In 1954 Oliver Messel especially awakened Tony to all the possibilities of the stage, from portraiture of the stars to the publicity photographs of a production displayed outside the theatre. This was an attractive sideline that Tony particularly longed to conquer, and he discussed it with such enthusiasm at Pelham Place one evening that Uncle Oliver grew thoughtful.

A few days later, an invitation arrived from Peter Glenville, the producer, to photograph the scenes of the new Terence Rattigan play *Separate Tables* during its try-out at Newcastle, and Tony was overjoyed. "This is either the beginning of the beginning or the beginning of the end," he excitedly told his assistants. A photo call, with the scenes set and the players in stage clothes, is always a long and arduous chore; and Margaret Leighton and Eric Portman, who were playing the leads, both considered they had never faced a young cameraman at once so self-assured and yet demanding. "Tony worked like fury all day, even when everyone else was finally exhausted," Keith Croft recalled afterwards.

Mr. Glenville had prudently stipulated that Tony was only on trial, and the stills used would in any case be charged at not more than 25s. each, but Margaret Leighton thought them "terrific" and the set embellished the front of the St. James's Theatre throughout the run. The house photographs for the productions of *Hotel Paradiso*, *The Desperate Hours*, *Tea and Sympathy* and *Family Reunion* and the stills for the film *A View From the Bridge* all followed in due order.

III

When old Colonel Messel died in February, 1953, Tony already knew that his grandfather had left Nymans to the National Trust, with provisions to permit a family tenancy of certain cottages on the estate and of the wing of the old house left undamaged in the fire. The matter had been discussed in front of him with the utmost candour but the irrevocable passage of events made him realise how dearly he had loved the place. During the summer he photographed the garden from every vantage point—the gazebo, the pergola clouded with wistaria, the borders and topiary—anxious for his camera to give him some souvenirs and unaware how jealously the new custodians would guard every tree in the grounds. A moral might be drawn from the fundamental change in the status of Nymans at the very moment when the grandson of the house was establishing himself in Pimlico. But a more crucial change of scene was to come his way in the summer of 1954 when Tony literally went through the floor at 20 Pimlico Road.

The basement store beneath the studio at last fell vacant and Tony took possession of that dingy grimy L-shaped cellar, little knowing how close he was to the royal friendship and the ensuing love affair that was to invest the place with world celebrity. Having knocked a hole through the floor near his wardrobe-bunk and lowered a ladder into the depths, his first act as proprietor was to photograph the abyss for a set of "before" and "after" photographs.

Friends looking at those pictures a few months later could scarcely believe the contrast. Instead of the mouldering cellar walls, Tony created an all-white sitting-room, a bedroom with violet coloured wallpaper and a kitchen-dinette embellished with a bamboo wallpaper to echo the delicate bamboo chairs. There were soft candelabra wall-lights, a Regency mirror to double space a stripped pinewood console, and a marble-stemmed lamp of Empire style. Two gratings that had formerly disclosed the hurrying legs and feet of passers-by were now veiled clerestory windows, patterned with passing shadows. And destined to be best-known of all was the spiral staircase, with gleaming wooden treads around a central pillar of polished copper which Tony had cleverly fabricated from copper plumbing.

It became Tony's habit to take promising sitters down this stairway, an amusing and surprising novelty so that they forgot their tensions completely and presently faced the camera relaxed and unguarded. His dinner-parties similarly became casually easy and pleasant affairs around the little round table. His friends not only admired his flat but paid young Tony the genuine compliment of consulting him on matters of good taste. A girl whom he had first met at Baron's discovered, on the eve of her marriage, a splendid four-poster in an antique shop in Sloane Street but cautiously refused to purchase this matrimonial bed until she had taken Tony along to vet and approve it.

Tony in turn, as his friend Stella King has noted, incessantly sought "other people's opinions whether on his wallpaper, his car or even his backyard carpentry", though he was apt to brood over an unenthusiastic or adverse viewpoint until able to convince himself that his critic was wrong. Even in those days the irrepressible jaunty extrovert Dr. Jekyll had a lone wolf Mr. Hyde in his character with a deep need of tranquillity and seclusion. The sociable friends who saw the flat in gay party mood, when they all chatted away about cars "going like crazy", movies one was "mad about" or "super" vacation spots . . . the sociable probably never imagined the hours and even weekends Tony spent there quite alone. The basement then became a monastic retreat, enclosed and shut away from the world, the faint tremor of passing traffic itself emphasising the silence. One of the few intimate friends of this time who understood Tony's need of solitude was Jacqueline Chan, the actress, and her pastel portrait by Oliver Messel presently hung in a place of honour over the mantelshelf in the little upstairs sitting-room. And

one of the few intruders in his sanctuary was the telephone, growing more insistent as his success became definitive.

As early as 1955, Tony was beginning to think of somewhere
where he could get away for a day or a weekend, not as far as Birr,
a Shangri-la beyond the horizon of the Pimlico house-tops, metropolitan yet peaceful, romantic and yet close at hand. His search
presently concentrated on the river, and the mysterious downstream
regions of Wapping, Greenwich and the Isle of Dogs. A pleasant
summer evening would be the signal for yet another jaunt of
exploration into the East End in the Morris 1000 that had now
replaced the Fiat. His companions were such close friends as Roger
Gilliat, a young doctor whom he had met a year or two earlier, or
Dominic Elwes, or Jacqui Chan. His Cambridge friend, Dan
Farson, happened to be engaged at the same time on a similar
house-hunt and from time to time they compared notes: on a flat
above a Limehouse barge yard, on the streets that bordered the
river around the Surrey Commercial Docks and on still more
remote regions that his stepfather's friend, John Betjeman, had
recommended as possible hunting grounds.

Tony loved the streets of London and when a prospect for
fashion photography came his way, he found the ever-necessary
freshness by posing his models by night under the street-lamps of
Piccadilly. For another original ploy he rounded up some of the
best of his debutante sitters and persuaded them to model haute
couture clothes against shabby industrial backgrounds in the East
End. "Is it fresh? Is it original?" editors would say. He took
models slipping on banana-skins and haughty ladies, who obviously
owned the earth, were shown peering hungrily into empty shop-
windows. At a risk of life and limb he posed a model in a summer
frock high in the branches of a wintry fir tree and another perfectly
groomed lady was seen steeped to the neck in a transparent water-
tank. With sample sets of his fashion photographs, Tony sought—
and sometimes obtained—commissions from wholesale manufacturers but the work was usually very much on a freelance "on
approval" basis. One of Tony's advantages over other photographers was his readiness often to back his own ideas regardless of
expense. The studio sittings were grist to the mill but the cost of
"magazine assignments", as young Tony sometimes termed the
tasks he had set himself, not infrequently outran the fees that
editors paid.

A typical instance occurred when the opening of the State Opera

House in Vienna was announced for the autumn of 1955 after nearly ten years of rebuilding. Tony convinced himself that back-stage photographs of the leading singers rehearsing for this great occasion would be a major magazine scoop, and pictures of the opening night, he was naively sure, would be a certainty for *Life* or *Look*. Reassuring reply cables across the Atlantic probably height-ened his optimism. His sole concession to economy on the project was to stay with his old friends, the Star-Busmans, at the Netherlands Embassy on the Ringstrasse, regardless that the extravagant flowers he sent to his hostess probably cost far more than a hotel bill. Unluckily, in his enthusiasm, he had overlooked a prime essential. The press passes for foreign photographers were strictly rationed and he failed to persuade anyone that he qualified.

He was summarily denied admission at the stage door and ejected from the front of the house, but then Tony bought a bouquet of yellow roses at a nearby florist's, and ordered them to be sent at once to the leading soprano, Sena Jurinac. By dint of walking in the wake of the flowers, he managed to reach the wings and was again on the point of being thrown out when he shouted to the *diva*, "I'm the man who sent the roses!" She received him, the watchdogs retreated and Tony's camera was given freedom at both the rehear-sals and premiere. Unluckily the major publications scorned the fruit of all this effort and expense. The pictures were eventually sold to Lord Harewood's magazine *Opera* for two or three guineas.

On the other hand, Tony took his cameras almost as an after-thought that same year on a winter sports holiday in Davos and earned almost enough to pay for the trip. In Switzerland, Austria, France and Italy, the earning power of his camera helped to fill his vacuum of travel. His wartime childhood had deprived him of the normal experience of holidays abroad and, indeed, Tony was seven-teen before he first crossed the Channel for a family holiday in Porto Fino. Now the whole world was becoming his photo-album, especially in 1956—his year of fate in so many ways—when he made a New Year resolution to stage a frontal attack upon the glossy pages of *Vogue*.

IV

A year or so previously Tony had produced a Victorian family group as a Christmas card, with the stern Papa in stovepipe trousers and muttonchop whiskers, the Mama in high-necked lace, and their ungainly child in a sailor-suit and large straw hat . . . and in reality all three were Tony in comic disguise. It was a skilful example of multiple exposure, and yet one of his closest friends felt that the card reflected an inner truth, for Tony has always managed to appear remarkably different to different people.

To Marlene Dietrich, when she made her cabaret appearance in the West End, he appeared a handsome but helpless public school type who did not know how to touch up her photograph until she said, "I will tell you how to do it, dear boy . . ." Her impresario, Major Neville-Willing, claims that Tony made him feel like a benevolent uncle: a discreet young man who showed him some shots of Marlene taken by telephoto lens during the show and pleaded, "These are simply not good enough. Please may I not have a private sitting? I promise I won't upset her." When the Press clamoured for the resulting pictures of the actress, in top hat and white tie, the impresario also admired Tony's skilful diplomacy. "I wouldn't want to trespass on Miss Dietrich's hospitality," he said, playing it cool, before giving way with every show of reluctance.

To Bert Swaebe, the veteran Society photographer, Tony seemed a complete professional, whom he occasionally met in Fleet Street "on his way to sell more pictures and who at an early stage believed in personal contact with editors". One day, when Swaebe had been lunching with the picture editor of the *Daily Express*, Frank Spooner, they both bumped into Tony, who thereupon made one of his characteristic gambits. "I'd like to take some pictures of you, Pop. Come down to the studio sometime." Spooner thought that the pictures could be used in the *Express* as a tribute from one photographer to another, and so through Swaebe's keen eyes we see Tony as seen by his sitters "searching around in his mind for new angles . . . He looked at me thoughtfully and then seemed to go into a trance . . ." Though Swaebe was then in his eighty-third year, Tony persuasively argued that a picture of him falling backwards through a paper screen would have irresistible news appeal and the picture of Swaebe tumbling "through the hoop" duly made the grade.

To Mark Boxer, who had known Tony from Cambridge days, he was a type who had escaped from convention and never wore an Old Etonian tie, all of whose abilities "his quickness, his sensitivity, his wit, his cheek, his sense of timing, his inquisitive interest in people" were making him one of the most original of English photographers. The then art editor of the *Sunday Times*, Mr. H. J.

Deverson, once wrote "The likeable thing about Armstrong-Jones is his quite uncalled-for modesty about his own work". With no inkling that Tony would ever join the staff, Deverson sometimes sat in the Pimlico studio surrounded by pictures while their originator anxiously enquired, "Do you think they'll do? Should this one have been cropped differently? Can you see *why* I photographed her this way?"

Actors and actresses, copy writers, theatre critics, publicists, artists, dancers, interior decorators—including David Hicks—now swirled around Tony. For fun, and a little for flattery, he asked them imperishably to autograph a mirror with a diamond stylus. For amusement they often descended upon him for breakfast, talking until put to flight by the brooms and dusters of his char, Mrs. Peabody. If talk often took up too much of Tony's day, he worked into the small hours to compensate. If a late night or a particularly trying session caused him to be temperamental with his secretary, he would signal his contrition with a huge box of chocolates, as well as apologies, or sweep her out to a special lunch. In those days, it hardly mattered to Tony if a secretary could not type as long as she was what he called "a super-person".

One doubts whether Tony ever fired a secretary. Anrobin Banks never found her job too demanding; and the resourceful Dorothy Everard who was with him during the later Pimlico phase is still Lord Snowdon's secretary today at Kensington Palace. Perhaps fluffier girls left because they found him too hard a taskmaster. Stella King has noted that, like his camera, Tony seemed to have the gift of reflecting the personality of whoever he was concerned with at a particular moment. Tommy Steele thought him as friendly a character as anyone in Camden Town and, incidentally, Tony to him was the only cameraman who ever edged out of the wings on to the stage during a performance in his anxiety to get the right shot. Later on, when Tony was photographing such celebrities as Somerset Maugham, Sir Ralph Vaughan-Williams and Sir Bertrand Russell, he confessed that he found the best way to make his sitters unbend was to appear "terribly embarrassed" . . . so that they lost their embarrassment in putting him at his ease.

And Jacqui Chan . . . what did the tiny Jacqueline Chan see with her dark almond eyes? She at first saw in Tony a photographer, like her father. She saw an air of mystery that he liked to create about himself, mirroring her own Oriental inscrutability. To her embarrassment, Jacqui Chan—now Mrs. David Salomon—was much in the news at the time of Tony's engagement, perhaps because she loyally refused to discuss her friendship, and so heightened hungry public speculation. The newspapers dug out photographs of Tony greeting her with an enthusiastic hug at London Airport, an affectionate greeting that inevitably looked more significant in Cardiff or Harrogate than in the theatrical artistic West End world where gestures were invariably exaggerated beyond life size.

Jacqui was in fact only eighteen when she first met Tony in 1954, while appearing in *Teahouse of the August Moon*. Born in Trinidad, the daughter of a Russian-Chinese father and a Chinese mother, she had studied as a dancer at a ballet school in Camberley "three generations from China", as she said, "the nearest I've ever been to it is Hong Kong". Tony was fascinated by her exotic, elfin quality; the porcelain delicacy of her figure; her tiny charm as a model. "I think she's the most beautiful person I've ever seen," he once told his stepmother but, according to Carol Coombe, "the fire went out of their friendship" after about two years, and the sweetness of any early infatuation or imagined romance was replaced by a more calm and yet steadfast camaraderie.

Probably their friendship was at its zenith early in 1956 when Tony first placed a portfolio of photographs before Penny Conner, subsequently to be better known as Penelope Gilliat and then the feature editor of *Vogue*. On the desk Tony spread an array of pictures of Jacqui Chan which Miss Conner discussed and politely discarded, and then Tony produced two portraits—of Edith Evans and Alec Guinness—of such striking insight that the editress decided to use them in the next issue going to press, that of May, 1956. Warming to this strange young man, "with his quick light voice, his energy, his jumpy charm", Miss Conner talked of the prospect of getting a really good picture of John Cranko, the gifted Sadlers' Wells choreographer, whose revue *Cranks* seemed about to take the town by storm. Talking in the busy Conde-Nast offices in Hanover Square, Penny Conner did not realise she was opening the first chink in the door of a royal romance or, indeed, that her then husband, Dr. Roger Gilliat, would one day be Tony's best man in Westminster Abbey.

With the credit-line of "Tony Armstrong Jones"—no hyphen, one notices—an action photograph of John Cranko, rehearsing his ballet *The Prince of Pagodas* at Covent Garden, appeared in the magazine in September, 1956, an accurate unusual study of the choreographer in a moment of perplexity, pondering, one lean finger to nose. Through the immensely satisfying years that Tony worked as a contributor to *Vogue* under the chief editorship of Audrey Withers, as an editorial summed up, "the ordinary was the last thing we expected or got". *Vogue* offered an ideal metier for nearly every aspect of his craft, and Tony worked at each new possibility with the dynamism that only his intimates know. By March, 1957, he was rivalling Norman Parkinson in the field of colour fashion photography. In June of that year his conquest was so complete that page upon page of the magazine carried a set of intensely clever conversation pieces of his in which fashion was subtly second to action. A pretty girl in a summer frock sits at an al fresco luncheon table while a young man unexpectedly kisses her. A young couple dance with abandon to lure the eye to an attractive dance-frock.Tony's models often looked like socialites because they were, and the natural effect was perhaps a single shot selected from a hundred wasted wooden negatives.

For the two years before his marriage, *Vogue* had the prescience to sign up Tony for his "exclusive" fashion photographs. "Clothes he loves," an editorial ultimately noted, "but, as he sees it, clothes are for people to live in, dance in, run in, eat in and drink in. So what is known as a sitting became, where Tony Armstrong-Jones was concerned, a running, standing and jumping . . . He persuaded models, actors, porters, head waiters . . . that the whole thing was rather a lark . . . All the fooling about, the moving of furniture, the piling of flowers, the pouring of drinks, had one end in view—a professional picture."

In arranging a photo lay-out around the show *Irma La Douce* Tony found that an actor was absent, so he himself dressed up the part for one of the rare Armstrong-Jones photographs when his eye was not actually at the shutter. *Vogue's* sophisticated pages also gave scope for his most ambitious portraiture, his net widening from Robert Morley and Spike Milligan, Mai Zetterling, Ralph Richardson and John Gielgud to studies of Eugene Ionesco, Tamara Karsavina, and Adelina de Lara, classic in the repose of her old age. All the portraits compel attention in appearing to carve an accurate cross-section of character. Tony once said that one of the most glib tricks anyone can do with a camera is to be cutting or sardonic. Truth nevertheless lurked in photographic surgery, as when he presented Somerset Maugham, not in profile, but by cutting the full face in half, from hair to chin, depicting only the sardonic and watchful left side, or when he similarly trimmed his portrait of Vaughan-Williams to show massive eyes, nose and mouth alone.

One of the pictures that Penny Conner particularly wanted was a portrait study of Christian Dior, who rarely gave a sitting and who replied with the usual refusal when Tony wrote from London suggesting an appointment. Undismayed, Tony caught the next plane to Paris, hired a car to Dior's country home and, as he said, "talked like crazy" in his fairly good but rather rusty French. The couturier consented to one photograph which necessarily entailed, as his persistent visitor explained, a choice of negatives. The resulting full-page portrait of Dior appeared in the April, 1957, *Vogue* and caught the interested eye, among others, of Princess Margaret, who had now met and was intrigued by the amusing, audacious Antony Armstrong-Jones.

7 *Friendship with the Princess*

I

In the enraptured international surprise that greeted the announcement of Antony Armstrong-Jones' engagement to Princess Margaret in 1960, the fascinating riddle for the majority of people was how they had first met. In the public mind, a fairy story had come true in modern style and, as *The Observer* commented, the Princess in her palace had "taken the hand, if not exactly of a woodcutter, of the lad who came to take the photographs". This view still prevails and yet, within the private scene, the remarkable factor is not that they met and fell in love but that they did not meet earlier.

When Lord Snowdon was born, his mother shared many social acquaintances with the then Duchess of York, the present Queen Mother, including the Duffs and Duff-Coopers, the Herberts of Wilton, Airlies and Hambledens, Pagets and Cecils, the Countess of Seafield and kinsfolk of the Duke of Buccleuch. At Sandroyd School, the slightest shift in the current of boyhood friendships could have linked Tony more firmly with the young princes Tomislav and Andrea of Yugoslavia; and it appears that, one mid-term, Prince "Tommy" was indeed within an ace of introducing him to his aunt-in-law, Princess Marina, the Duchess of Kent, for a visit to Coppins, where Prince Philip was soon to court Princess Elizabeth. One remembers Prince Philip's first youthful meeting with his own future bride at Dartmouth; and when Princess Margaret in her teens paid her two visits to Eton with her parents, the pattern might readily have been repeated, save perhaps for the stardust in the cogs of chance. Many of Tony's fellow Etonians were already established within the circle that presently became known as the Princess Margaret set, youngsters such as Dominic Elliott, Colin Tennant, Dominic and Peter Elwes and even Billy Wallace, if one includes the somewhat senior group with Angus Ogilvy and John Worsley.

In Coronation year, Simon Elwes painted a particularly delightful portrait of Princess Margaret, and the Princess went to a party in his studio in St. John's Wood to mark its completion. As a close friend of the artist since their Slade days, Oliver Messel was among the fifty or sixty guests, and so were the painter's two sons, Dominic and Peter, and their friend, Tony. In the crowded studio, Tony was not presented to the guest of honour and in all probability she never noticed him. Yet he came away with a revived impression of her beauty, heightened and echoed by the wide blue eyes and pearl-transparent skin of her painted likeness. Had they met then, had they fallen in love at first sight, the Princess might have been spared all the anguish and the tempest of publicity that centred in the following year around her affection for Group-Captain Peter Townsend. But it was not to be.

The fates similarly missed their cue a year later when Princess Margaret was concerned with the charity production of *The Frog* as an understudy and assistant producer. Tony might have been expected to photograph the amateur cast, including as it did his godfather, Sir Michael Duff, his schoolfellow Colin Tennant and his studio sitters and clients, Douglas Fairbanks, Jnr. and Mrs. Gerald Legge (Lady Dartmouth). *The Tatler* or *Sketch* would have snapped up pictures of the histrionics of the young Duke of Devonshire or Billy Wallace; but where Princess Margaret was concerned Tony was too diffident and insufficiently opportunist or brash to push himself forward.

Again, circumstances could have reasonably provided an alternative meeting in 1955, when Princess Margaret made her first cruise to the Caribbean, that intriguing foretaste of her honeymoon, and the royal yacht *Britannia* put into Nassau, where Tony's godmother, the Countess of Seafield, had an island home. Lady Seafield could readily have entertained the Princess ashore, and she would even have had a special reason for inviting Tony, for her young kinsman, Mark Ogilvie-Grant, was at that very time a house-guest of Lord and Lady Rosse at 25 Eaton Terrace. Yet one pursues this attractive will o' the wisp in vain, for the make-believe meeting never happened. Lady Seafield was not in Nassau at the time and Tony remained no nearer the royal cruising area than Rotherhithe.

Then, on a dreary February afternoon in 1956, Princess Margaret sat in the shrouded stalls of the St. Martin's Theatre, watching a rehearsal of John Cranko's revue, *Cranks*. Less than four months had passed since radio and television programmes had been interrupted for her personal statement, "I would like it to be known that I have decided not to marry Group-Captain Peter Townsend . . . I am deeply grateful for the concern of all those who have constantly prayed for my happiness." On the stage of the little theatre a girl was singing what was to prove the hit of the show, "Who is it always there?" and at that moment Tony was walking in at the stage-door.

The door-keeper, who knew that he was taking the house photographs, thought it right to mention that the Princess was inside.

"Oh, dear. Oh, thank you," said Tony, "Then I'll make myself scarce." He did not wish to intrude, and this was clearly not a convenient moment to roam around with his camera. It has been said that the Princess's close friend and extra lady in waiting, Lady Elizabeth Cavendish, had a financial interest in the show as one of eight or nine "angels" or part-backers who shared the production costs. Possibly Princess Margaret herself was involved, for she sat in at several rehearsals, making occasional suggestions. She proposed a rearrangement of two scenes, for example, because the stage settings by John Piper were too much alike, and the necessary changes were carried out.

Taking his production photographs during ordinary rehearsals, Tony missed the Princess by minutes more than once. She was firmly in focus, however, in April, 1956, when the Princess and Lady Elizabeth Cavendish were at the wedding of Lady Anne Coke and Colin Tennant at Holkham Hall. Tony had been invited as a personal friend of the bridegroom when the bride asked him to take her wedding photographs as well, and a charming photograph shows Princess Margaret on the steps of Holkham, smiling out at the cameramen, her eyes assuredly bright with amusement at the shadow-boxing of a morning-coated young man in the group, bobbing, weaving and ducking with his Leica.

It were as if their lives were moving closer, their affairs gradually mingling, like pebble circles across the pool of events. *Cranks* ran until the autumn, its fashionable success heightened by the Princess's repeated visits, and Tony and the tall blonde Lady Elizabeth already knew one another fairly well when they met one night at a supper-party John Cranko gave just after the show. They talked, I think, of John Betjeman, whom they both knew. Occupied a great deal as she is with social work in the East End, Elizabeth Cavendish had heard with interest of Tony's room at Rotherhithe. Gradually, as acquaintance deepened, trivial gossipy details of the charming and interesting Antony Armstrong-Jones were casually mentioned at Clarence House. Tony's recommendation of *Hotel Paradiso*, for example, indirectly led to Princess Margaret's visit to the Winter Garden to see the show.

Paying a visit to the studio, Lady Elizabeth greatly admired Tony's studies of the youngest generation. "He is at his nicest with children," a friend had said, and Lady Elizabeth suggested that he might perhaps care to photograph some children she knew, without hinting that she was thinking of the family of Lord and Lady Rupert Nevill, the close friends of the Queen. As it happened, her discretion was unnecessary for Tony had also known the Nevills for some time.

Tony's quick, questing mind was in fact already darting over the possibilities of royal photography, though his ideas were running on quite a different line. The sudden death of Baron had left a gap in the ranks of royal portraitists. Tony brooded over both the prospects and the ethics of the matter for some months and then, in the summer of 1956, he carefully composed a letter to the Duke of Kent to suggest a sitting.

As all Fleet Street knows, the Armstrong-Jones photograph of the Duke of Kent in the regimental full-dress of the Royal Scots Greys was issued, State portrait style, for the Duke's twenty-first birthday, and Tony modestly explained his break-through by saying that all he had to do was write his letter. Jealous rivals were more inclined to suspect an old boy network. Was not Tony an old friend of Jane Sheffield, who was also a friend of the Duke of Kent, and had not both the Duke and Tony been guests at the festivities of Jane's wedding to Jocelyn Stevens, to whose Cambridge magazine *Cameo* Tony had contributed only a year or two earlier? (The family link with the Sheffields in fact dated from their grandparents' shared gardening enthusiasms.) Again, the Duke frequently went dancing with Emma Tennant, whose cousins were among Tony's closest cronies. It was nevertheless undeniable that none of Tony's professional competitors had approached the Duke of Kent in the first place. In reality, the photograph was taken four months before release, and was supposed to be kept a secret. Tony was seriously alarmed when a casual question by his publicity friend, Major

Willing, one day suggested that premature whispers of his scoop were leaking out.

Meanwhile, the Queen similarly admired Tony's photographs of young Guy and Angela Nevill, and Tony was presented to Her Majesty at a cocktail party at the Nevills' home near Uckfield, when she complimented him on the Duke of Kent pictures. Godfrey Winn, too, recalls a dance at the Nevills' when the Queen was staying the weekend, and Tony, he noticed, "was the shyest guest in the room".

The vetting of Antony Armstrong-Jones as a photographer was, in fact, pleasant, thorough and entirely unobtrusive. In the early autumn, his return from Birr coincided with a telephone call from Commander Colville, the Queen's press secretary at Buckingham Palace, enquiring whether he would like to photograph Prince Charles and Princess Anne. Tony tried not to sound too astonished as he replied that he would indeed appreciate such an honour very much. And so, thirty-two years after his mother had first entered Buckingham Palace as a debutante, Tony was also invited there, with his lights and his camera.

"That makes two Q.C.s in the family," Ronald Armstrong-Jones quipped when he eventually heard the news, "Queen's Counsel and Queen's Cameraman." The resulting pictures were criticised by some, especially one showing the figures of the royal children, in shadowy profile, bending over a geographic sphere. This repeated a silhouette effect in a photograph of the younger Nevills used for a Christmas card, which the Queen had admired, but in general the originality and unconventional quality of the photographs was widely praised. The eighth birthday portrait of Prince Charles shows him leaning negligently against a piano, his boyish grin disclosing that Tony had won his complete confidence.

Tony had posed the two children in the White Drawing Room and the Picture Gallery, with these opulent backgrounds in soft-focus. Altogether he presented thirty photographs for the Queen's final selection. He has never described his first impressions of the Palace and when would-be interviewers telephoned he answered their questions only in general terms. Yes, he had talked to Prince Charles "like a grown-up. Children hate being talked down to . . ." and he had taken the children in silhouette because "they had such beautiful profiles". As a not uncharacteristic gesture behind this nonsense, he sent a huge blow-up of the best photograph to Commander Colville, and it was accepted, for Tony had fulfilled the foremost royal requirement, that of absolute discretion.

Moreover, it had nothing to do with photography when, early in 1957, Tony first met Princess Margaret at a dinner-party given by Lady Elizabeth Cavendish at her mother's house in Chelsea, 5 Cheyne Walk. Their perceptive hostess had felt sure he would prove an interesting and amusing guest, and so it turned out. He fully understood the Princess's position without being intimidated by it and, as the evening wore on, the two young people established that they shared the same sense of humour. From start to finish, indeed, the evening went with a zing which Lord Snowdon and his wife have never forgotten.

II

A few weeks later Tony Armstrong-Jones was included in one of the theatre parties which the Princess enjoyed so much at this time. The show cannot now be identified with certainty, but, it was perhaps Noel Coward's play *Nude with Violin* or the thriller, *A Dead Secret* or else the two-man revue *At the Drop of a Hat* in which Michael Flanders, who had been in hospital for polio at the same time as Tony, triumphantly proved from his wheelchair his command of an audience. A private visit to a theatre involved an agreed strategy between the Princess and her companions. Friends such as Billy Wallace, Mark Bonham-Carter, Lady Elizabeth Cavendish or Iris Peake usually arranged the tickets; theatre managers were no longer invariably informed in advance and, arriving practically unheralded the Princess's presence was seldom noticed by the audience until the interval. To confuse the inquisitive, her party was usually of six or eight people, not all of whom were readily recognised, so that her name was no longer repeatedly linked with any one escort.

The prudence of Princess Margaret's friends had become vitally necessary and, to understand it, we need only to recollect the climate of undue, unsought publicity that still pursued every turn of her private life five years after her sister had come to the Throne. Fully aware of Bagehot's dictum that a royal marriage was the representation of a great universal truth, the newspapers doggedly followed every clue to a potential courtship, and this symptom of affectionate public curiosity became at times an intemperate inquisition.

In her teens Princess Margaret had thought it tragically unfair that her sister could be occasioned hurtful embarrassment by the

113

widespread speculation about Prince Philip long before he proposed. "Poor Lil, nothing of your own," she once said, in her governess, Marion Crawford's hearing. "Not even your love affair." Then the unrelaxing interest centred upon her own friendships, until the gossip culminated in what Malcolm Muggeridge termed the "orgy of vulgar and sentimental speculation" around her own youthful and possibly immature love for Peter Townsend.

Group-Captain Peter Townsend was sixteen years her senior and had divorced his wife. Briefly, then, the Royal Family had confronted a variant of the dilemma that bedevilled the passion of King Edward VIII (the Duke of Windsor) for Mrs. Simpson, namely that the Church of England regarded Christian marriage as indissoluble and the Queen could not therefore constitutionally approve the wedding of her sister to a man whose former wife was still living. Princess Margaret's uncle had found that his own emotional crisis could be assuaged only by abdication. His niece chose the painful alternative of renunciation, "conscious of my duty to the Commonwealth", as she said, a solution that her ultimately happy marriage was completely to vindicate.

In 1957, however, Princess Margaret had emerged from the Townsend trauma and, in her twenty-seventh year, she found herself surrounded by understanding friends who had soothed the nostalgia and regret. As if remorse for piling on the Townsend agony had watered the printing ink, even the newspaper columnists were beginning to pay less attention to "rumours of romance". Tony Armstrong-Jones was one of several newcomers to the royal circle, both young men and women, whose early acquaintance began flowering in unpublicised friendship. In the early days there was no watcher to analyse every mutual interest, every reciprocal understanding, that gradually drew Tony and the Princess so close together. In any stocktaking of friendship, over many months, he would have been entered as little more than a pleasant acquaintance.

Tony deeply enjoyed getting to know the Princess, with the audacious delight of a man who had long admired her from afar and found at last that he could ask her to dance with him. Behind the "Ma'am" was Margaret. Behind the formality was a beautiful girl of his own age, lonely and oddly vulnerable, waiting to be rescued from the icy fortress of protocol, though neither had any inkling that Tony was to be the unorthodox knight errant.

A bridge was crossed early in their friendship when Tony sought Princess Margaret's advice. The Princess was accustomed to being flattered, amused, coaxed and counselled, but rarely to being consulted outside her own regal ambience. Tony no doubt sought her opinion as an expert on exhibitions, she who had opened and visited so many. Should a display be arranged in a series of small rooms or compartments, like a jewelled belt, or was it better to be seen at once in a single setting, bursting with dazzling and undivided impact on the visitor's view?

Although there were hints of the approach that his father might have made in cross-examination, Tony genuinely wanted to know. Oliver Messel had been urging him for some time to stage an exhibition of his photographic work; only thus could he invite critical attention and now the time was ripe. The iron must be struck, unless he was to be regarded merely as a social or royal photographer. "An exhibition must have a name and I should like to call it Photocall," Tony would have explained, and with its suggestion of show business, publicity and urgency, the phrase won Princess Margaret's approval. The arrangements for the exhibition went forward, and Tony solicited the practical advice of other experienced friends in devising the publicity handouts: "The idea is to show a young man's way with a camera, in his first four years as a professional."

Leslie Caron opened the exhibition at Kodak House—the London headquarters of that company—in June, 1957, and for two months it alternately astonished or annoyed London photophobes. Tony found his name spread lavishly across the gossip columns and, for serious attention, the official journal of the Royal Photographic Society accorded it six pages, quoting some of the totally contrasting remarks overheard at the opening: "The beginning of a new era . . . Precocious trivialities . . . Pictures only for the detached aesthetic eye . . . Life itself! . . . They're not even in focus"—this from a Fleet Street picture editor who valued clarity above all else.

Other reviewers similarly spoke of the photographic artist's "concern to snatch the living instant" and his "abhorrence of the photographic cliché". If this praise was sweet to a creative artist's ears, Tony bore the criticisms in mind much longer. The official organ of the Institute of British Photographers deftly complained that "the method of presentation was, in most cases, very unorthodox" and this indeed struck the note of common accord.

Exhibitions of photographs were usually regimented arrays of black-framed squares, all of nearly equal size. But Tony had a huge leaping mural of Anya Linden, the ballerina, nineteen feet high, curbed only by the height of the ceiling. There were cut-outs and colour pics, prints from 35 mm. negatives magnified to colossal size, emphasising the grain, so that guests at a Buckingham Palace garden-party seemed to move through a snowstorm. The versatility and variety of the exhibition struck the sympathetic as cheeky and provocative. Blameless landscapes contrasted with slum close-ups of point and candour, fashion photographs and theatrical scenes. The gallery of celebrities both demanded and received attention, ranging as it did from the treble life-size Edith Evans to Annigoni, Dior and Ingrid Bergman, Paul Scofield, Humphrey Lyttelton and Laurence Olivier.

Princess Margaret would dearly have loved to have had a private view but apparently contented herself with a fleeting visit to the Pimlico studio one afternoon with Elizabeth Cavendish after the Kodak show had closed and the dismantled pictures were set out for her inspection. The two ladies descended the spiral staircase while Tony made tea, and the conversation no doubt turned to holidays. Tony had been invited to join his Uncle Oliver in Venice, and he could explain that he was then going on to Malta to help Sacheverell Sitwell with photographs for a book. Princess Margaret was travelling north as usual to Balmoral. On the journey to Scotland, the impressions of Tony's basement flat and the versatility of his talent were vivid-fresh in her mind and she must already have decided that he was indeed an extraordinary young man.

III

Tony wrote to a friend that Venice reminded him of Rotherhithe. There was the same surge and gurgle of the tide, the wash of passing traffic, the similar decaying timber baulks and lichened stone, the same airy expanses of sea-grey waves. All these formed part of the prospect from his Rotherhithe window, and all are now part of the indelible impression of a lost sanctuary that will remain for ever with the Snowdons.

Tony expended at least thirty reels of film in Venice. He photographed it ecstatically—or was the ecastsy already flowering for another reason in his deeper self? He rose at dawn to capture the Piazza San Marco while still free of a single tourist, but he found a gowned priest already at work painting, and his study of the solitary human figure among the pigeons finally afforded the best composition of all. Venice was Rotherhithe—and of course rather more—with its beauty given colour and clarity. Months later, when *Vogue* wanted a photograph of a girl as if sunning at the Lido for a sun-basking feature, Tony persuaded a model to sit in an old wooden chair in the tidal wavelets beneath his Rotherhithe window and created the identical effect.

After two years of house-hunting, his dream of a down-river retreat had been suddenly fulfilled in 1956. By dint of enquiries in every riverside pub, he had followed up one futile trail after another until, unexpectedly, he heard that a journalist named Bill Glenton might know of something in Rotherhithe Street. About a mile down-stream from Tower Bridge, on the south bank of the river, there stood a line of nine eighteenth-century merchants' houses which still incredibly survived, askew, lurching, rickety, presenting a variety of pleasant Georgian windows to the river view. Some of the houses still retained their unpretentious original panelling; some enjoyed overhanging balconies or tiny rooftop terraces, and all this row of astonishing survivors, Numbers 51 to 59, occupied on the landward side a tranquil semi cul-de-sac. Beyond, to the east, only the narrowest thoroughfare wriggled between warehouses to the old parish church of St. Mary's, in which the Pilgrim Fathers were reputed to have offered their last prayers in England, with a tiny churchyard where some of the crew of the *Mayflower* lay buried.

Naturally, all these forgotten dwellings, with their long low rooms and sloping floors, found their devotees, content to ignore the whisper that the old houses were one day to be demolished by the L.C.C. A doctor lived in one, and an artist, an author and a social worker were his neighbours. Mr. Glenton occupied No. 59 at the end of the row, alongside a bomb site. His house had first been rescued from dereliction by Geoffrey Fletcher, the London artist and writer, who had stripped away layers of rotting paper to find the walls still lined with beautiful pine, and had jollied the place a little by giving it the name "The Little Midshipman', culled from *Dombey and Son*. Not that the house had any known link with Dickens or had ever been a pub, but the name enjoyed a romantic ring that heightened Tony's sense of discovery. Scrutinising the house from the street and the river, without approaching the occupant, he bubbled with excitement. The ground-floor back room directly overlooked the water, beneath a big first-floor bay window, and he was practically sure that the room was empty.

Having established this, Tony handled the matter with astonishing tact. Night after night, by virtue of his local knowledge, Bill Glenton was persuaded to help him scour dockland in search of something suitable until it became obvious that the hunt would yield no results. Then, having made Mr. Glenton his ally, Tony admitted that the search was fruitless, and he drove back to Pimlico, only to return a week or two later. "Would it perhaps be possible for me to stay here in this house?" he said.

As he had feared, he saw that his intended host was reluctant, and he pressed the point home. "I'm as quiet as a church mouse. You'd hardly know I was here. I thought perhaps your room on the ground floor was empty?"

Mr. Glenton admitted that the room was used only as a storeroom, and under the pressure of Tony's enthusiasm he conducted him down the passage. Tony's first view of the room was unforgettable. The wide window commanded a prospect of the river to the turrets and spires of Tower Bridge and across to the warehouses of Wapping, above the islets of moored barges and the traffic in midstream.

"There's a concrete floor," Tony continued his persuasions, "that means it's dry. I could use rush matting. I could paint the walls and scour the beams. It would help improve the house to convert this one room." And he obviously wanted the room so much that Mr. Glenton gave way, for a trial period and for no rent save the cost of electricity. The journalist did not know what astonishing secrets would eventually result from this bargain and how he would one day find himself an arch-conspirator in Tony's married romance.

For weeks after that, Tony spent every hour of his free time immersed in carpentry and painting, running back and forth to Rotherhithe with car-loads of prepared timber and paint. When Bill Glenton at last inspected the finished effect, he found that a mass of unsightly pipes along one wall were masked with a line of cupboards of pine polished with beeswax, containing a kitchenette and an electric cooker. Elsewhere the stone walls gleamed with white emulsion paint, and were fitted with shelves for ornaments and books, while the open shelves of a Georgian corner cupboard filled the angle of the inner wall near the door.

When the floor was ready, Tony and one of his friends sat cross-legged like tailors, arduously stitching squares of rush matting together with needle and thread. Facing north, the room constantly danced with light reflected from the river, and Tony heightened the cottage atmosphere with an old round deal table from which he had stripped the paint, a bentwood rocking chair that may have come from the Nymans nursery, two small basketwork chairs, a brass-bound wooden chest and an ancient divan.

These requisites were then enriched with a painted wall clock trailing its chain and pendulum, a cane-seated japanned Victorian chair, a gilded cage containing three stuffed lovebirds, a carved and painted blackamoor and a clutter of varied ornaments. Among the earliest visitors, Tony's father and stepmother were amused to note his ship-in-a-bottle from Eton days, and a china model of a night-capped couple primly in a bed bearing the motto, "The last in bed to put out the light". Carol recalls in her memoirs that Tony shared a "bathroom" with the other occupants of the house, though this was, I think, a euphemism for the antiquated lavatory at the top of the stairs, with its rusting cistern and obstinate chain. A cause for more general mirth was the stout cable chain that hung down the slimy embankment wall outside Tony's window, by which he per-suaded friends to descend to the strip of tide-washed shingle that he called his private beach.

"Of course you can do it, you're so nimble and clever and supple," he wheedled Carol. Tony, she knew, liked to demonstrate his agility but she successfully reached the beach. Not to be outdone, Ronnie Armstrong-Jones made the descent one night without get-ting a speck of Thames mud or green slime on his dinner-jacket, only to spoil the effect by lingering until the tide was already lap-ping the beach. Laughing helplessly, he and Tony had to complete the return journey in bare feet, paddling along to the nearby steps.

At first Tony had intended the room partly as a retreat where he would rest when prolonged over-exertion caused the nerves of his old polio leg to throb and pain, but before long he could not resist showing his delectable hideaway to a wider circle of friends. The room then grew more nautical in atmosphere, with a hammock slung to hooks in the ceiling, a picture of Grace Darling rowing frantically towards her shipwreck, and a huge painting of a wide-whiskered old admiral which glowered against almost the whole of the back wall opposite the river. Tony said he had been unable to resist buying him for thirty shillings, "At that price, the old boy was a bargain". The implacable grandeur of this personage, however, proved somewhat daunting and Tony ultimately pushed a borrowed old upright piano in front, over which the head of the admiral glared in choleric indignation.

This personage was also confronted, one might say, by a serene sculptured head of Jacqui Chan, and flanked by white china candlesticks and specimens of Victorian glass. Tony began discovering the loot of the local junk-shops, and his collection met an appreciative eye when John Betjeman stayed in the room for a few weeks, after the fire in his own house at Smithfield that made him temporarily homeless. Tony naturally enquired if Bill Glenton would mind but he did not immediately explain that he had first met John through Lady Elizabeth Cavendish, whom he brought to Rotherhithe a few weeks later. Yet the poet was, of course, already an associate of the Earl and Countess of Rosse in founding the Victorian Society. Everything conspired to strengthen the meshwork of new friendships that formed around Tony and Princess Margaret.

IV

A biographer may wish to be impersonal, but I perhaps should mention that I first saw Princess Margaret in Tony's company on a drear February evening in 1958. We all went to the Metropole, the local cinema behind Buckingham Palace, and Tony was "one of the group". The film was the Hitchcock–Agatha Christie movie, *Witness for the Prosecution*, which tempts me to add that I had no wish to play witness for the persecution. Editors were apt to phone or cable me on the merest bubble of gossip, and were seldom content if I expressed doubts upon the latest "escort" around whom they flung wild romantic speculation.

Even close friends scarcely realised, that evening at the cinema, that Princess Margaret included Tony Armstrong-Jones in her party because she sympathetically knew he needed cheering up. This set the seal on six months friendship, there was no attempt at concealment and yet a clue was inadvertently dropped into the heart of Fleet Street—and overlooked—at the very same time. A Clarence House official asked his press-clipping service to include reviews of Sacheverell Sitwell's book on Malta and notices of the new Cranko revue *Keep Your Hair On* . . . and in both of these the single common denominator was Tony Armstrong-Jones.

Tony basked in Malta in September, 1957, taking photographs for the Sitwell book. He was conscientious and, finding the light too harsh in the middle of the day, he asked to be called at five a.m. so that he could be up betimes for the best effects. Presently, too, he asked Mr. Sitwell's permission to show the pictures to a friend,

without stipulating whom. Mr. Sitwell himself was so pleased with
the illustrations that he insisted Tony should share the credit with
his name on both the binding and title-page. When Princess
Margaret returned from Balmoral that autumn and next met Tony,
it was to share interest and amusement in his impressions of both
Venice and Malta, and his photographs especially recaptured the
happiness of the Princess's own first visit to the island when her
sister was living there as a young wife at the Villa Guardamangia.
Here were the Oriental vistas across Grand Harbour, the stairways
and tunnels, the wandering cats and chickens, the dghajsas and
donkeys, the siestas and sailors, the tiled floors and curious cabs, the
white walls of Medina and its evening silhouette, the children and
statuary, the nights of fiesta and moments of prayer, a photogene's
Malta which reviewers were presently to say perfectly captured and
set off the spirit of the Sitwell text.

But for Tony, having mailed his photographs to Clarence House,
at the Princess's bidding, enthusiasm swept on to the next project,
which was nothing less promising than to do the scenery and
costumes, with Desmond Heeley, of Cranko's revue. Tony had in
mind a series of stage designs and scenic surprises based on photography: an enormous enlargement of an enigmatic eye to gaze at
the audience as they assembled before the show, a low-level shot to
give a strutting pigeon's view of Trafalgar Square, a hairdressing
salon with a backdrop like a book page which would swing over
whenever a customer entered. There was also a highly impressive
effect of Victoria Station and, at one point, an enormous ten-foot
enlargement of a beribboned plait of hair . . . and all this to the
requirements of a musical comedy plot.

"I shall buy every seat," Princess Margaret said with a smile. In
the event, the dress rehearsal was held under what seemed to Tony
the happy augury of his sister's birthday . . . but the show opened on
February 13th at the Apollo to a complete debacle. *The Times* mentioned that "the gallery booed". In dire reality, during the final
chorus, the din from the gallery swelled to such an uproar that the
startled cast on the stage could no longer hear the orchestra. Alas,
on hastily seeking *The Times'* impressions of Tony's stage designs,
Princess Margaret could only read that "the scenery consisting for
the most part of screens, transparent or painted, hoisted up and
down . . . amusing in the German style fashionable in the 1920s".
One may wonder whether a young man of twenty-seven could be
expected to remember the Berlin stage fashions of the year before

he was born, but *The Stage* was equally trenchant. "The blown-up photographic settings of Tony Armstrong-Jones help to emphasise the staleness of the show," it asserted, and after fourteen performances the revue was taken off.

And so Tony presumably needed cheering up. The film show was a prescribed tonic and the party went back to Clarence House afterwards. A buffet supper would have been set out in the small library or dining-room, and the company wandered, glass in hand, between the library and the Princess's sitting-room at garden level. This was probably the first time Tony saw the Princess's room, grey-carpeted, decorated in pale green, with her stacked magazine table, the stereo, the pink armchairs, and he would have instantly registered the unexpected details, the electric fire, the small carved wooden crucifix above her desk, the leather bindings in the formal bookcase. Listening to records, talking in ever-changing groups, casually dancing, the Princess must have discovered with astonishment that, far from needing cheering up, Tony's disappointment was forgotten.

On admiring his Malta photographs, she had said encouragingly that he should do another book, all by himself. Now he could tell her that Weidenfeld and Nicolson had already commissioned the book and that it had to be completed terribly quickly. It was planned to include about one hundred and fifty photographs, and the title would simply be *London*.

8 *"Inside the Circle"*

"This is a book about people—London people—and the way they behave," wrote Tony Armstrong-Jones in the Introduction of his book. "Londoners are essentially locals. There are locals of Victoria and Chelsea. Of Portobello Road, of Cable Street and of Rotherhithe; all with a language that's as private as a patois, relaxed when they're inside the circle and a bit guarded with non-members." One catches the pause in his thoughts, at the brink of his innermost feelings. He was inside the circle now, where people were "most themselves—their most normal, and in a way their most strange". In retrospect, one realises that *London* was a talisman, smoothing each new stage of deepening friendship as Tony and Princess Margaret met at friends' houses through the first six months of 1958.

The book was to reflect every facet of London life, every aspect and its opposite, a theme affording Tony and the Princess a fabulous guessing-game at every meeting, a constant challenge in ideas and contrasts. The idea was that the different sections should show Londoners in every activity: going, waiting, working, feeding, adorning, judging—"And what else?" Tony would enquire in his light, lilting voice.

"Talking, Reading, Dancing . . ." one can hear the proposals. "Watching—that's a good one! Loving—why not?" What photograph could illustrate The End . . . except garbage outside Cartier's? What was the opposite of cleaning lamps in Whitehall . . . if not the glass roof of Paddington Station? What expressed Performing better than Piccadilly buskers, actors at the Open Air Theatre, strip-tease in a music-hall? What better antithesis of a dockers' strip cabaret in Canning Town other than Mme. Vacani's dancing class? "Ending" could be expressed by the last minute litter at Caledonian Market, the empty car of the last train to Cockfosters . . . and an enthusiast carrying plants from the Chelsea Flower Show.

The game went on for weeks while Tony roamed London. For "posing" he photographed John Betjeman in a City graveyard and Jacqui Chan peeping from behind a horticultural signboard in Kew Gardens that announced "A native of China . . . This specimen is one of five of the original importations . . ." And from all the four corners of London, as he made his forages, Tony brought back stories for Princess Margaret. An Irish girl was being tattooed at the parlour in the Waterloo Road "because she had toothache very badly the night before and the pain of the tattooing would take away the pain of the toothache". A plump headless torso back-stage at Madame Tussaud's, for whose identity Tony invited guesses, was joyfully disclosed as none other than the Archbishop of Canterbury.

Elizabeth Cavendish assured him there was one London scene he would never get—an action shot inside the Ladies' Turkish Baths. Tony duly produced a set of photographs of wonderfully convincing seraglio atmosphere and swore that he had taken the pictures himself. "You can see the empty deckchair I was sitting in!" And it was true, for the management had allowed him to take over the bath late at night and he had filled the place with his own models.

Tony dedicated his book to "my sister Susan, who lives in Dublin". The frontispiece depicts the view from his Rotherhithe room but otherwise the first illustration shows a small indistinct muffled figure who may well have been Princess Margaret incognito, engaged in the incredible adventure of crossing the Thames on the Woolwich ferry.

This exploit was perhaps to come later, but the Princess visited the Rotherhithe branch of the Dockland Settlement with Elizabeth Cavendish one evening that March, and no doubt availed herself of an early opportunity for her first brief visit to the Room. Mr. Glenton noticed at about this time that Tony was gradually becoming not only a little more conventional in his dress but also rather more secretive about the friends he brought to No. 59, whom he did not always introduce as of old.

In April, when the Princess flew off on a three-week tour of the Caribbean, Tony got down to work with Mark Boxer, then art editor of *The Queen*, who was helping him with the lay-out of *London*. On her return, Princess Margaret no doubt leafed through the latest *Vogue*, alert for picture credits, and a bulky package initialled T.A.J. awaited her homecoming. This would have contained the best of his current output, which at that time included his publicity pictures of Peter Sellers, his stage photographs of *Irma La Douce*, a set of studies of Beatrice Lillie in *Auntie Mame* and some fashion photographs of people grandly dining at home while oblivious of a supine husband laid out on two chairs.

Except in the most casual way, Lord Snowdon has never confided his inward early impressions of Princess Margaret to a soul. "A man only really falls in love once," he once said in a serious moment to Bill Glenton. "If I fell in love, I'd marry the girl, whoever she was." He was fascinated, enthralled, but never intoxicated by finding himself "inside the circle", the charmed magic circle around the girl he had always admired. Like many genial extroverts, he has never been able to recall every detail in steering his ship through the cataract of events. "It's no good saying 'hold it' to a moment of real life," he once wrote. "Like trying to hold a breath, you find you've lost it."

He was content—and perhaps a little flattered at first—to find that he could amuse and even genuinely win the interest of the Queen's sister. While willing to conform to the gulf of her royal status to the last "Ma'am", he could readily, in the Queen Mother's phrase, "find a way round it". Laughter was the great catalyst. Scrutinising some summer fashion pictures taken at David Hicks' house in Essex, the Princess detected something odd about an oak tree in the background which seemed to be sprouting horse chestnut leaves. Tony chuckled and admitted the photographs had been taken in early spring before the oak leaves were out, so he had stuck chestnut leaves on the tree with adhesive tape.

Then there were the hilarious stories he told about a journey into the Italian Alps to photograph winter sports fashions in summer when there was no snow lower than 11,000 feet and the only snow within sight of a hotel terrace was lipped on the edge of a crevasse. Tony wanted the chef to hover benignly in the snowy background but the poor man had to step back farther and farther, towards the abyss, to get it just right. The models looked wonderfully relaxed, though in reality they were all terribly frightened. Tony thought it would be fun to show a number of elegant young men in dinner-jackets ski-ing with the girls. "Don't they all look wonderful?" he said. "But they're all just the Italian hotel waiters—and they couldn't ski a yard!" He was full of such stories, told with his infectious giggle, and so he crossed the crevasses of social acquaintance, all but unaware that they existed.

In the summer of 1957, he was invited to photograph the Queen, Prince Philip and the children at Buckingham Palace. Tony discovered that no portraits had ever been taken in the garden and, having asked permission to wander about beforehand, looking for settings, he submitted sketches of what he had in mind. This resulted in the highly effective set of informal photographs issued for the royal visit to Canada and the U.S.A. that year. Tony had prepared himself so rigorously that he occupied only fifteen minutes of the Queen and Prince Philip's time, and one picture, showing the Queen and Prince Philip looking down from a rustic bridge at their children, was eventually reproduced in nearly every newspaper of the western world.

Princess Margaret was naturally curious about the session and Tony teased her about the need for absolute secrecy and discretion. It was equally fun for the Princess to know in advance what would be appearing in the Christmas number of *Vogue*, especially so since the 1957 issue, for example, was a T.A.J. lay-out with Jacqui Chan, Anna Massey and Heather Sears in modern variants of Cinderella. It was Tony's idea to replace the pumpkin not with a gilded coach but with a bubble-car in the kitchen of the Cavendish Hotel, and the Princess laughed at his comic tale of the difficulty of getting the car into the kitchen, manhandled by a battery of chefs. The fairy godmother's wand was a fish-frying implement topped with firework sparklers.

Princess Margaret was indeed one of the few people whom Tony knew he could trust implicitly with an editorial secret. On one occasion, when he had been to Dublin to photograph Brendan Behan, one of the pictures subsequently appeared in *Vogue* credited to "Oswald Jones". Tony explained that editors sometimes tired of using the same name. "I often wish they would tire of using mine," said Princess Margaret, pensively.

II

In the days of chivalry a noble knight was supposed to perform all manner of unusual feats to win the regard of his lady, but is it merely coincidental that Tony launched into a string of different exploits as his friendship with Princess Margaret deepened? His photographic exhibition, the whirlwind publicity of his royal photographs, his scenery for the Cranko show, his book on London, all followed in quick succession. If some experiments met with indifferent success, this very uncertainty possibly heightened the piquant interest of Clarence House. If in the early summer of 1958, or before, Princess Margaret asked Tony's opinion as a man on some of the dress designs selected for her first Canadian tour, one may conjecture that Tony in turn sought the Princess's views for his own entirely new ideas on women's winter-sports design. In the opinion of one dress-trade friend whom he consulted, "He went off the deep end about it. He had a whole series of revolutionary but probably premature ideas, rather like the very young Mary Quant. He had talents in every direction and wanted to demonstrate everything." Tony had considered for a long time that sports tailoring methods were absurdly obsolete. Why should clothes have seams, why should pieces of cloth be sewn together, when surely they could be *stuck* together? A winter sports visit to Arosa convinced him that Englishwomen in the Alps looked fearful frumps, all in the same tailored ski-pants and anoraks. Surely they would welcome new *fun clothes*, clothes that would look vividly adventurous, mad and terrific in the snow? Tony's reputation as a royal photographer, and the quality of his portraiture in the glossy magazines, saw all his time fully filled in Pimlico, but he always slashed every routine project to do the things he really wanted. Friends found him experimenting with tailoring samples and a glue-pot, and he spent every free evening sketching designs.

Altogether he drew some eighteen outfits: knickerbockers in leather, a ballooning anorak in silk with yellow and orange spiral stripes, an anorak of white leather matched with an enormous fox-fur collar and a detachable hood lined with white fox, a smock in pale-blue leather, and so on. Tony knew that sketching was still not his strong suit; he could scarcely express his ideas, but he got a fashion-artist friend to re-draw his roughs with more style. Princess Margaret reviewed the designs enthusiastically and probably re-drew some of the sketches herself, for fashion-drawing has always been a side-interest for which she has an exceptional flair. Unaware of this potential royal imprint, the first manufacturer to whom Tony showed the designs expressed some interest but added excuses, "We've already designed our winter models" he explained, "Can you come back next year?"

In the end Tony impatiently joined forces with Miss Kiki Byrne, who ran an exclusive boutique in Sloane Street and welcomed a business alliance with a young man already strongly entrenched in the editorial hearts of *Harper's*, *Vogue* and *The Queen*. The indefatigable Jacqui suggested a couturier for the making-up. When an unforeseen difficulty arose because they had no knickerbocker cutter, Tony, quite unperturbed, went round to his own tailors, Denman and Goddards, and was soon telling an apocryphal new story of the Savile Row trousers cutter who blushed scarlet on being asked to fit a girl model.

When all was ready, the collection was shown with all the chi-chi and publicity that Tony could muster. Lady Elizabeth Cavendish sat beside Tony and, although they missed the real point, the fashion writers could not have hoped for a better news angle than to find the little show attended by Princess Margaret's lady in waiting. The applause in the packed salon was polite and Tony puckered his brow with anxiety only when he overheard some of the comments. He could not sleep that night until he had impatiently rushed down to Fleet Street to collect the first editions of the morning papers.

The reviews were superficially pleasant but, as usual, the would-be couturier was more aware of the criticisms. He read that his styles were "exaggerated and impractical". His leather knickerbockers would absorb the snow, his balloon smock bloused to the hip "gave a pregnant look" . . .

Curious customers went to Kiki's to inspect, grimaced at the prices and went away. It did not materially help Tony and his partner to discover that the Norwegian press publicised his collection to such effect that knickerbockers enlivened the Scandinavian ski-slopes a season or two later. But Tony was still trying to dig himself out of the snowdrift of defeat when the telephone rang. Penelope Gilliat, the Penny Conner who had married Dr. Roger Gilliat four years before, telephoned him and enquired, "Tony, how would you like to go to New York?"

III

Princess Margaret had returned home from Canada full of stories of her tour across to the West Coast. Although the diplomatic bag does not divulge its secrets, one may suspect that she wrote Tony a treasured letter or two from Vancouver, still bubbling with enquiries and ideas about his "snow show". And certainly Tony experienced, for the first time, a forlorn sense of missing her companionship. Absurd though this inkling of his inner emotions must still have seemed, at this stage, he felt bereft of one of the few people with whom he could always be wholly candid and totally sincere. Then, as 1958 ebbed, the Princess also felt the gentle ache of separation, for Tony flew to New York in mid-November and did not return to London until after he had seen in the New Year as usual at Birr.

But first the Princess had the pleasure of reading the reviews on *London* and *Malta*, which were both published by different firms almost within the same week. *The Times Literary Supplement* admired the photographer's virtuosity, containing elements of "fantasy, drama, the exotic, the strange", and praised, in *Malta*, his "memorable effects of light and shade . . . his photographs make the book what it is". *The Daily Telegraph* agreed by claiming that the "illustrations share the distinction of the text". *The New York Herald Tribune* hailed Tony as "Britain's most original candid photographer". The *Daily Express* said, with some reason, that *London* was "brilliantly observed".

Before Tony's departure for the U.S., incidentally, the Commissioner-General for Malta gave a reception in London to help launch the Malta book, collecting such notable guests as Lord Perth, then Minister of State for Colonial Affairs and the then Mr. Alan Lennox-Boyd, Secretary of State for Colonial Affairs. The latter asked both the author and illustrator to autograph the book, unaware that he would meet Tony at a luncheon at Clarence House, given for the High Commissioner of Rhodesia, nine months later.

Nor was this the only coincidence, for Mr. Sitwell had flown home from Japan to attend the Malta reception. "That's odd," said Tony. "I'm just flying off to New York—and among other things I'm doing the photographs for the Japanese play, *Rashomon*, opening in Philadelphia!" His Uncle Oliver was designing the décor and costumes, and events dovetailed so propitiously that the mercurial Tony began to toy with dizzy dreams of a rich extra career in theatrical photography in America.

Mrs. Gilliat had organised the transatlantic trip as a fourteen-page layout for *Vogue* to illustrate British clothes against New York backgrounds, and Tony was joined at London airport by Pagan Grigg, the model, and her architect husband, John Taylor. No conjuring trick of travel is more exhilarating, flying west, than the eight-hour change in hemispheres. With the prestige of press V.I.P.s, the four flew out in the midday Comet which dropped them magically into a New York sunset of banked clouds and jewelled lights, and the reception hall of Idlewild greeted them with a steam-heat atmosphere, "hot enough to force orchids" as Penny said. Then they were on their way . . . "to get the message" in a hail-storm of impressions . . . the explicit traffic lights that flashed "Walk . . . Don't Walk" . . . the menu cards large as newspapers with their gigantic imagery of Jumbo Shrimps and ;Two-Man Steaks . . . the "zingy air" . . . the noise and dazzle of Times Square. They breakfasted next morning in an automat and Tony wasted a film on the Staten Island ferry, frustrated to discover that the Manhattan skyline indeed all but defied an original approach. The top of the Empire State Building, where Pagan was scheduled to model a coat, is itself curiously confined and meaningless unless the camera points outward. But Tony improvised a game of paper darts, a group of sight-seeing sailors joined in, and the Leica clicked merrily.

Penny's notes, and Tony's fashion pictures, still ring with the fun and zest of the visit: the dollar lunch in the "sculpture garden" at the Museum of Modern Art; Penny window-shopping for antiques along Third Avenue; Pagan posing precariously in a red dance dress on the ice-rink at Rockefeller Plaza while her husband, for-mally dressed British-style in a dinner jacket, skated rings around her under the bemused eyes of the local populace. They arranged a camera session, too, for a day dress modelled in the Peerless Dis-count Store on Lexington Avenue, where everything in the racks is half-price. They sampled the ice hockey fans at Madison Square Garden and the schoolgirl culture-seekers at the Metropolitan Museum. They explored the Seagram's skyscraper (new as it was that year) and appraised, with English astonishment, the "good red meat of a New York hamburger".

Tony's camera caught the anxious scowls of an art auction at the Parke Bernet Galleries and the jealously-guarded agonies of a rehearsal of the New York Philharmonic Orchestra at Carnegie Hall and, if there are City regulations forbidding photographers and their models to hold up the traffic, here was one photographer who had never heard of them.

To a policeman who politely enquired why he was lying down in the middle of West 45th Street, Tony explained with embarrassment but equal politeness that he was trying to photograph the steam arising from a heating grid: extra atmosphere, he pointed out for his photograph of the girl posed at the entrance of the Knicker-bocker Hotel. After this exploit, they had dinner at the Serendipity General Store in Chinatown, supping on lobster impaled on pink paper parasols. And then Tony spent another twenty minutes lying in the road to get just the effect he wanted of high fashion against the exotic orientalism of East Sixtieth Street ...

"Whaddya think ya doing?" asked a cop.

"I'm photographing a pretty girl. I've just finished, officer!"

Friends were to be hilariously regaled with New York stories for weeks afterwards. Tony's most impressive location was a car dump way up town where old wrecks were stacked six or seven high to await their nemesis. Tony sought out the foreman, asked him impeccably if he could please take pictures, and then set Pagan mountaineering up the pile of wreckage in an immaculate two-piece suiting: two cars, three cars, four scrap storeys high until she began wailing miserably, "But how shall I ever get down?"

The last picture to be taken was in fact the first illustration in the *Vogue* set, supposedly taken at Idlewild on arrival. They went back to the airfield in daylight when a Comet had just landed. The steps were wheeled away, and Pagan struck a flying pose in the aircraft doorway, as if she were leaping into space, just right for the caption, "Making a perfect landing ... a jersey suit ..."

Tony is said to have spent the Thanksgiving Day holiday in the Condé-Nast dark-room, making sure that his negs showed the results he wanted. But there was time, too, to meet New York friends—Hermione Gingold, James Thurber, Charles Laughton—before Tony joined his uncle in Philadelphia. The extremely high wages of stage-hands and electricians made the management wince when Tony wanted scenes set with full stage lighting, and he learned why American theatrical photography often falls short of London standards. The determined young photographer from London, what was more, said that he would do the job properly, or not at all. Even stranger, he refused to hand over his unprocessed films to allow the management to take their own choice of what they thought best. With this impressive firmness wedded to his own diplomatic charm, all went well, and the labours of production for Oliver Messel and his exacting nephew culminated in a Christmas dinner with Mr. Messel's Danish-born manager, where they remember being regaled with nearly as much caviar as turkey.

IV

As we have noted, Tony observed the happy custom of spending the New Year at Birr. His two half-brothers, Lord Oxmantown and

Martin Parsons, invariably met him at Dublin airport, full of so much laughter and talk, so much family news, that the sixty green miles motoring across Ireland into Offaly County passed in a flash. Yet the New Year of 1959 was sharply different, for Tony landed for the first time direct from New York at Shannon airport, as if change were in the air. William and Martin found him bubbling with American impressions and bursting with eagerness to see his sister, Susan, his suitcase stuffed with toys for her babies, Tom and Emma and Catherine.

As it does for so many visitors, Ireland always gave Tony a sense of coming home, recapturing the essence of past childhood, and especially Birr. As a boy, he had always found the castle, with its towers and battlements, a wonderland of adventure. As a young man he responded with sensitive admiration to the beauty and peace of his mother's home, the rooms massed with flowers, the walls shining with rococo mirrors and gilt-framed paintings, every detail imbued with her delicate care. For Tony, and especially when he was there, Birr was always "the most beautiful place in the world".

The leopards of the Rosse coat-of-arms on the wrought-iron entrance gates are creatures of playful charm who might have been elaborated by Oliver Messel but were in reality designed by an earlier Countess of Rosse, whose amusing touches still fleck the castle here and there. The Gothic ceiling of the entrance hall recalls the atmosphere of Nymans, with its broad high window and deep-hued tapestries and wall-hung swords. As at Nymans, there is always the aura of hospitality and, in those days, Tony always seemed to arrive in time for tea in the yellow drawing-room or the library, rooms both grounded in eighteenth-century atmosphere though different in texture, each with their welcoming log fires burning beyond the brass fenders.

By the eccentricities of castle architecture, both these rooms open into the splendour of the Gothic saloon, the largest and perhaps most beautiful of all the apartments at Birr, unique in Ireland. Save for the cosy charm of his bedroom, this was—and remains—Tony's favourite room. "There's no other like it anywhere," he used to assure his friends, with affectionate pride, before discovering that he was strangely mistaken.

In attempting to describe the saloon, he talked vaguely of Strawberry Hill Gothic. It is, in fact, a long and lofty apartment, octagonal at each end, the green-gold walls broken by slim white and gold Gothic shafts that, rising to the vaulted plaster ceiling, give the effect of a light and elegant tent. Along one wall, moreover, three arched Gothic windows, command the view across the river to the distant hills, enriching the room with the constant interplay of light from green leaves and flashing water. More than anywhere else, the saloon gave scope for Lady Rosse's flower arrangements, space for the white and gold chairs that she had bought for Lord Rosse as a wedding gift and space for fine pieces from her father's collection . . . and vaulted height to set off the most intricate Waterford glass chandelier imaginable.

We have lingered in this lovely and individual room, in the heart of Ireland, for reasons that will soon become apparent. In choosing it as the setting for one of his early professional photographs in the *Tatler*, his conversation piece of the Countess of Rosse "looking at a photograph album with her son, Lord Oxmantown", Tony unwittingly carved a tracery for the future. Pleased as he was with the photograph, he perhaps showed it to Princess Margaret shortly before the Kodak exhibition of 1958 and she must have regarded it with astonishment. The Gothic Saloon at Birr? But there was also a Gothic saloon, almost identical, at Royal Lodge and Tony "must see it at some time".

The invitation was lightly given and as lightly, conventionally, accepted and half-forgotten. Yet all the world has wondered how Tony first "mixed in" with the Royal Family, and what his early impressions were, and the simple answer emerges from his first visit to Royal Lodge, at the Queen Mother's invitation, one Saturday afternoon early in 1959. Just as Princess Margaret was gaily astonished by the Pimlico basement and the Little Midshipman, so Tony entered the big drawing-room or saloon of her home with astonished recognition, and found that he had seldom felt more at home in a new environment in his life.

For it was simply his mother's saloon all over again. It was like stepping through the looking-glass, magically, into a counterpart room, with the same high Gothic windows, except that there were five instead of three, and the same slender Gothic columns, save that the ornamentation was picked out in delicate silver instead of gold. There was the all but identical chimney-piece, similarly decked at each end with candelabra, so alike that one might well be reduced to counting the sconces, five apiece at Royal Lodge to Birr Castle's seven. Birr has its sumptuous chandelier of Waterford crystal, and the larger saloon of Royal Lodge has the sparkle of three such chandeliers.

In both rooms paintings and, everywhere, flowers contribute to the urbane and feminine atmosphere. The Queen Mother was accustomed to admiration of her saloon, and no doubt amused to find her guest and her daughter lost in this hilarious storm of comparison. To heighten the coincidences, Tony remembered a desk in the Birr saloon placed, like a desk at Royal Lodge, sidelong to the window. There was, besides, one similarity of which Tony said nothing, though it has been mentioned elsewhere. Petite and like sisters in age and build, Tony perhaps found that Princess Margaret's mother curiously resembled his own mother, a resemblance making her all the more sympathetic and endearing.

As at Birr Castle, on a wintry Saturday afternoon, tea at Royal Lodge was served beside the log-fire in the smaller, comfortable octagonal sitting-room adjoining. Princess Margaret was eager to hear Tony's American adventures. Had he seen *West Side Story*? Tony could admit to seeing nothing lighter than *Ivanov*. Presently the Princess put on a record and in the sunset light the songs from the new musical—which had recently opened in London—surged through the room. "*I feel pretty . . . oh, so pretty*" . . . "*Tonight, tonight,*—the world is mine tonight" and "*Maria, Maria . . .* I'm in love with a girl named Maria . . ." One cannot chart all the incidents of a friendship, and only in imagination can we capture the glow of two people who are falling in love.

V

Princess Margaret had first seen *West Side Story* as guest of honour at the charity premiére. She went to see it again in February, with the Queen and Elizabeth Cavendish, and with Tony inconspicuous in the trio of escorts. When the Queen Mother attended a performance, she told Walter Clarke, the theatre manager, "Princess Margaret is always playing the records", and Her Majesty needed no maternal intuition when she discovered that the story was a Manhattan version of Romeo and Juliet in modern dress, and that the Romeo role was named Tony.

People in love are apt to build their own world around them, a world in which every event and circumstance fall into place like scenery in the slots of a toy theatre, and for Margaret and Tony the songs of *West Side Story* and the melodies of the film *Gigi* will for ever capture the first pristine magic of their early romance. Tony did not immediately see himself as the Princess's suitor. The mood was more a deepening of affectionate friendship, each discovering the other at a new and more sincere level of candour. Tony once said to a studio friend, "You can know so many people and not know anyone at all." Perhaps in exploring the true personality of Princess Margaret he learned how vulnerable to hurt she still was beneath the superficial gaiety, and all his tender protective instincts were aroused. "At a deeper emotional level, both have had disadvantages to overcome, have suffered setbacks, are gay," one observer noted. "Both have a touch of immaturity still; are sociable yet paradoxically solitary. Both have been a long time getting settled down."

Across the flowing stream there were still stepping-stones to be crossed. In February, Princess Margaret paid a visit to Lord and Lady Rupert Nevill at Uckfield. Tony proposed himself for a visit to his grandmama Messel at Cuckfield, not a dozen miles away. At about this time Tony had acquired another motor-bike, a useful asset when photographers were apt to peer into cars turning into the Nevills' drive but paid no attention to anyone arriving on a motor-bike by a back lane from the A272. Artlessly, Tony mentioned to Mrs. Messel that he was going to see someone he liked very much. Then he gently broke the surprise by saying "It's someone you already know . . . in a way—it's Princess Margaret", and thus the old lady and her trusted companion, Miss Dengate, were among the first to be prepared for the official betrothal, still a year distant.

They may have been a trifle bewildered, the following month, to read that Tony was in Davos with Jacqui Chan although, to be sure, the columnist reporting this event made it clear that they were staying at different ends of the town. Tony, in fact, continued his usual photographic assignments and the discreet Miss Chan has never indicated whether she actively assisted in the smoke-screen that Tony increasingly threw around his movements as the months passed. In 1957, when she appeared as principal boy in pantomime at the little Theatre Royal in Windsor, Tony had booked the entire front row for his friends and begged his columnist acquaintances to take note that this might make a good story. Now, in 1959, when Bill Glenton enquired about Jacqui, Tony seemed to him "to skate around the subject". Her bronze head nevertheless continued to hold its premier place in the little Rotherhithe room, gazing inscrutably across the Thames.

Others thought that they detected a new restlessness. Tony began saying that he was becoming bored with photography and thought of giving it up, although he still did photo-call work, competing with David Sim, for example, in the little magazine *Plays and*

Players. Taking photographs of *A Midsummer Night's Dream* at the Old Vic, he startled the players by being able to quote their lines by heart. He photographed Julie Andrews, Jacqui Chan, Natasha Parry and Mrs. Bluey Mavroleon modelling head-dresses; and it has become a curiosity that he photographed the Earl and Countess of Harewood at Harewood Hall for the March, 1959, issue of *Vogue* (as well as the cartoonist Giles and his Bentley on another page). Planning a photo layout of jiving youngsters in party kit, he involved Princess Margaret in a fever of hep-cat slang, and a royal dinner-party was enlivened by guests vying in bringing zingy phrases to mind, "Dig!... I got the message. Man, I've flipped ... acting like a cool cat ... having a ball ... strictly from outer space ... acting real gone ... "

The Queen Mother had arranged to pay a private visit to Italy at the end of April and Princess Margaret's sudden decision to join her was charged with significance. Perhaps this holiday, brief as it was, was the equivalent of the separation, the sea change, traditionally expected of a princess when taking the most momentous decision of her life.

Not that the romantic atmosphere of Italy was able to quell love in bloom. The Duke of Edinburgh returned home from a three-month world tour on April 30th and I believe that the Queen and he were privately told of Princess Margaret's "growing fondness for Tony" that weekend at Windsor.

A growing fondness ... but, as yet, no more. Tony himself faced a painful private preoccupation at this time in the breakdown of his father's marriage after twenty-three years. Carol had left her husband, after involving herself with a new group of friends, and had given Ronnie grounds for divorce, and it decidedly grieved Tony to find his father confronting solitude when just turning sixty and by no means in good health. This solicitude for his father gnawed at the bud of his happiness with Princess Margaret, and yet her consoling sympathy obviously served in turn to bring them still closer together. A salient occasion was the photo-session at Royal Lodge when Tony took the official photographs for the Princess's twenty-ninth birthday. The pictures were in reality taken three months ahead of time and evoke the perfect happiness of that radiant summer day.

Besides, Tony now enjoyed an excuse to carry a photograph of Princess Margaret around in his wallet, for why should a photographer not find a mascot in his own current work? There is a story, too, that when shopping in Cartier's the Princess greatly admired a gold replica of a walnut which, on being opened, proved to be a holder for a dozen tiny photographs. Billy Wallace, always a willing aide, is said to have quietly purchased the walnut a day or two later. In similar vein, understanding friends are supposed to have invited the Princess and Tony to dinner and then quietly left them to themselves, although neither were so unmindful of the courtesies.

"It just so happened that we had a nursery crisis one night—and then my husband remembered the overseas telephone calls he had to make in his study," one married friend recalls. Like many young couples, in fact, the two found that opportunities to be alone together were all too few. A penthouse terrace at treetop level in Belgravia and a tiny secluded back-garden in Chelsea were early settings of their whispered conversations. Like any young couple, they held hands in the back row at the pictures. It made no difference that the cinema was the private theatre in the basement of Clarence House or that the movie was the then-banned Marlon Brando film *The Wild Ones*. It is melancholy to add that a footman sharply noted the occasion and later narrated it in print.

The story is told of two workmen who argued for an hour on whether a petite figure seen hurrying from a car across the pavement of the Pimlico Road was Princess Margaret. Ultimately they adjourned with their unlikely tale to a pub and deservedly met the general derision of the incredulous company. According to Bill Glenton, Tony once drove the Princess to his studio "but the sudden and unexpected arrival of a group of friends made them wary of returning". On the other hand, it was some while before Mr. Glenton realised that Princess Margaret was a guest incognito in his own Rotherhithe home. He was puzzled that Elizabeth Cavendish sometimes visited Tony's river room to "tidy a little" until he discovered by chance that she was Princess Margaret's lady in waiting and an unbelievable possibility entered his thoughts. Then, one evening, returning from a newspaper assignment, he was about to climb the staircase when the door of the ground-floor room opened enquiringly and "against the softly candle-lit background was the unmistakable figure" of the Princess.

Now Mr. Glenton was a Fleet Street journalist and here, in his own home, within a few feet of his typewriter, was the "lead" of the greatest romantic scoop story of the century. It says much for the loyalty of ordinary folk to the Royal Family that he said nothing at the time . . . and indeed kept every secret until after 59 Rotherhithe Street had met the axes of the demolition men and had been reduced to rubble.

9 *The Phenomenal Marriage*

The passage of time readily embellishes the private lives of royalty
with a patina of legend, but in the romance of Princess Margaret
and Lord Snowdon in 1959 nothing was more remarkable than the
reality itself. For the then Tony Armstrong-Jones, at the gate of his
thirties, the adventures of the year assumed an Arabian Nights
quality, as he moved from the basement of Coleshill Buildings to
Clarence House or from Royal Lodge to Rotherhithe.If cameramen
were inclined to loiter at the formal sentry-guarded western
entrance to Clarence House, he drove in by the little-known eastern
gate on the far side of St. James's Palace. When the Queen Mother
invited him to Royal Lodge, he often made his way there circuit-
ously, by way of an entrance gate on the far side of Windsor Great
Park.

Long before he first met Princess Margaret, Tony had always
enjoyed provoking his closer friends with an air of mystery or
teasing them with his deliberate vagueness but now they noticed, as
one said, "a cautious secrecy quite unlike the old Tony". He would
mention that he was going away for the weekend without saying
where, or suddenly apologise and dash away, merely saying that he
had an appointment. In conversation, casual enquiries about his
movements were met at times with "a curious deafness, a dreamy
stare". And yet if anyone had been inquisitive enough to follow
Tony, they might have discovered nothing more surprising than his
Borgwald shooting brake parked at the back of Clarence House, an
unsuspicious circumstance for a young man drawing a four-figure
income from the copyright fees of royal photography. Indeed, when
a newspaper correspondent noticed Tony sitting in the Queen's

pavilion, watching polo at Smith's Lawn, he concluded it was an instance of a Court photographer enjoying royal privileges.

Another acquaintance believes she saw Tony window-shopping one rainy night in Chelsea with "a girl in a head-scarf wearing a raincoat too big for her" and still cannot be sure whether in fact she saw Princess Margaret on one of her Haroun al Raschid adventures. The Princess had drawn Tony into her innermost world but Tony in turn continually "got a kick" out of showing that the ordinary enjoyments of everyday life were by no means out of reach of the Queen's sister.

Always eager to hear news of Tony's Pimlico "digs", both the Queen and her mother could venture to satisfy their curiosity, in that populous district, only by driving past in a car. Prince Philip is said to have strolled in by a back way, through the Coleshill court-yard and down the steps, to have a drink one night, and we can imagine him discussing the merits of Tony's cameras—his Leica and Nikon, Rolliflex and Hasleblad—or looking round the basement to express his sailorly appreciation of the space-saving and gadgetry. Far from the two future brothers-in-law being at odds, they early laid foundations of mutual understanding and sympathy with one another. Yet it was Princess Margaret herself whom Tony liberated from the exclusive confining royal orbit, introducing her to the homes of his own trusted intimates and kinsfolk, taking her to meet his Aunt Gwendy, his father's younger sister, for example, or stopping for an impromptu lunch at some favourite country inn of his, where she was seldom recognised. The Princess evinced a phobia about snooping cameramen and at Balmoral had more than once been reduced to tears by the unwelcome insistence of one of the more importunate photographers. Tony eloquently persuaded her, I think, that save for the millionth chance cameras lurk only where royalty is anticipated and that people usually see only what they expect to see. And a pair of sunglasses was usually a sufficient disguise.

At Rotherhithe, strangers occasionally disturbed the Princess by mistake but never realised her identity. "I hope you don't mind," one of Bill Glenton's visitors said to him afterwards, "I wandered into your lodger's room. She must have wondered who I was." At a hotel restaurant not far from Maidenhead, a waiter reminisced, "The lady was quite a lot like Princess Margaret. But when she called him 'Tony' and he called her 'Ducky' I knew I must be wrong." At another restaurant, an American paused beside the table. "Forgive me staring," she said. "I've never seen such a resemblance. You remind me of beautiful Princess Margaret!"

"Thank you. I'm flattered," came the reply.

Though one takes some of these stories with a grain of salt, they echo the spirit of masquerade or romantic operetta in which Tony and his princess indulged with great gaiety and fun. When booking a table for six at a Soho restaurant, Dominic Elliot over-stressed that there would be "an important guest". Princess Margaret was, of course, unfailingly recognised and so was Mr. Elliot who had sat next to her, but no attention was paid to Tony who had sat opposite. When dancing with the Princess at a charity ball, Tony was careful to accord his partner a strictly formal bow as the dance ended. And so their romance remained off the record, their affection concealed from Fleet Street and thus from the world long after it became known to the concourse of their closer friends.

Yet straws blew in the wind. In June the Queen Mother appointed a press secretary for herself and Princess Margaret for the first time, as if anticipating that the normal flow of newspaper enquiries at Clarence House might one day swell into a torrent. In that month, too, Tony darkly hinted of going to America to start a new career and began to talk of selling his business, pretending that he was bored with photography. At Royal Lodge one day Princess Margaret horrified the gardeners by seizing a pair of shears and cutting her way through a yew hedge that, in its perfection, had divided the house from the sunlight and freedom of the swimming pool. The Princess had been to Portugal on a private visit and there are indications that the Queen consulted her advisers at this time with a view to a message to be passed to her Commonwealth Prime Ministers.

Then suddenly the skies cleared. In mid-July, Mr. Antony Armstrong-Jones was among the guests at an informal luncheon party at Clarence House given by Queen Elizabeth the Queen Mother in honour of the High Commissioner for Rhodesia and Nyasaland, Sir Gilbert Rennie. The Rennies' elder son was getting married later in the month and, with romance in her Scottish maternal heart, Lady Rennie wondered a little about the handsome young man of about her son's age who spent much of his time talking to his neighbour, Princess Alexandra, but cast an occasional deeply mischievous glance along the table towards Princess Margaret. I, too, had occasion to note that the Sussex festivities of Goodwood week were "like a series of pre-engagement parties". For part of the time

Princess Margaret stayed with her friends, the Parker-Bowles, at their seaside house near Aldwick and the extent of anonymity possible to the Queen's sister was seldom better defined. Tony stayed inland at Billy Wallace's home near Petworth and usually made an early start in his car to motor the few miles to the coast. And there was no reason why anyone should pay any particular attention to a young man hand-in-hand with a girl in a yellow swimsuit scampering happily along the beach.

II

The possibilities of marriage had been "in the air", as we have seen, since the early spring, after little more than a year of swift-growing friendship. The prospect subtly surmised between the two young people in March or April had become ardently desired by early May, when Tony took up a very clear position as an intending suitor and had "a serious talk" first with the Queen Mother and then with the Queen. There were of course no constitutional or legal objections and no family difficulties of any kind. At that time, however, Princess Margaret was third in succession to the Throne and, on her own initiative, the Queen decided to consult her Ministers on the conjectural situation that might arise if her sister should wish to marry a commoner. The question was necessarily couched in impersonal terms and in the meantime Tony was sympathetically counselled to wait a little, much in the pattern of Prince Philip when he first approached King George VI for his elder daughter's hand.

There are hints that the Queen personally mentioned the matter to Mr. John Diefenbaker, the Prime Minister of Canada, and Mrs. Diefenbaker, expressing her own happiness, in July, during the six-weeks tour of Canada. This was the journey from which the Queen returned radiant with the anticipation that she was to have another child, and the circumstance was to be well summarised in a letter from a royal lady many months later. "People are saying that Elizabeth does not favour the match between Margaret and Armstrong-Jones—what nonsense! As if one cannot gauge her emotional response to her sister's happiness by the advent of the new baby—and this after nine years of hoping for more children!"

Next, in mid-August, Tony was the Queen Mother's guest at the Castle of Mey for a couple of days before he joined the royal house-party at Balmoral for the first time. The announcement that the Queen was expecting a baby caused one of those extraordinary deliriums of public curiosity, so much so that the customary Sunday drive from Balmoral Castle to Crathie Church had to be cancelled and Divine Service was held in a drawing-room instead. The newspapers reported that yards of camouflage netting had been erected "to defeat anyone who trained binoculars on the Queen's guests" and a *Paris-Match* photographer who crawled through the tussocks and swamps of Glen Muick was all but devoured by midges before he ran into a cordon of alert Scottish troops. Trained in the difference between wood-smoke and fire, local folk had the impression that something was about to happen but nobody knew what.

According to John Payne, then a member of Princess Margaret's staff, Tony must have been conspicuous riding or walking on the moors with Princess Margaret in his non-conforming kit, "plus fours ... suede boots ... a loose fitting corduroy jacket and a sharp-peaked cap ... they both carried cameras wherever they went". The Queen was as determined as her sister that not the slightest hint of rumour should mar private felicity. The Princess had planned to celebrate her twenty-ninth birthday on Friday, August 21st, with a family picnic and an evening dance, but it poured with rain all day and the royal party stayed indoors. Unusually exotic bouquets of flowers from America were delivered to the Princess, though whether they came from Earl Mountbatten, who was in New York, or from Uncle Oliver Messel or deviously from Tony himself one cannot say.

It may be that, in the end, Tony and the Princess mischievously kept their private betrothal secret from everyone for just a few hours. When at last they broke their news to the royal circle, the Queen was not unprepared and had indeed a little surprise in readiness of her own. A Western had been booked for the movie programme in the Castle ballroom but the Queen had arranged for the George Cole film *The Bridal Path* to be kept in reserve and it was shown instead. It was a homely Scottish story of love and marriage, and the happy-ever-after ending was received with a roar of applause from the royals, an outburst highly mystifying to members of the Household not in the know.

This private betrothal, as I have termed it, might be better defined as an understanding. The two had agreed to follow the traditional prudent system of the Royal Family and wait six months before a formal engagement and, although they had endured separations enough already, they even undertook to part for a month or two in the late autumn. There is some evidence that March 1st, St.

David's Day, was considered for an announcement, a date highly appropriate for the first Welshman to marry into the Royal Family since Owen Glendower. Then it was pointed out that this perhaps unwisely indicated a Leap Year proposal on February 29th. Tony is said to have favoured St. Valentine's day on February 14th and Lady Rosse's birthday on February 8th was also considered, but then it seemed better to defer the decision until after the arrival of the Queen's baby.

Returning to London after ten days at Balmoral, Tony busied himself with photographs for his last *Vogue* magazine cover which was to show a girl embowered in roses. Armfuls and pyramids of roses filled the studio until Tony found that the scene in his view-finder reeked of sentiment and the final shot showed a blonde in profile with only a single rose nestling below her ear. This was the picture that "sang from the bookstalls", as one editress thought, just at the time of the engagement announcement.

But first the young people enjoyed the warm dry Indian summer when Princess Margaret returned from Scotland. The radiogram at Royal Lodge was seldom silent, and the two could sup alone, with small tables drawn up to their armchairs, watching television, like a cosy domestic foretaste of the future. They disappeared into the moonlight in the garden or sat watching the moths fluttering against the lamps near the swimming-pool, planning and confiding. The Princess amused Tony, I think, by choosing her bridesmaids chiefly on the premise that they should be the prettiest group of bridesmaids ever seen, and Tony amused his future bride by revealing that he had given scarcely any thought to the all-important question of who should be his best man.

Although Tony had brought many couples together, no one had ever asked him to be a best man, and so there was no prospect of "returning a compliment". Many a suitable young man, moreover, might have expressed horror at the prospect of acting as best man at a semi-State wedding in Westminster Abbey. The dark and jaunty Jeremy Fry, when first asked as a trusted friend, agreed however without demur. Son of a former chairman of the chocolate firm, Jeremy had met his own wife, Camilla Grinling, through Tony. Besides, he had been at Gordonstoun with Prince Philip and so had gone through the same mill of discipline and *savoir faire*. It was characteristic of the Frys that when Tony suggested talking it over, they at once suggested he should come down for the weekend and nonchalantly added that he should bring the Princess.

Their home, Widcombe Manor, was a small early eighteenth-century house, formerly celebrated as the home of H. A. Vachell, the novelist, of "Quinneys" fame, and locally renowned for the ornamental staircase, fountains and cascades of its gardens. Princess Margaret was enchanted and dreamed, as a bride will, of just such a house for herself and Tony, in or near London. During that happy unfettered weekend right away from the world of royalty she had besides the fun of paying secret visits with Tony to Bath and Bristol without being recognised. If their time dimensions could have crossed, it was surely an escapade that would have danced through the romantic dreams of Elizabeth Linley nearly 250 years distant.

In London, too, the Queen Mother indulged the betrothed couple by arranging a party for them at Clarence House, which turned out to be probably the greatest evening of gaiety witnessed in that staid old mansion this century. The footmen wore the scarlet coats of semi-State livery; more than two hundred and fifty guests danced to Ray Ellington's band until 3 a.m. and bacon-and-egg breakfasts were served at the tables arranged along the main corridor until nearly dawn. If, as one participant noted, "Princess Margaret positively bounced with excitement", there was the added fun that fewer than half the guests suspected the real reason for the party. The Princess and Tony were careful to change partners. The culminating moment came when the Queen Mother headed a conga line that swayed and curled from the first-floor drawing-room, down and around the house and back—and who should notice that Princess Margaret and Tony in fact headed the noisy laughing line behind their hostess and the Queen?

Another evening, when a dinner and dance was given at Buckingham Palace, Princess Alexandra delighted in being a fellow-conspirator by pretending that the whole brilliant affair was staged-simply to welcome her home from Australia. Then the lovers parted, as they had agreed, Princess Margaret to take up a stream of official duties while Tony flew to Ireland to join his sister, Susan, at Abbey Leix. A thick mantle of snow, seldom seen so early in winter in central Ireland, covered the Slieve Bloom mountains that divide Leix from Birr, thirty miles distant. Tony improvised toboggans for the delectation of his two young Vesey nieces and their brother, Tom, and spent hours swishing down the white hills with the laughing, shrieking children, his unfettered happiness absurdly obvious.

Tony and Susan also shared another private cause for contentment. They had worried over their father's solitude—now that he had divorced Carol and she had married her Italian—and instead, all had come right and Ronnie Armstrong-Jones sent word that he hoped to beat Tony, if not to the altar, at least to the marriage registrar. In London, Ronnie had hesitantly mentioned to his son that Jenifer Unite was the same age as Susan... "and she's a honey". They had met at a party when Jenifer was between trips as a B.O.A.C. air-hostess; they discovered that they both knew the same people in the Bahamas, where Ronnie had investment interests, and they planned to honeymoon in Bermuda. Tony and Susan, though quietly amused at the prospect of having a stepmother as young as themselves, were delighted for their father. If Susan faced an inner perplexity (for she had embraced her husband's Roman Catholic faith on marriage) Tony's view was quite uncomplicated. When his sister and brother-in-law attended Mass, he went by himself to Holy Communion at the Protestant parish church in the village. Tony's sincere religious faith is known only to his closest friends.

III

Tony's younger half-brother, Martin Parsons, celebrated his coming-of-age on December 23rd, enlivening Tony's last bachelor Christmas at Abbey Leix and Birr with still greater festivity. Tony saw the New Year in at Birr, his all-important New Year of 1960, and then went straight to Sandringham.

He knew already that his Princess had not changed her mind. The whole house-party, the children, the dogs, joined in the happiest welcome and, although this was his first visit, Tony once again—as at Royal Lodge—felt strangely at home. Though so different in size, Sandringham shared much of the atmosphere of his Grandmama Messel's home at Holmsted Manor, with the keepsakes of delicate glass and china, the bleached oak and white paintwork. As so often at his grandmama's, Tony also realised that there had been much discussion about his future.

Despite the Queen Mother's buoyant assurance that all would come right, that "a way would be found", one suspects that the preliminaries of closing his photographic business had left Tony with a sense of disorientation. Now the intangible prospects of the Arts Council, the British Council, the Civic Trust, the Council of Industrial Design, the idea of a gallery of photographic art, drifted

145

as unresolved as the blue smoke of the log fires. Suggestions on where they were to live were no less desultory. The couple had firmly made up their minds that they wished for a small house, and clearly there was no questioning Tony's assumption that he would pay the bills and would indeed be master in his own home.

One evening the young couple kept the table joyously aglow with their vision of the siege of Pimlico by all the forces of press and television once their engagement was announced. Several friends had generously offered sanctuary but Tony readily accepted the Queen and Prince Philip's suggestion that it would be better to take up residence in Buckingham Palace. On another important question, however, one can add with the surest authority that he was less amenable. The Queen drew him aside one day to discuss her sister's married name and touched on the question of Tony's future rank and style. Her future brother-in-law was taken aback; he had never thought of himself as anything but an unvarnished Armstrong-Jones. The Queen tacitly suggested an earldom and Tony, while thanking her and expressing his appreciation, undertook to think about the possibility—*but then he declined*.

Since nothing in Lord Snowdon's career has been more sharply criticised than his acceptance of a title, one considers that it might have been wiser if his early refusal had been permitted to become public knowledge. As Kingsley Martin has said, his insistence on marrying as a commoner was to prove a welcome modern asset to the monarchy. Perhaps one of the Queen's advisers was committed to persuading Tony and, skirting around the ambiguous marriages of some of George III's daughters, he could point out that no British princess so close in the Succession had married a commoner since a daughter of Edward IV married Thomas Kymbe in 1503. There were suggestions that the Armstrong-Jones connection with Caernarvonshire could be commemorated at least by a peerage, say, perhaps, the title of Lord Arvon. But Tony was politely adamant, and a suggestion that a style and title should be devised for his children evoked an unexpected response from the puritanic Welsh strain deep in his make-up, for he unmistakably showed that he thought it inappropriate to discuss children before he was married.

The Sandringham group dispersed early, for Princess Margaret had an official and well-timed engagement at the Royal Docks, downstream from Rotherhithe, and since Elizabeth Cavendish was her lady in waiting that day we may infer that they subsequently changed cars and made their way through the Blackwall Tunnel to the Little Midshipman. Tony would have brought things in for tea and lit the oilstove in readiness so that they basked in a pleasant fug as they watched the sunset view of the river. The next day, January 13th, all the Royal Family—except the Queen, who was anticipating her baby in February—went to Romsey for the wedding of Lady Pamela Mountbatten and David Hicks; and Tony was there, too, unnoticed but rightfully included among the 1,200 guests, for he had known David since his earliest days in Pimlico.

Only six weeks remained before Tony's name became a household word in every home of the western world, and he divided his time between his Princess's company back at Sandringham, and the essential maintenance of their smoke-screen. He asked Swaebe, one day, whether he would like to take over the lease of the Pimlico studio because, Tony reiterated, "I'm thinking of making a complete break . . . and going to America." He was conspicuous at the rehearsals of a John Cranko ballet at Covent Garden, clambering around the stage and over the seats, looking for camera angles, giving an impression of business as usual. The story spread that attendants suggested throwing him out as an intruder until he explained that he had the ballet-master's permission. Again, he pretended to be anxious to photograph a dress rehearsal at the Shakespeare Memorial Theatre at Stratford-on-Avon scheduled for the end of February; he initiated correspondence with B.B.C. television on the prospects of working creatively in television films and went along to see Huw Wheldon, producer of the cultural programme *Monitor*.

Here and there was a wisp of true intention. He went along to view a house for sale in London's 'Little Venice', overlooking the Regent's Canal, and one surmises Tony's dream that a home might yet be found overlooking the water, as at Rotherhithe. Early one morning he went along to the Little Midshipman to collect a few treasures and mysteriously explained to Bill Glenton, "It may be a while before I see you again. Do please look after the room. *Don't let anyone in!*"

For the chase was quickening. On the last day at Sandringham, January 31st, most of the royals walked through the park to Sandringham Church but Margaret and Tony put their secrecy at hazard by reverently going together to the little church at West Newton. Pamela Mountbatten's wedding had renewed the old press speculation about Princess Margaret, and in Commander Colville's office at Buckingham Palace every visitor tried sooner or later to glean a clue to the Princess's future. The Queen's press secretary invariably gazed inscrutably back at his questioner, and never by a flicker indicated the outsize clue hanging beside him on the wall, the most obvious object in the room, the huge photograph of Prince Charles and Princess Anne taken, as everyone knew, by Antony Armstrong-Jones.

Tony himself made one slip. Overhearing the novelist Kingsley Amis airing some adverse views on Princess Margaret at a reception, his impulse to defend her proved irresistible. "You are absolutely wrong . . ." he began, warmly.

"But how do you know?" Kingsley Amis demanded. "Do you know her? Are you a friend?" In the heat of the moment, Tony could not but say that he was, and ears round about were cocked and alert and listening.

The Queen had agreed that the engagement should be announced seven days after the advent of her baby, and Prince Andrew was born on February 19th. This was no doubt the day when Tony telephoned Carol Coombe in Chelsea to say that Susan was in town and that they would both like to drop round. His stepmother had noticed his happy gaiety only a few weeks before and had teased him with having a new girl friend but found he was not to be drawn. But when Tony and Sue—as Carol always called her—arrived that afternoon, she at once knew there was "some excitement in the air, some secret they wanted to share . . ."

"Carol," said Tony, diffidently, "I'm engaged!"

Naturally, Carol congratulated him and kissed him and wanted to know the name of the lucky girl.

"Princess Margaret!"

"Don't be silly, Tone. You really must tell me whom you're going to marry."

"It's true—Princess Margaret!"

"It's true," Susan in turn assured her, and they solemnly adjured their stupefied stepmother that their news must remain in absolute confidence. Princess Margaret was deeply anxious lest in the remaining seven days her secret should still be spoiled. But then a series of extraordinary, dismaying and unforeseen events occurred.

On Sunday morning, the 21st, came the incredible news that the Countess Mountbatten, who was visiting North Borneo and was only fifty-eight, had died during the night. Within forty-eight hours, on the 23rd, the Royal Family also learned that the elderly Marquess of Carisbrooke, Queen Victoria's last surviving grandson, had died at his home in Kensington Palace. The extraordinary conjunction of events threw Tony and the Princess into alternate sadness and alarm. While Mr. Macmillan, as Prime Minister, was officially expressing his condolences, he was also privately informing Mr. Hugh Gaitskell, as Leader of the Opposition, of the impending betrothal. The Queen had decreed a week of family mourning but decided equally that prearranged events should not be affected.

Her special concern was particularly for a wedding within the Queen Mother's family, that of Diana Bowes-Lyon to Peter Somervell in Westminster Abbey on February 24th. The Queen Mother and Princess Margaret were among the guests in the splendour of the Henry VII Chapel and there, too—unnoticed for the last time—was Tony. We can imagine the glances that he and the Princess exchanged in the church where within three months they would be made man and wife. At the reception in St. James's Palace afterwards one guest thought them "sweetly and quite absurdly in love".

Next day Tony motored down to Sussex with Susan to see their grandmother. They found her suddenly aged and ailing, and indeed both Oliver Messel and Lady Rosse were staying with her and were greatly concerned. Mrs. Messel was anxious that her illness should not "cast a shadow", as she said, over the engagement but Tony inevitably returned to London in some gloom. Yet nothing now could hold back the full joy of events. On Friday the 26th the betrothed couple were waiting together at Royal Lodge when the announcement from Clarence House came over the radio:

It is with the greatest pleasure that Queen Elizabeth The Queen Mother announces the betrothal of her beloved daughter The Princess Margaret to Mr. Antony Charles Robert Armstrong-Jones, son of Mr. R. O. L. Armstrong-Jones Q.C., and the Countess of Rosse, to which union The Queen has gladly given her consent.

One story is that the Queen Mother had secretly filled the house with family guests who, at this signal, burst upon the couple with their rejoicing. Another tale is that the Princess forgot to wear her engagement ring next morning, so accustomed was she to concealing it. The ring had been specially made to Tony's own design, a ruby like a rosebud set within a marguerite of diamonds on a gold band. Certainly the couple had their own private joke about displaying the ring next day when they posed in the saloon and walked in the garden for *The Times* and television cameramen . . . and for the first time in his life Tony tried hard not to be the impresario of the photo-session.

IV

For the next ten weeks Tony made his home in Buckingham Palace in a first-floor guest suite notable for its heavy mahogany furniture, old-fashioned pictures, gilt-and-white décor and a handwritten card "Armstrong-Jones" inserted into a slot on his door. Apart from a standing order for a bowl of fruit and a jug of orange juice to be taken to his room every evening, the staff scarcely knew he was there. He had his own latchkey for an inner door of the courtyard and no one attended his comings and goings, although a detective was allocated "in case required". As the Queen and her husband had foreseen, the immunity of the Palace—alternating with the guest room above the porch at Royal Lodge—afforded welcome protection from the world's fervent, almost hysterical attention.

Commander Colville's office was in a state of telephone siege as he explained, over and over again, that "both the Queen and Prince Philip were delighted because this is such an obviously happy match". Without exception, the press of the democratic world jubilantly decided that the engagement was a royal story as phenomenal as the Coronation or Abdication, with the added strength that this was a popular romantic bombshell surprise. And certainly the leader writers and commentators were as right as could be when they agreed that the announcement gave universal pleasure.

Tony and his Princess, one gathers, studied the newspapers with a mixture of happy interest, humour and horror. It was dismaying to read that Carol had once sold razor-blades outside Olympia exhibition: she had indeed, as a promotion girl, years before, once joined in a razor-blade advertising campaign. Tony discovered that a host of writers, quite unknown to him, could write "with intimacy" as his "personal friends". It was news to himself to read that his own tankard was kept at a Pimlico pub, that his favourite lunch was a meat pie washed down with ale, and that he was an Adonis with "a direct and dazzling blue regard". Tracked down on his honeymoon in Bermuda, Ronnie Armstrong-Jones contributed to the joy of nations when he told a reporter, "I've known about my son and Princess Margaret for months. But naturally I never interfered."

Writing an exceptionally accurate profile, Mark Boxer concluded that friends in future would "not drop in quite so casually for breakfast" and he summed up, "But what will his life be from now on? He is too bright, too alert, too conscious of his talents to do nothing . . . It would be sad if Tony spent the next eight years living down his past." In fairness, it must be added that other writers were taken aback by editorial exuberance. I contributed a hurriedly-written series to a Sunday newspaper and was startled to find it advertised by enormous posters "Scoops the World! . . . Exclusive! The romance . . . the full inside story . . ." The series was accorded a similar treatment across North America and throughout the Commonwealth, in Berlin, Tokyo, Rome and so on, and a friend not given to exaggeration phoned me from Paris to tell me that the boulevards were placarded with "Le Roman d'Amour de Tony—par Helen Cathcart"!

Every household in Britain was glued to its television screen when Tony made his first appearance in public with Princess Margaret and the Queen Mother at a gala performance at the Royal Opera House, Covent Garden. Tony knew the great theatre so well when it was dark and empty. Now it blazed with television arc-lamps, and glittered with the diamonds and decorations of a full dress occasion. Tony had never noticed, I think, how steep was the grand staircase, how difficult to climb with an aching left leg, without putting out a hand to the balustrade, while the insatiable television cameras watched him relentlessly. He stepped into the royal box unaware that the Queen Mother had moved aside so that she should not diminish her daughter's tumultuous reception. He stood behind his Princess, smiling at her in love and pride, and quite failed to realise—the nice man that he is!—that the applause, breaking into cheers, were as much in confident welcome to him as in affectionate well-wishing to his future bride.

The following week, there were plans to celebrate Tony's thirtieth birthday on March 7th with a luncheon party at Clarence House to include Mr. and Mrs. Ronald Armstrong-Jones, newly returned from their honeymoon, and with a dinner party to include Lord and Lady Rosse in the evening. But when Tony's mother telephoned her birthday greetings she had to break the sad news that his grandmother's illness had taken a grave turn. Making his apologies to the Queen Mother, Tony left immediately after lunch for Holmsted Manor, and Mrs. Messel died there the following day. Grief was thus once again strangely mingled with happiness and with the severance of that beloved link with an older generation, a firmer maturity settled on Tony's shoulders.

Henceforth, like man and shadow, there were to be two Tonys; the grown man of practical sense and single-mind whom his kinsfolk observed with understanding and the fantasy Tony of the public image who had become the dream-boy of the western world. There was the real Tony, unconventional though sufficiently orthodox inside, the man who held the Etonian view of public duty and yet disliked to be bound to discipline, superficial and yet determined, his personality blending the polar opposites of his parents. And there was the Tony of contemporary folklore and illusion, the peasant boy who was marrying the beautiful Princess and so appealing to the deepest atavistic instincts of man and womankind.

Tony was not the dupe of his own publicity. His attitude was demonstrated when he read a profile of himself that an editorial friend, John Barber, who had once written his photo captions, had contributed to the *Daily Mail*. Tony impulsively rang up Mr. Barber from Buckingham Palace to thank him, adding "I hope I can live up to the high opinion you have of me". It is instructive to check what drew this response. Mr. Barber had written, "His marriage means that the Establishment acquires a gifted professional in creative work . . . He may well find his career in working for the visual arts in the tradition of Queen Victoria's consort . . . He will not be trapped in any gilded coach if only because he is too aware of his gifts. He is free for ever from what has been his insatiable need to fight for the limelight. The best of his life is yet to come."

Tony also noticed, with a droll and ironic eye, that the newspapers brashly discussed whether he should have a title and that they found it a vexed issue on which they were about evenly divided. The editor of *Burke's Peerage* opined that a peerage seemed more fitting than a knighthood and thought it "not inconceivable" that Mr. Armstrong-Jones might change his name to Windsor. The editor of *Debrett* maintained that to make Mr. Armstrong-Jones a marquis—"and one imagines the title would not be less"—implied that a Princess in a democracy still might not marry outside the nobility. An official of the College of Arms admitted guardedly that a royal bridegroom could become a Knight of the Garter, and thus hold the highest Order of Chivalry, though becoming no more than a "Sir". More ingeniously, Peterborough of the *Daily Telegraph* discovered that Princess Margaret could be created a duchess or a marchioness in her own right and so be gifted with secondary titles to bestow on the children while Mr. Armstrong-Jones might still remain a commoner.

To the public, attracted by the newcomer's good looks and engaging smile, these were hazy issues. It was more debatable that the Princess's Civil List allowance of £6,000 would be increased on marriage to £15,000, although Parliament had fixed no real provision for her husband. Was the husband, then, to live off his wife? Was there indeed any alternative if he had no great wealth of his own and were denied his own career? The wits even seized upon the family motto of the Armstrong-Jones, "*A noddo Duw a Noddir*— To Support God is to be Supported". As the plans for the wedding went forward, the sensitive barometer of public opinion indicated a mood of anxiety on what Tony might find to do in royal circles and on what might become of him.

It was natural, thought the public, that he should snatch a time of happiness in his betrothal, pleasing to hear of him spending a day at Newbury races with his fiancée, and fun to catch glimpses of him on television following the boat-race with Princess Margaret in the Cambridge launch—and what a pity that year that Oxford won! It was amusing that the press cameras caught him a conventional step behind the Princess at the so-appropriate first night of *Follow That Girl*. (In private life, Tony had closely followed the fortunes of the show before production, for one of his Buckley cousins, Aunt Gwendy's daughter, was married to the brother of the composer, Julian Slade, and Tony had known Julian at Cambridge.) A month after his public debut on the royal scene, Tony also accompanied Princess Margaret on a duty visit to a students' club in Bayswater. The newspapers reported that he appeared "a trifle nervous at first" but was soon "chatting informally". We can judge for ourselves the discrepancy between the public image of the shy handsome newcomer and the Tony whom we know was equal to any task.

In April he participated in the royal occasions centred upon the State Visit of President de Gaulle: the State banquet at Buckingham Palace, the gala performance at Covent Garden and the dinner to the Queen and Prince Philip at the French Embassy. The masts and stands erected for the President's ceremonial drives were, in fact, left in place for the wedding. Meanwhile, like any other engaged couple, Tony and his Princess made a round of visits to their friends. They went to stay with the Frys at Widcombe Manor; they visited the Nevills and the Wills; they were at Badminton and went to tea with Cecil Beaton at Broadchalke and asked him if he would take the wedding pictures. With his own appreciative eye and sense of fun, Uncle Oliver visited Tony at Buckingham Palace and then they both went round to tea at Clarence House. Tony is widely supposed to have taken the photographs at the christening of Prince Andrew at Buckingham Palace, but this was regarded as a completely private occasion and none of the pictures was ever published.

V

The wedding date was fixed for May 6th, seven weeks after the Queen in Council had given her formal consent to the marriage. The honeymoon was to be a Caribbean cruise on the royal yacht *Britannia*, with no ports of destination known and apparently nothing fixed. This preserved the bridegroom's budget, though Tony was determined to meet every extra expense ashore, and I understand that he had to be approached with the utmost diplomacy in being persuaded not to buy the wedding-ring. Part of the Welsh gold from which the Queen's wedding-ring had been made had been set aside for her sister. Tony quietly attempted to pay the goldsmith's bill but discovered that the charge was waived. From the same firm, however, he bought eight small gold travelling clocks, inscribed with the wedding date, as his gift to each of the bridesmaids. The bride's greatest problem was to keep her Hartnell wedding-gown a complete surprise for her bridegroom and for the world, but otherwise she and Tony solved all their problems together.

Both bride and groom wished for part of the service of the old Prayer Book, with the promise to obey, and they asked if the Beatitudes could be read instead of an address. Both agreed to share their wedding with the world by television, except for stipulating that there should be no close-ups in the sacred moments when they exchanged their vows. They also realised that the thousand wedding guests in the Abbey nave would see nothing of the ceremony at the high altar, owing to the intervening organ screen, and for the first time television monitor sets were installed to help share the full ritual of the service with everyone present.

Among the least substantiated of the snide stories that were to spring up around Tony, perhaps as a counter-irritant to glamour, was the legend that he was deserting his friends. The texture of friendship is always changing and fortunate indeed are they who can keep as many as five or six firm friends throughout their lives. Yet Buckingham Palace could have proved Tony's loyalties if they had published the list of the thousand guests invited to the Queen's reception for the young couple on May 4th. For here were his school friends, John and Simon Sainsbury, together with Dominic Elwes from more remote boyhood, and Julian More who had known him at Cambridge, and his wife, who had posed for Tony in the early Baron days. And here was Rory McEwen, whose guitar had often strummed at the Pimlico parties, and friends whom Tony had first gained through his camera, such as Anna Massey, Margaret Leighton and Leslie Caron. There were show folk first known through Oliver Messel, including Margot Fonteyn, Joyce Grenfell and Noel Coward . . .

Again, in a sense, all London was there, for the crowds had decided to have a night out and were in a carnival mood as Tony drove out from Clarence House with the Queen Mother and Princess Margaret in the illuminated royal limousine. The only significant absentee at the Palace, indeed, was the intended best man, Jeremy Fry. He had for some time been subject to attacks of jaundice and early in April, when it became clear that his presence at the Abbey ceremony was at hazard, he had to withdraw on the advice of his doctors. As all the world knows, Dr. Roger Gilliat agreed to step into the breach and all was well. Or nearly well. What the world did not know was that Tony himself was vulnerable to strain, and had been under the orthopaedic surgeon, Mr. Osmond-Clarke, and taking physio-therapy for some months. As a consultant neurologist, Dr. Gilliat had powers in reserve other than the responsibility of producing a ring from his pocket.

But the wedding went off, of course, with royal precision. London was garlanded with flags and flowers. The Mall was decorated with white banners with the monogram M-A for Margaret and Antony, and an arch of real roses soared sixty feet above the bridal way. In Westminster Abbey itself were touches of happy symbolism. White roses and marguerites were included ahead of season in the cascades of white flowers at the altar because they had been used to decorate the font at Princess Margaret's christening; and the procession of royal guests was headed by none other than Prince Tomislav of Yugoslavia, that fellow pupil and friend from Sandroyd.

After the ceremony, when the groom had led his bride down the aisle to the triumphant trumpet tune and air by Purcell, the processions re-formed and the Countess of Rosse and Ronald Armstrong-Jones walked side by side behind the Queen and the Duke of Edinburgh, the Prince of Wales, the Queen Mother and the Queen of Denmark. They had married thirty-five years earlier in "the little church next door" and the most impulsive reach of imagination could not have shown that—although divorced—they would ride once again over their own wedding route through the gay and happy crowds, in the wake of the cheers for their son and his wife in the bridal glass coach. In the journeys of their own wedding day past Buckingham Palace they had not dreamed they would one day stand on the balcony looking down at the sea of upturned faces in the tumult of sound that greeted Tony and his bride.

In the end it had turned out best after all, for Ronnie and Anne, that for the children's sake they had maintained a level friendship. (Yet was it for the children, or a deeper sentiment, that Ronnie still kept a painting of Anne in his drawing-room?) The wedding photographs in the Palace suggest occasional embarrassments. But when the honeymooners took their departure and the laughing guests showered them with rose petals and ran from the Palace courtyard to speed them on their way, Ronnie took Anne's hand to help her forward. Thus the two, hand in hand, shared Tony's farewell waves and beaming smile as the car drove away.

The crowds had eagerly waited in the Mall and gathered along the route to Tower Pier, where the couple were to embark for the royal yacht. After the morning's pageantry of the Glass Coach and the clattering, jingling Captain's Escort of the Household Cavalry, it was difficult to foresee what the leave-taking would be. From the viewpoint of the crowds and television cameras, what happened was dramatic and entirely unexpected. A royal Rolls emerged from the Palace with only a single escort car, as if husband and wife had dropped the royal trappings from that moment and were on their own.

Down the Mall and along the Embankment, the tiny procession was able to progress at fair pace but, in the City, the five o'clock crowds joined the throngs patiently waiting on the pavements and the honeymoon car became engulfed in well-wishers breaking through, twenty deep, on either side. There were too few police, the crowds themselves were enclosed and helpless, and the car moved at snail's pace through a sea of smiling faces.

Tower Pier was reached an hour late, and church bells, hooters and ships' sirens saluted the couple with a joyous clamour as the royal yacht got under way. All the world now knew of the Rotherhithe room; Bill Glenton had been in Westminster Abbey that morning—although he had not yet been introduced to the Princess—and it was a culminating moment of romance of that extraordinary day when Tony and his bride scampered across to the near side of the bridge of *Britannia*, frantically waving to him until his window had slipped astern.

10 *Kensington and Rotherhithe*

I

As the royal yacht *Britannia* headed west into the Atlantic with the honeymooners, the Admiralty transmitted a radio warning of a floating mine, an apt symbol of the fringe difficulties of Mr. Antony Armstrong-Jones's new status. On his wedding-day he heard that his Aunt Elaine (Mrs. Edward Wauchope) had been robbed of her jewellery at her London hotel, a theft that he ruefully knew might not have occurred but for his celebrity . . . or was it notoriety? The newspapers seemed ready to transpose the two with a vexing facility; and this embarrassing incident posed for everyone the problem of what might lie in store for the couple who now became universally known as the Joneses.

The British press treated the honeymoon with marked restraint but the French infested the Caribbean with photographers and reporters, and the yacht continually had to change course to avoid discovery. One newspaper reported—it is difficult to know on what evidence—that the couple were queasy when the *Britannia* rolled in mid-Atlantic. Later, although republican readers were regaled with the twin discomforts of inadequate air-conditioning and hot vibrating metal, the newly-weds' privacy was in fact successfully maintained. Their public landings in Trinidad, Dominica and Antigua evoked a prolonged and happy mood of flower-pelting and calypsos, but the couple spent much of their time sunbathing, swimming and picnicking on tiny islands where they were put ashore and left alone.

"It was so very wonderful," Princess Margaret was to tell a friend, "both of us just lying on those empty beaches without a soul in sight. Neither of us ever wanted to be 'rescued' in the evening—

158

we would have gladly stayed for ever and lived in a little grass hut."
One of her favourite honeymoon snapshots shows Tony wildly
struggling to climb a palm-tree, while her husband's favourite
memento is framed in crystal in his dressing-room at Kensington
Palace, the photograph of a girl with bare shoulders and windblown
hair, her eyes puckered in sunlight, a photograph not of a Princess
but of a woman in love.

The newly-weds returned aboard *Britannia* to Portsmouth on
June 18th, "a quiet homecoming", as the press noted, "with no
bands, no guard of honour". A rumour that Princess Margaret
intended permanently to retire from public life was quickly put to
flight by her appearance on official duties in Lincolnshire scarcely a
week later. The Princess had indeed maintained engagements on the
day before the wedding and the world now waited expectantly to
see what Mr. Armstrong-Jones would do. There was a noticeable
lull of indecision as the Queen and her advisers cautiously sought to
define a fresh field of public duty for the new recruit. More by
chance than intention, Tony was present with a family party at the
Royal Tournament and he then accompanied his wife to a Girl
Guides' Festival at Wembley Stadium. Possibly these events were
not the happiest choice but Tony's appearance with Princess Margaret at a string of smaller official occasions were an indication that
he had been advised to gain experience of royal protocol gradually.

A major initiation came on July 29th when he flew to Dartmouth
with his Princess in an aircraft of the Queen's Flight and officially
accompanied her on a visit of inspection to the Royal Naval College, playing the role of escort under the critical eyes of the assembled cadets and naval officers. With this event, one cannot but
admire the felicity of royal timing, and the Queen's over-all supervi-
sion was again in evidence. It was just twenty-one years, within a
week, since Princess Margaret had visited Dartmouth as a child on
the historic occasion when the then Princess Elizabeth had first met
Prince Philip.

Behind the scenes, too, the indefatigable Mrs. Everard, Tony's
secretary from Pimlico, was coping with innumerable invitations
for her employer to join a vast array of organisations, some wildly
inappropriate and others with built-in hazards. Tony first agreed to
become a council member on the governing body of the Royal
Academy of Dramatic Art in succession to Countess Mountbatten
of Burma; and one need hardly add that a similar invitation to join
the council of the Polio Research Fund was accepted with alacrity.

Meanwhile, a congenial preoccupation immediately presented itself in setting up the first married home in the far northern wing of Kensington Palace known as No. 10. For a month, on returning from their honeymoon, the newly-weds lived at Clarence House, running over to Kensington in Tony's new Sunbeam Rapier every few days. The house had only recently been refurbished for the former tenant, the Marquis of Carisbrooke, to the customary Office of Works specifications and so there could be no criticism on the grounds of public expense. It was in any case a grace-and-favour residence that the Princess had always admired. Visiting it for the first time, two months before their wedding, Tony found it to be wonderfully secluded, near the old Palace stables, facing a grassy corner where clusters of early daffodils were in bloom, as if on an immaculate village green.

Princess Margaret had first known it when visiting her retired governess at a cottage across the way. "It's just like a doll's house," she said, and curiously enough this was nearly the truth. The house is said to have been built as a nursery for King George III's elder children and when his eldest daughter, Princess Charlotte, wanted a doll's house the King gave her an exact miniature replica of the building scaled down to doll's size. With its red-brick double-fronted façade, and five entrance steps, toymakers everywhere copied the style, which still influenced dolls' houses into our present century.

Yet the house had an equally personal and attractive link with Tony's family. When he first inspected it with Princess Margaret, Lord Carisbrooke's furnishings were still in place, including the family portrait of his Battenberg grandfather, Prince Alexander, that founder of the line who had been a friend of the Messels in distant Darmstadt. One likes to think of the painted eyes of the portrait gazing in welcome as the royally-married scion of the Messels explored the house.

But Tony's visits were strictly practical. While Princess Margaret was charmed by the two "doll's house" living-rooms demurely facing across the white-painted hall, Tony's imagination was challenged by an empty and bomb-damaged house next door where the window-cleaners and maintenance staff of Kensington Palace kept ladders and scaffolding. One gathers that he scraped away shabby paint to discover honey-toned panelling and brushed away cobwebs to disclose beautiful carved eighteenth-century architraves. He perhaps bewildered his Princess a little by mentally knocking holes through the walls and sketching a floor plan that created a new private world in what would be a cosily separate suite of apartments on the first floor. The scheme was swiftly set in action. As the weeks passed and the wedding-gifts were assembled in St. James's Palace, the couple decided where each piece should ultimately stand with a remarkable certainty and precision, from Uncle Oliver's seventeenth-century Flemish screen to the antique Chinese coromandel table that was the gift of the British Cabinet.

The white drawing-room housed Princess Margaret's piano and a new wedding-gift hi-fi, but its principal feature was also an expression of Tony's family affections, for he installed the beautiful escritoire from the home of his Messel grandmama. The adjacent dining-room could seat ten—with a little crowding—at the eighteenth-century oval table; and Princess Margaret's pink-painted bedroom, her husband's dressing-room—replete with fitted wardrobes—a bathroom and a small guest room completed the suite. The ground-floor comprised a small reception-room for visitors, a business suite for Princess Margaret's staff, an office for Mrs. Everard and a workroom for Tony overlooking a southern tree-studded courtyard that resembled a college close.

The newly-weds were to move in during the first week of July and, on the appointed day, Tony arrived early and busied himself upstairs hanging pictures and moving the furniture around, carrying ornaments and vases of flowers from one spot to another. The staff were under the impression that Princess Margaret would arrive direct from an official engagement and might perhaps be carried over the threshold. Instead, Tony impatiently returned to Clarence House and his wife arrived at No. 10 to learn that she had just missed him. While a telephone call hurriedly re-arranged matters, Princess Margaret went upstairs and then returned, it was noted, "pink with pleasure".

"Please let it seem that I haven't been upstairs at all yet," she said. "My husband's arranged everything so beautifully to surprise me." And perhaps Lord Snowdon will only learn as he reads these words that his wife's apparently unfeigned surprise, her delicious delight at the way everything was arranged had already had a dress rehearsal.

II

Within modern history the Royal Family had never before had a non-royal male recruit so close to the Throne, let alone a newcomer not of the landed aristocracy, lacking the traditional lustre of Army rank or great wealth. Princess Mary, King George V's only daughter, might well have remained a spinster if her suitor, the then Viscount Lascelles, had thought that the match might require him to close down his business interests, in his case the family sugar plantations in Barbados. In an earlier generation, Queen Mary had considered it "rather strange" for a princess "to marry a subject", even though the bridegroom in question was the Earl of Fife, highly approved by Queen Victoria "as he is immensely rich". Many people assumed that Tony Armstrong-Jones was under pressure to close his Pimlico studio and sever his Fleet Street interests. In reality, he needed a lull from photography, as we have seen, and his studio was transferred to his agent, Tom Blau of Camera Press, but Tony continued to draw his income from copyrights.

We may note that Viscount Lascelles was created a Knight of the Garter on his wedding to Princess Mary and, as we have seen, Tony was very probably offered this honour and begged to be allowed to decline. The Monarchy, in fact, had never before acquired a new member of the Royal Family so stubbornly wishful to remain a commoner and yet so eager to share his wife's royal interests in married equality, essentially non-royal and yet willing to learn.

This led to some early mistakes and confusion. Royal servants were usually required to sign a covenant not to divulge information acquired by virtue of their employment, but the undertaking was not at first sought when new staff were taken on at Clarence House for Mr. Armstrong-Jones' household. The sequel of this curious muddle was the affair of the ineffable butler who remained at Kensington Palace for twenty-five days and afterwards sold his royal reminiscences to a Sunday newspaper reputedly for thousands of pounds. In pained and skilfully ghosted accents the butler claimed to have been astonished when his employer suggested he should help him build some wine racks with a little home carpentry. Instead, without consulting anyone, he had made haste to install not only "proper racks" but also a store of "inexpensive" vintage wines. He found it "intolerable" to be questioned for having purchased £20 worth of cutlery for the staff table without the authority of the master of the house, and "undignified" not to be permitted a float of £100 for petty disbursements at the kitchen door. In the public mind the young couple's early married life was thus thought to be marred by a series of dismal troubles with domestic staff.

One may sympathise if Tony disliked the ensuing headlines,

although they became as trivial in retrospect as the bother about his wax effigy, which was kidnapped from Madame Tussaud's and found some days later propped up in a telephone box. Princess Margaret fretted lest the privacy and anonymity that they had enjoyed in the days of courtship should now be denied them. Tony's method of reassuring his wife was to take her walking through the crowd at the Royal Ascot race-meeting and, without a phalanx of officials to clear the way, no one recognised the young man in spectacles or the girl on his arm. (Some years later, they were barred from the Royal Enclosure by a gateman who was busily looking at badges rather than faces. "It's us," Princess Margaret quietly had to say, before they gained admission.) It was similarly reassuring on their way to Balmoral that August to be able to stop off at Womersley and visit Lord and Lady Rosse without attracting attention.

While the young couple adjusted to married life, in other words, they also had to adjust to the undeniable distortion of public images that capered in a world of illusion with total irrelevance to their actual hopes and ideals. When Princess Margaret presented new Colours to a battalion of the Highland Light Infantry, Tony accompanied her in mufti as his first involvement in military ceremonial. But this merely elicited a silly season argument in the press on his right to wear a kilt, although Innes' standard work on Clan tartans readily showed that he was entitled to wear the tartan of Armstrong of Mangerton and Whitelaugh . . . (not that he did). The columnists who reported that Tony had been practising shooting with clay pigeons and that he acquitted himself as "an excellent marksman on the grouse moors" would have found it difficult to believe that he had long enjoyed shooting: it might have been better if they had been briefed that he had handled a gun at an early age.

The Scottish summer, besides, produced days of torrential rain when Tony got out his drawing-board. Psychoanalysts profess it significant that his temporary abandonment of photography was succeeded by a phase of designing aviaries, as if an obsession with cages lurked in his new happiness. He had however designed a small aviary for Jeremy Fry at Widcombe Manor the year before and created a fanciful cage as a garden gift to Royal Lodge. Elizabeth Cavendish's brother-in-law, Michael Tree, had admired the Widcombe effort and Tony designed an amusing cage like a Chinese pagoda to grace his Mereworth Castle home in Kent. One thing led to another, for it was on Mr. and Mrs. Tree's earnest recommendation that Tony ultimately designed his more celebrated aviary for the London Zoo. The prospect caught his fancy, indeed, of reviving an art neglected since Regency times. But it must be added that other interests were already being hammered out behind the scenes in recognition of the married couple's anxiety that they should share each other's interests and undergo similar compulsions in one another's working lives.

By the autumn Tony had participated in the ceremonial of two further State visits, those of the President of Argentina and the King and Queen of Thailand, and students of royal protocol therefore found significance in an announcement concerning the wedding of King Baudouin of the Belgians to Dona Fabiola in Brussels that "Princess Margaret accompanied by Mr. Antony Armstrong-Jones would be present on behalf of The Queen". The occasion provided Tony with his first vivid experience of an airport scrimmage when the crowds yelled "Vive Tonee!" and scores of milling photographers surrounded him, the security men having all trooped off to accompany the Princess as she inspected a guard of honour. "Give me a break, you boys," he pleaded, his every word now newsworthy.

Later, the young couple ventured out from their hotel to explore the city but were recognised and had to scamper away hand-in-hand like children through the first escape route that offered, an underground garage. At the Palace ball that evening Tony was seen to be wearing his first decoration, the star of a Grand Officer of the Order of Leopold II. That same month, in London, Tony also undertook his first public engagement alone, and made his first speech, after rehearsing for days, when he presented the prizes in a national photographic competition at a luncheon at the Dorchester. "A camera must be part of one, an extra limb capable of freezing a situation," he told the assembled enthusiasts.

He had to learn as he went along, and he ruefully wondered whether speechmaking was in his line, but that same week he laboured over two other speeches that he foresaw he would shortly make for the Council of Industrial Design. Remembering that six months had passed since the wedding, the newspapers now began enquiring whether he would be content to spend the rest of his life doing nothing. His critics were unaware that the plans for his Design Centre job had already been settled and nothing was known of his commissioned work for the London Zoo, for several months were to elapse before the "imaginative and provocative" design for his Zoo aviary could be displayed at a press conference. "I was doing it," Tony then said with satisfaction, "when I was described as hanging around doing nothing."

III

After Christmas at Sandringham, Tony and his Princess saw the New Year in at Birr Castle, Lord and Lady Rosse had also invited Jeremy and Camilla Fry and Billy Wallace to help usher in 1961; Tony had so looked forward to showing his wife his boyhood home, and the visit was a great success, despite the unforeseen nuisance of unexpected publicity. Tony had not imagined that Birr town could be anything other than its normal sleepy self. It was only on the Queen Mother's urgent entreaty that they decided to take their detective, Fred Crocker, along ... and Chief Inspector Crocker, they considered, was needlessly worried about a conversation he had with the chief of the Birr police.

Yet Crocker's presence proved more than welcome. They had expected to fly over, little noticed, on excursion tickets; and Aer Lingus instead tore the seats out of the first-class compartment to create a drawing-room while the rest of the plane was fully booked with reporters and cameramen travelling as passengers. Halfway on the journey the captain invited the Princess to visit the crew deck, and her appearance was the signal for such a scrimmage of photographers and onlookers in the gangway that she had to retreat. Yet this set the key for the scenes at the airport and the fierce race of cars on the normally quiet road through Kildare. In the scrum at the gates of the Castle, Crocker appealed to the crowd for the Princess to be left alone. "But it's our first royal visit since the troubles—and it's a great day for the Irish," piped up a voice of unmistakable brogue.

Fortunately, Birr Castle could withstand even this siege. Tony found it disconcerting to be cautious and wary when he showed his wife round the grounds he knew so well, and on Sunday morning the pleasant parish church became like Craithie in August. But nothing marred the pleasure of country friends and neighbours when they gathered in the Gothic saloon as usual for sherry, and Princess Margaret so obviously shared Tony's delight that the large room at Birr was indeed the counterpart of the saloon at Royal Lodge. Tony tenderly noted his mother's happiness at playing hostess to all her family: his own wife and friends, Sue and her husband, John, his own two half-brothers and sundry kinsfolk of the de Vescis. The Rupert Nevills came over while visiting nearby friends; and in the dining-room, with its high-backed oak chairs, the two big tables were put together in baronial style to create the festivity at which Lady Rosse excelled. Finally, leaving Birr by a distant estate gate, Tony and his Princess motored with Susan and John to spend a few days at Abbey Leix. The following week, Princess Margaret and Tony went to Oslo for the wedding of Princess Astrid to Johan Ferner and enjoyed the private joke that it was "so quiet after Birr".

But the true satisfaction for Tony was that Birr was no longer something he merely described to his wife; it now had a place, real and tangible, in her heart as well. All his past had to be shared with her, as well as present happiness: a visit to the little garden of 25 Eaton Terrace as well as a nostalgic return to Eton. Tony telephoned his former housemaster to enquire whether he could "show his wife around", and Mr. Wilkinson absently expected another customary old boy's visit, until he remembered that the wife was Princess Margaret.

They arrived late one Sunday afternoon when Tony's old room reeked of the teatime flavour of sardines on toast, and he took her to School Yard and Weston's Yard to show her the very spot where he had stood on her two previous visits sixteen and fourteen years earlier. Did this third sentimental visit have a special sacrament? They went to evensong in College Chapel, and one wonders whether, against the sweet voices of the choir, Tony also remembered his grandmama's voice with her gentle counsel, "You must do everything three times . . ."

All through the winter months, however, Tony also pursued an objective having nothing to do with family sentiment: a simple wish to get cracking with a worthwhile job that, he must have discovered with dismay, first involved acceptance at committee meetings and even the public agreement of the President of the Board of Trade. His unpaid but reasonably professional role with the Council of Industrial Design was announced early in January with nothing more definite than the cautious phrase that he had "accepted an invitation to assist in the work of the Council".

It was five years since Prince Philip had opened the Design Centre as a showplace of well-designed British consumer goods; the annual awards for good design presented by the Prince had successfully maintained public interest, and Tony could see an expanding outlet for his own energies. He could evolve new ideas in exhibition lay-out, advise on the making of films and filmstrips and visual teaching aids to good design, perhaps improve the lay-out and impact of the C.I.D. monthly magazine *Design* and so forth. In general he would be expending his talents in a vital field of British prestige and it was dismaying that sections of the press seemed more interested in whether he would clock-in or have an insurance card and whether the brew of the office tea would be improved.

The post had been announced as subject to other duties and within two days a gossip-writer discovered that the new assistant had taken time off to attend a council meeting at the R.A.D.A. Within a week, however, he was able to visit a furnishing trades exhibition which had received a hostile press for its atrocities, and chaffed the managing directors of some of the offending firms with a subtle variant of Prince Philip's style. He attended a display of Swedish furnishing on the axiom that ready publicity for good modern design might deter perpetrators of the shoddy. He was to find himself, later on, visiting potteries and carpet-factories, making speeches to antique dealers and architects. The latter occasion was, in fact, a congress of international architects where he originally offered to deputise for Princess Margaret, and then gave an excellent speech pleading for excitement, boldness and originality in architecture. Lord Snowdon's life is full of events that no one imagined could possibly occur, but nothing could have seemed more unlikely than that a failed architectural student would after ten years have the courage to address an audience of two thousand architects filling the Royal Festival Hall. Lady Rosse considered the occasion a triumph and greeted her son radiantly as he came from the platform.

IV

There were other improbabilities which were to crystallise in public knowledge only in the fulness of time. The onlookers who clustered about the C.o.I.D. doorway, the gateway peepers of Kensington Palace and the chroniclers of Tony's public appearances would all have been surprised could they have known that he spent many of his evenings in his workroom at No. 10 carefully cutting lengths of balsa wood with a razor-blade, snipping and soldering tiny lengths of copper tubing and picture wire and conning over mathematical tables. The public read of his visits both to battleships and art exhibitions with Princess Margaret, and the addicts of glamour noted his role in the events of the State Visit of the King and Queen of Nepal. But meanwhile the private man was having "hundreds of meetings"—as he negligently put it—with an architect, Mr. Cedric Price, who lectured at London University, and with Mr. Frank Newby, the consulting engineer who designed the structure of the American Embassy in Grosvenor Square, threshing out the problems of their new aviary at the London Zoo.

This was especially so in March, when Princess Margaret told Tony with radiant certainty that she was to have a baby; and the Queen, fresh from her tour of India, tried to visit her sister as often as possible. Tony knew how dearly the two sisters loved to be together, and how rare the opportunities of such sessions really were. There were times when the atmosphere seemed to vibrate with their sympathy and understanding of one another and, after dinner, Tony would tactfully leave them engrossed in their companionship. It was never the same, he no doubt remembered the Queen Mother once saying, when anyone else was around. And so in April the model of the new contemporary aviary was displayed at a press conference at the Zoo and Tony explained his vision of "an exciting exercise in architecture . . . an ideal enclosure for the birds to live as free a life as possible . . . a tension structure linked to the ground as little as possible to give a floating effect".

The reporters found the structure difficult to describe: two impacted pyramids of metal like the outline of competing yachts against the sky, the masts of an aviary of finest aluminium mesh through which the public could stroll as through a garden. The press reviews were puzzled, impressed, perhaps mildly derisive, and the aviary was henceforth to become a curious barometer of Tony's status in public opinion, veering between admiration and ridicule, veiled hostility and appreciation. The public did not always know what to make of Princess Margaret's husband; any difficulties experienced in constructing the full-scale aviary underlined the general opinion that Lord Snowdon was "perhaps a little impractical". The delay in the public opening of the expensive structure, caused by the discovery that gale winds were blowing holes in the wire, significantly coincided with criticism that too much public money was being spent at Kensington Palace.

"We can't do anything right," Tony said unhappily, at one stage, and he lacked Prince Philip's guard of withering sarcasm. The early days of marriage still found him unaware of the rhythmic tide of alternating popularity and disfavour familiar to more experienced members of the Royal Family. The aviary was successfully opened in 1965, a year when the solidity of Lord Snowdon's public work and his qualities of resilience, determination and courage were becoming better known. But the sensitivity of the barometer was demonstrated with firmer certainty in 1968 when an exceptional combination of wind and snow opened some of the horizontal joints of the aviary wire mesh. A few years earlier this might have caused a national gale of laughter. Instead, the *Guardian* was almost alone in featuring the story for its cultivated readers, and editors, generally, sympathetically soft-pedalled it with a reticence that reflected Lord Snowdon's rising personal prestige.

But this is looking ahead and, in 1961, as a young husband, Tony gloomily felt at times that his marriage must have upset the press. "They seem to be looking for faults," he once said, when downcast at a new burst of sniping. Meanwhile, he strove to dive into public duty at the deep end and, apart from his C.I.D. programme of visits and tours, it was a welcome token of appreciation that the Institute of British Photographers gave a luncheon in his honour.

Princess Margaret's happy anticipations were made known early in June, and on June 8th the Royal Family gathered for the wedding of the Duke of Kent to Miss Katherine Worsley in York Minister. For Tony it afforded an amusing reunion with old friends, such as Prince Tomislav of Yugoslavia, of his Sandroyd days, and Worsleys whom he had known at Eton. He had, however, undertaken to take care of the principal guest, Queen Ena of Spain, and her incisive, practised impressions are amusing. "He proved a charming escort during the journey (on the royal train)", she wrote. "He seemed far removed from the incorrigible eccentric described by the newspapers. He was the picture of correctness and of an English gentleman. His speech is soft, his gestures are pleasing and precise and he wears a pleasant and perpetual smile. My curiosity was satisfied on every point."

Tony had turned to the safe topic of modern Spanish painting, unaware that Queen Ena was grand-daughter of the Alexander of Hesse whom his Messel great-great-grandfather had known. From her wisdom, the elderly Queen talked of Princess Margaret and mentioned the need of relaxation for a mother-to-be—and her curiosity would have hungered indeed if Tony had dared to confide that he and his wife still found perfect relaxation, unbelievably, in his room in Rotherhithe.

V

Millions had read about The Room, the "love nest", the "hideaway", without a suspicion that Tony and his wife still used it and revelled in it as a wonderful escape hatch from the over-eventful and socially congested life of royalty. The penalty of having many friends and kinsfolk is that kindness and hospitality must be requited, and one evening, not long after their honeymoon, the newly-weds realised with dismay that they had not dined alone together for six weeks. At this, Tony packed a picnic basket and, having telephoned Bill Glenton in the old way, they darted down the Old Kent Road in the Mini and were in Rotherhithe thirty minutes later.

In the narrow, shabby hall Tony introduced his wife to his journalist "landlord" for the first time, "Have you met the Princess?" he said with a twinkle, and from that moment, incredibly, the romantic saga of the room was resumed for another three years. Royalty had two faces and the crowds who admired the diamond-decked glamorous duty Princess had no inkling of the girl in skirt and jumper who climbed the stairs in a dockland house to ask timidly if she could borrow a cup of sugar. The bo'suns of sightseeing launches on the Thames used to point out the house as one of the new sights of London. "There it is," bellowed a loudspeaker one summer evening, "that's where the romance occurred, right where that young couple are sitting now." In the fading light of dusk, Tony and his wife hurriedly shrank back into the shadows, but the sightseers hardly cast them a glance.

Fascinated by the river traffic, Princess Margaret would lean farther and farther out of the window until passing bargemen sometimes shouted endearments and she suddenly realised that she might be recognised and quickly withdrew. Tony was never more content than to sit there just watching her, talking, as the river lights twinkled in the gloaming. For them both the room continued to recapture, two and three years after their marriage, the tenderness and enchantment of their betrothal.

To say that life in Rotherhithe was quite unlike Kensington Palace would be more than an understatement. One evening a neighbour tried to empty a bin of ashes into the river. Blown by the wind, the ashes drifted in at the open window, filling the Princess's hair, covering Tony and herself with grey. Brushing frantically at each other, yelling, laughing, the noise brought Mr. Glenton down, but there was nothing to be done save get their brooms and brushes out of their cupboard and spend an hour or two cleaning up.

They continually planned to buy a vacuum-cleaner but never got around to this luxury. Tony loved to cook steaks with new and inventive ingredients. Princess Margaret would wash up afterwards, with a squirt of detergent, while Tony sometimes dried and stacked away. On one occasion, Tony's grilling pan caught fire, and they dashed it into a sink of cold water, filling the house with pungent smoke. The incident was described and talked about long after a fire in the attics of Kensington Palace had been forgotten. As a married couple, Tony and his Princess made no changes in the room except to have an adjacent cupboard converted into a cramped but modern toilet. "It is magnificently convenient," Noel Coward agreed one evening, when they held a sing-song that went on long into the night. What the neighbours thought on hearing Noel Coward's distinctive light tenor raised in "Mad Dogs and Englishmen" will presumably never be known.

Even the Queen Mother visited the room, although this was admittedly an event calling for special preparation. Mrs. Everard, Tony's trusted secretary, went down beforehand to clean and polish and set the table with a bowl of roses. No detail was overlooked, from clean tea towels to the aerosol purifier to help cleanse the atmosphere of reminders of Mr. Glenton's cats. "Would you mind if I bring my mother-in-law down?" Tony had telephoned beforehand, and it was not until replacing the phone that his host realised who his mother-in-law was. When the Queen Mother arrived, early in the evening, her large Clarence House car had no space to stop opposite the door. The house was overlooked by all the dozens of windows of the opposite block of tenement flats, and anyone who chanced to glance out would have seen that unmistakable figure moving along the pavement of Rotherhithe Street without the slightest hurry or fluster.

All was well. The familiar smell of sizzling steaks presently poured from the room. The swans afterwards crowded beneath the windows, like a mob before a revolution, aware of the special scraps that were being thrown and the cheerful roar of a sing-song presently drifted over the water, undistinguishable in tone from a sing-song in the river pub further along the road. More remarkable still, the Queen Mother insisted on going exploring after midnight in the nearby churchyard of St. Mary's, looking for the graves of the *Mayflower* sailors. "I haven't enjoyed myself so much since I was a girl of twenty," she told Tony happily, at the end of the evening.

As the date for the arrival of the baby drew near, Tony and the Princess renewed their visits on the old footing of being alone together, just looking out at the river and sitting around. A few months later Mrs. Glenton herself expected a baby, and Princess Margaret by then was full of experienced and practical advice. The baby in the house made no difference to the romantic enchantment of the room. It merely meant that, if Tony and Margaret arrived unannounced, they often had to squeeze past the pram and duck under a string of nappies airing in the hall.

VI

If contrast is the spice of life, it might be said that Tony took his decision to accept a title during the long talks with his wife at Rotherhithe. The question was much in the air as the summer of 1961 progressed and, behind the scenes, the smoke of rumour was not without fire. The public at large had considered Tony courageous and contemporary for not accepting a title on his marriage, taking it very much for granted that one had been offered. As the *Daily Telegraph* summed up, "Considerable admiration was expressed in widely differing circles at the reported disinclination of Mr. Antony Armstrong-Jones to accept ennoblement . . . There was felt to be great dignity in his reluctance to accept honours conferred in respect of entry by marriage into the Royal Family." And in the same newspaper, with the deed accomplished, Peterborough expressed a considerable element of opinion when he wrote, "With all the goodwill in the world, it is difficult to greet the bestowal of a peerage on Mr. Armstrong-Jones with great enthusiasm."

The announcement that the Queen had conferred an earldom on her sister's husband was eventually made from Balmoral on Monday October 1st. He would henceforward be known as the Earl of Snowdon, with the subsidiary title of Viscount Linley of Nymans. The first signal indeed had come on the Saturday evening when Tony telephoned his mother while she was at dinner in a Wexford hotel: her excitement and pleasure could not be entirely kept from others. By coincidence of timing, his father had been appointed Deputy Lieutenant of Caernarvonshire only the previous week and, in a day or so, the young commoner had been due to open an art exhibition in Glasgow, his first public duty in Scotland without Princess Margaret. In confusion, I once claimed that Lord Snowdon had chosen his title from the slopes of Snow Hill or Snowdon, the original name of the site of Royal Lodge, but this added coincidence proved a source of annoyance, for Tony had indeed been at pains to compliment his father's native region.

Why did Lord Snowdon at last accept a title? Was it merely because the Queen wished it and had offered the earldom, according to custom, on her Prime Minister's advice? The forthright John Gordon asserted that the royal decision was out of step with public opinion. When commoners, particularly in the arts, decline a title, they often give a reason for their refusal, but explanations are rare when honours are accepted. If the obvious explanation is that Tony could not reject the opportunity to cast the mantle of nobility upon his children, this could have been overcome, as we have noted, by creating Princess Margaret a royal duchess in her own right. But perhaps the young husband was disposed to prefer a title that conferred the same style of "Countess" upon his wife as on his mother and, in the last analysis, perhaps his disinclination was overcome because his wife wished it so.

Commander Colville, the Queen's press secretary, was careful to stress that "when the title was offered Mr. Armstrong-Jones accepted with great pleasure". Yet nothing was to prove more difficult for Tony to live down than his elevation to the peerage.

11 *The Tumult and the Shouting*

I

On the morning of November 3rd, 1961, Lord Snowdon awaited the birth of Princess Margaret's first baby, as eager and anxious as his own father had been more than thirty-one years earlier. The doctors had suggested that Clarence House was more convenient than the cramped apartments of 10 Kensington Palace and, "nervous as a kitten", the young husband spent much time on the telephone, ringing up his mother, his sister, his father, his Aunt Gwendy and others, faithfully observing his promise to keep them informed. Queen Elizabeth the Queen Mother kept her son-in-law company in his vigil, occasionally peeping down from the windows at the gathering crowd, sharing the joke when, whether by accident or some joker's intention, a Stork Margarine van briefly parked near the kerb. The prospective father noticed the stamp of the sentries, crashing their hob-nailed boots as they turned about, and a message was passed to the Guards' officer so that presently they stamped in dumb show. The baby, a six-pound four-ounce son, was born at 10.45 a.m., and Lord Snowdon impulsively sent out a message to the waiting reporters, "We're absolutely thrilled and delighted".

His son was born fifth in succession to the British Throne and, added to the romantic element, the arrival of the child attracted world-wide attention: an excitement for breakfast-time radio in the United States and an excuse for another round of drinks in late-night Sydney. A few days earlier, the expectant parents had attended morning service at Westminster Abbey and before the baby was twenty-fours hours old the Earl of Snowdon quietly went to early morning Holy Communion "to give thanks", as the Dean said.

"Tony took to the baby at once . . . I didn't know if he would," Princess Margaret told Bill Glenton. Tony's romantic heart was indeed deeply touched by the tender poetry of nativity, and in this adoring mood his camera was as sensitive as the painter's brush. He is said to have photographed his son every day: in the cradle which Lady Rosse had lovingly sewn and trimmed and embroidered at Birr, and receiving his first sponge-bath in the capable hands of his Sussex nanny, Verona Sumner. His imagination was fired with the prospect of creating a perfect photographic triptych of mother and child, and with this thought he took a set of pictures when the baby was three weeks old, "waiting around half the night for the right expression," as he said.

The Queen Mother mischievously suggested that with a little trick photography he could create a wonderful sensation by pretending that twins had been born. The Royal Family among themselves naturally enjoyed a little private fun at the expense of the commentators. Still embarrassed by the hostility of those who considered his title archaic and absurd, Lord Snowdon imagined that his critics might think it quite ridiculous if he called in another photographer to take the first official pictures of his son. His own three photographs were therefore released through his customary agency, Camera Press, to the astonishment of the pundits who imagined he had undergone an enforced permanent retirement from his profession.

The pictures sold like hot cakes, and all the world's newspapers clamoured for rights. Princess Margaret had never looked more serene and beautiful than in these madonna-like studies. The photographs were widely praised and yet sniping was immediately resumed from the underbrush. How much money was the Earl of Snowdon making from "snapping his son"? Was it ethical that a royal husband should earn fees for photographing his wife? Every modern Junius joined in the controversy. Lord Snowdon did not care to answer the fault-finders, who might otherwise have discovered that in reality he was giving all the proceeds of the photographs to charity, dividing them equally between the Polio Research Fund and the Invalid Children's Aid Association, organisations that still benefit to this day.

Little Viscount Linley was baptised in the blue-and-gold Music Room at Buckingham Palace when he was six weeks old. The Queen as sponsor named him David Albert Charles. The other godparents were Lady Elizabeth Cavendish, who had first brought

the parents together, Lord Plunket—a great friend to them both—
Lord Rupert Nevill, and the Rev. Simon Phipps. The tiny central
figure of this ceremony wore the fragile robe of Honiton lace
reserved for Queen Victoria's descendants and yelled lustily
throughout, dismaying the parents who had told everyone how
good and quiet he always was. Ronnie Armstrong-Jones and Lady
Rosse were also there, one of those rare and happy occasions when
Lord Snowdon could see his own parents together, but if he took
any photographs of the subsequent Palace assembly for tea, none
were released to the press. Instead, a rival outburst of critical fire,
an ambuscade on another flank, sprang from the discovery that the
young parents were treating themselves to a three-weeks holiday in
Antigua . . . as if it were setting a shocking moral example to the
nation by leaving a two-month-old babe at Sandringham in the care
of a skilled nurse and a devoted royal grandmama.

Tony and his Princess revelled in a second honeymoon of fishing,
swimming, collecting seashells, sunning and relaxing and, in view
of all the gunning that had been going on, Lord Snowdon may
have been a diplomatic absentee when, on January 5th, 1962, it was
announced that he had accepted a post as an artistic adviser of the
Sunday Times.

Three years had elapsed since Toronto-born Roy Thomson had
added Lord Kemsley's eighteen newspapers to his own television,
radio and newspaper empire; and now the rosy bespectacled Canadian was about to enhance the most important of the papers, the
Sunday Times, with Britain's first colour magazine supplement.
Thomson had first met Lord Snowdon at a Clarence House luncheon, when his mind was dwelling at the time on the unpalatable
fact that the rival *Observer* appealed more to young people than the
Sunday Times, which was being outsold in the university towns. He
had appointed Denis Hamilton, just turned forty, as his editor, and
Hamilton in turn approached Snowdon in due course as a prospective artistic adviser.

At the hub of the wheel was Mark Boxer, who was to edit the
colour supplement and had known Tony from Cambridge days.
Lord Snowdon was immediately interested but the formalities
before he could accept the appointment were considerable. The
Queen was consulted, and she in turn sought the opinions of her
advisers, including the Prime Minister. Some safeguards were suggested: that her brother-in-law would not be involved in political
journalism and that his name should not be directly used in the

newspaper's own advertising. The priority of his public engage-ments would be reserved; he would continue to be available to the Council of Industrial Design and he would not service the *Sunday Times* with exclusive royal photographs.

Roy Thomson may have looked crestfallen at times as the difficul-ties were hammered out and he no doubt saw some of his wilder hopes smoothed away in the process. He was in Canada for Christmas when Hamilton telephoned that Snowdon had finally accepted the offer. A day or two after the announcement, he enquired how the London newspapers were taking it and was told they had taken it very well indeed.

A hush before battle occurred, in fact, before the opposition *Observer* weighed in with its heavy guns and enquired whether "the Monarchy had been well-advised to become involved, even indirect-ly" in the Fleet Street battle for advertising and circulation. The fuss about the fees for the baby photographs was now nothing to the outcry taken up on all sides. The *Sunday Express* even hinted that Lord Snowdon was being paid for his royal connections rather than his work, and that he might "bring the Throne into greater indignity and disrepute than at any time since the Abdication". But the wider issues somewhat puzzled Tony, who had seen it argued for months that he should take a proper job, and now that he had taken a salaried post for the first time in his life saw only that they "still were not satisfied".

II

A storm moves away, leaving the sky all the clearer, and in Lord Snowdon's personal life the successive points of controversy were no more than heavy rain-showers. As Oliver Messel summed up with directness and simplicity, his nephew was "quite happy about the new job. It is something within his scope and understanding." Due to take up his post on February 1st, Lord Snowdon turned up beforehand to accustom himself to the clime of the Thomson edi-torial offices in Gray's Inn Road. It was to be typical of his life from then on that he attended his first conference of the *Sunday Times* editorial board at 11 a.m. on February 6th and dashed off afterwards to the family lunch at Buckingham Palace that commemorated the Queen's tenth anniversary of her Accession.

He was a cog in an editorial team; and the colour supplement was costly but successful, judging by public response. At an early stage,

Lord Snowdon's special field was defined as the features on "art, architecture and design" and the new recruit took a spare-time professional refresher course on the latest technicalities of colour photography. In the helter-skelter of journalism it is already difficult to be sure of the features that he wholly initiated and supervised, but an early essay with his camera involved a sally into the East End with Sean Kenny and Lionel Bart to compare the air-raid scenes of their stage show *Blitz* with their 1962 counterpart, and at the top of the Vickers building on Millbank Oskar Kokoschka was photographed while painting a panorama of the Thames.

Lord Snowdon enjoyed an unquestioned freedom to develop his own ideas but found himself baffled, at times, by the rival cameramen who crowded around and wanted to photograph him taking photographs. There were other equally personal difficulties. Margot Fonteyn and Rudi Nureyev, for instance, invited him to photograph them at rehearsals at Covent Garden; and other photographers, who had asked for facilities and had been refused, inevitably raised a cry of "Privilege!"

Having always worked independently, Lord Snowdon found it curious to be asked to join the National Union of Journalists. He had however never before been "on the staff" and as soon as his first staff photograph appeared in print it was pointed out that he was "eligible" for trade union membership. On advice from his seniors, Snowdon duly joined, but this was no sooner done than the professional Institute of Journalists expressed "profound regret" at his concurrence.

It was like fire-walking without knowing the knack, yet Lord Snowdon's difficulties might have been eased if anyone had realised that he was not establishing royal precedents. It had in fact all happened before, nearly a century earlier, when Queen Victoria's nephew, Count Gleichen, decided to turn professional sculptor and the Queen not only gave him his first commission but also allowed him to build a studio in the gardens of St. James's Palace. Civic commissions flowed in, amid fierce protests from other sculptors at the "unfair" competition of a member of the Royal Family.

These not dissimilar eruptions around Lord Snowdon, of course, simmered down. His job was to win him new friendships and create a cause-and-effect of events—in new projects for books, films and other interests—that continue to this day. Within the year, he could slip out of the country on a three-day trip to Venice with a photographer colleague, Bob Belton, without attracting attention, footloose and free once again on returning home to entertain his Princess with amusing tales of his adventures. And meanwhile his salary, reputed to be rising to £10,000 a year, plus expenses, gave him more than parity with his wife's own net income, which in itself was not unimportant.

Princess Margaret's secretary, Major Francis Legh, and Lord Snowdon's faithful Mrs. Everard were often in consultation to ensure that Tony's professional engagements synchronised so far as possible with the Princess's programme of solo official duties, so that they might spend as much free time as possible together. Just before his thirty-second birthday, one of Lord Snowdon's more personal engagements involved at his request three brief rehearsals. This was the ceremony of his introduction as a peer to the House of Lords. The House was, in fact, crowded for the occasion and Princess Margaret, the Countess of Snowdon, sat in the Commonwealth Gallery as a spectator. The little procession to the Woolsack was, by tradition, headed by the Earl of Norfolk as Earl Marshal and Sir Brian Horrocks as Black Rod, with the richly clad Garter King of Arms. Her husband's new robes of red and white miniver, the Princess may have noted, looked rather fresher than the robes of his sponsors and friends, the Earls of Westmorland and Leicester.

"Considering the difficulties of the said affairs and the dangers impending, waiving all excuses," the new Lord was enjoined, "do you be personally present in our Parliament . . ." Then, retiring to a back bench with his escorts, he had to rise and doff his tricorne hat and bow to the Throne, and so be seated again, and rise again, bowing, three times.

A few minutes later, divested of his robes, a spruce and more familiar figure took his seat on the front cross-bench between his sponsors, and Lord Snowdon listened to a debate, not without personal interest, on tax relief for part-time professional married women. Meanwhile, in the House of Commons, Mr. Hamilton, the Scottish Labour Member for West Fife was putting down discordant questions about another personal difficulty, namely, the cost being occasioned the nation by the Earl and Countess of Snowdon's new home at Kensington Palace.

III

Royal couples always enter a target area when they choose their homes or, rather, have homes provided for them. Having elected to pay for a Monarchy, no matter how advantageous the terms of the Civil List, the nation has to decide whether or not it should pay the royal kinsfolk who devote much of their time to the service of the Crown and whether they should be housed in fitting state and style in traditional old palaces. It has to decide, too, whether the master-pieces of Wren architecture should be allowed to crumble or whether Georgian palaces should now all become uninhabited museums. With the fabric of Kensington Palace managed by the Ministry of Works and the finance annually reviewed by Parliament under the heading of Royal Palace Estimates, royalty has to be tough-skinned as well as gracious in enduring public discussion. As a young husband, not yet armoured against the arrows of enquiry and criticism, Lord Snowdon found that he had to face three years of constant fret in the conversion and repair of his ultimate home.

Very little had been spent on the south-west wing of Kensington Palace for nearly fifty years. As I mentioned in my recent book on Princess Alexandra, the large old-fashioned suite of Queen Victoria's daughter, Princess Louise, had been divided into two, to form Suites 1 and 1A. Suite 1 had become the London home of Princess Marina, the Duchess of Kent and, as part of the same scheme of rehabilitation, the Queen offered 1A to her sister as a grace-and-favour residence when it could be put into order.

The first plans and estimates were put in hand at the time of Princess Margaret's engagement, and she and Tony had originally planned to "make do" in rooms in Clarence House for a year or two. When little No. 10 unexpectedly fell empty, the young people naturally seized the opportunity. The doll's house that enchanted a newly married couple was, however, to prove impractical for a family.

Visitors to 10 Kensington Palace early in 1962 did not really receive the impression of unspoilt luxury which strangers invariably associated with the Snowdons' home. Ushered into a morning room where an Empire clock ticked in unsullied tranquillity, one might hear voices and footsteps drifting through the party wall, and indeed at times the sound of school-children visiting the State Apartments, and the London Museum next door resembled the noise of a tube train. From the not far distant nursery suite, the infant Lord Linley also made himself heard. "Babies do cry rather a lot," Lord Snowdon admitted, although his wife thought other-wise. It was possibly not a coincidence that when the baby was five months old, Princess Margaret's life-long maid, Ruby Gordon—the sister of the Queen's "Bobo"—decided to resign from royal service. Such adjustments occur in every new household and, for a time, the Princess replaced Ruby with Mrs. Parker, who had been his grand-mama Messel's maid and who now serves as a part-time reserve to Isobel Mathieson.

Like the summer thunder that seems to crash and echo in different quarters of the sky, the cost of restoring 1A Kensington Palace inevitably added to the clamour that had greeted Lord Snowdon's appointment to the *Sunday Times*. The headlines insisted that Princess Margaret and Tony were moving to "a bigger house . . . a larger home", even though Lord Snowdon himself read the estimates with the helpless surprise—and, I suspect, the same indignation—of any citizen on seeing the cost of a new government scheme. The lowest tender was for £70,000 and, difficult as it was for any layman to comprehend such a figure for making good the ravages of dry-rot, blitz ruin and damp in a building of some twenty rooms, this was presently increased by £15,000, as a Ministry of Works announcement phrased it, on account of "structural defects discovered on opening up".

This restoration—or, rather, rebuilding of part of Kensington Palace within the Christopher Wren shell—would have been needful even if the Snowdons had lived elsewhere. The Queen contributed £20,000 to the public cost, rather as a donation to the maintenance of tradition than directly towards her sister's home. The Ministry expected to hand over an interior, finished to standard specification, by the autumn of 1962, and the vicissitudes and gradual completion of the work inevitably became an ever more engrossing interest of the Snowdons' private horizon.

In May, 1962, Princess Margaret and Lord Snowdon made a short official tour together in North Wales, inspecting mills and factories and slate quarries. An occasion of light relief was provided when Tony's godfather, Sir Michael Duff, officially welcomed the couple as Lord Lieutenant of Caernarvon and introduced them to his Deputy Lieutenant who was none other than Ronnie Armstrong-Jones. The pair stayed at Plas Dinas, and the director of the Snowdon Mountain Railway suggested striking a gold medal to provide Lord Snowdon and "his heirs in perpetuity" with the right of free travel up and down the mountain. But this was also the occasion when the Snowdons officially visited the Dinorwic slate quarries and so discovered the perfect dark green paving to contrast against white paint in their new entrance hall. It was the time, too, when Clock Court was crammed with flagstones taken up from the basement, and they learned that a spring had welled up in vindictive triumph to flood the cellars. This would mean deeper concrete foundations and further delay.

In August, too, they visited Jamaica for the independence celebrations and, in a sense, the Earl of Snowdon played a State role as consort when Princess Margaret opened the first session of Jamaica's national Parliament. But on returning home they hurried to note the effect from the southern windows of 1A of a new brick wall which was creating a pleasant walled garden in a former enclosure of gloomy privet and laurel.

A private dream also came true for Tony when Princess Margaret celebrated her thirty-second birthday with Susan and John de Vesci and their children at Abbey Leix, a happy augury to Susan of how her brother's marriage was consolidating in the pleasant tempo of family life. Tony was as ebullient as ever, bubbling with topics: his plans for his workroom at 1A and a super kitchen; the fun of water skiing and the wonderful progress that "Margot" was making, and the interest of all his "jobs" with the *Sunday Times* He had been amused by the work of photographing all the women tycoons of the dress trade for a special feature and equally engrossed by taking on the furnishing and decorating of editor Denis Hamilton's office in contemporary style. And there was his book, *Art Scene*, as it was then provisionally called—*Private View* as it became—a complete photographic round-up of the modern art scene in London involving hundreds of pictures to illustrate the text by Bryan Robertson of the Whitechapel Art Gallery and John Russell of the *Sunday Times*.

So many enthusiasms and projects, now, and the autumn brought a millrace of plans and efficient accomplishment. Part of the "extra to specification" interior decoration of 1A would be drawn from Lord Snowdon's own pocket and, horrified by the professional estimates of veneering the two mahogany doors for the dining-room, he was convinced he could do them himself . . . and in fact did so with professional perfection. Meticulously measured to the last inch, he designed the run of modern louvred cupboards to be finished in polished deal and sycamore for his dressing room, and he made his own big working desk in teak and stainless steel.

There would be no drawers in the desk, he decided, to deter him from the temptation of shovelling urgent papers out of sight. (There was however to be a useful range of pine storage cupboards in Mrs. Everard's room.) Lord Snowdon also designed and carefully made the mock-up of an ultra-modern extractor hood for the kitchen, and he would have made the highly functional finished piece himself but for the admitted limitations in his practical know-ledge. The workshops of Eton had taught him how to weld steel but not aluminium.

He presently purchased a set of oxyacetylene welding equipment and enjoyed himself so much, making stainless steel shelving, cabinets and locks that his wife, who tremendously admired his efforts, felt called on to remind him they were planning a home, not a prison. The workmen at 1A got used to the man in a visor, whose identity had puzzled them when they first saw him wandering about, and presently it was their turn to admire a long, low built-in electric fire which Lord Snowdon had set in green Welsh Dinorwic slate and stainless steel.

Meticulously choosing the exact shade of pale brown for the kitchen floor tiles, the Snowdons decided there was only one way to show what they really wanted, and they sent the manufacturer the shell of a hard-boiled brown egg. In breaks from the handiwork and discussion, the Snowdons also went shopping, exploring the small antique shops around Ebury Street, visiting street markets and junk yards, and were recognised only once, in the celebrity-conscious Portobello Road.

Princess Margaret eagerly assented with Tony's idea that they wanted echoes of Birr Castle, difficult as it was to settle on details. The Countess of Rosse possesses a unique white-and-gold Gothic bedroom of furniture which she had found in the Castle attics, made by Italian craftsmen just before the Victorian era. Poking around Bristol during a weekend with the Frys at Widcombe Manor, the Snowdons found a Gothic dressing-table, doors and pillars that might have been made to match the Birr Gothic. They bought these for £15 and then discovered an equally appropriate Gothic cornice in a yard at Hammersmith. Painted off-white, the fragments trans-formed a room with Edwardian alcoves into a highly eclectic bathroom. For the middle of the bathroom Tony designed a glass-topped cabinet to display the Princess's honeymoon collection of sea-shells: a functional as well as ornamental novelty in that the cabinet nestles in a hexagon of hot-pipes draped with bath-towels.

The Snowdons moved into 1A in the spring of 1963, just after spending a winter sports holiday with the Frys at Davos. It was perhaps Tony's idea that every room should find a recurrent motif in flecks of blue. The blue glass of the dining-table could echo the

183

blue silks of the adjoining drawing-room, repeated again in the flasks and jars of the bathroom, renewed in the blue-and-gold of two apothecary jars, mounted on wrought iron stands, that stand like sentinels at a bedroom door. These in turn were to view with the Victoriana for which Tony loved to rummage in out-of-the-way shops: brass firemen's helmets, ancient tin-plate advertisements . . . and, as a most treasured souvenir, the line of Grandmama Messel's first alphabet cards, A a B b C c D d . . . regimented above the cabinets in his study.

IV

From the outset Lord Snowdon has kept two engagement books at Kensington Palace, one for his own professional life, the other for all the activities which he shares with his wife. They roughly match in content, as he once explained to Godfrey Winn. In practice the two sides of life frequently overlap, as when he visited Anthony Fry, Jeremy's brother, at the Camberwell School of Art and there met and photographed Patrick Procktor for his book, *Private View* and presently gave his wife the gift of a Procktor painting. When the Princess and Lord Snowdon set out one day by helicopter from Kensington Green on an official visit to Cambridge, Tony naturally observed the private sentiment of the occasion by wearing his Hawkes Club tie. At about the time of his thirty-third birthday the Queen approved the appointment of the Earl of Snowdon as Constable of Caernarvon Castle in succession to Lord Harlech. When Her Majesty visited Caernarvon in the summer it thus fell to him officially to welcome the Queen to the fortress by handing her the heavy fifteen-inch-long iron key with the traditional ritual, a useful dress rehearsal for the more important future ceremonial that would involve the Prince of Wales. But privately Tony and his wife spent a few days at Plas Dinas and, with still deeper privacy, Mrs. Armstrong-Jones also welcomed the Queen to her home.

In public, Lord Snowdon made speeches, his throat parched with nerves, his hands trembling so much that he could scarcely lift his glass. He addressed the annual luncheon of the British Jewellers' Association, for example, and spoke out, as his experience entitled him to do, about the unadventurous quality of most new designs. Visiting Northern Ireland with Sir Paul Reilly, the director of C.o.I.D., he successfully took the chair at a meeting of hundreds of manufacturers. He dutifully went through the routines of leadership, though "speech fright" was something he still found dreadfully hard to control. Yet in private his table talk was always effervescent with his impressions and plans.

He had a great deal of fun, for example, when Roy Thomson at last saw the new décor of Denis Hamilton's editorial office and asked plaintively whether Tony could fix up his old office as well. Roy grew alarmed when Lord Snowdon cast out his decrepit old desk and worn-out swivel chair and not only installed a new desk with expensive black leather trays but also glass-topped tables, low conversational settees and expensive Chinese table lamps. Lord Thomson talked of having a nude painting on the wall, but Tony bought him instead an African scene by Sidney Nolan of an elephant at a water-hole (which seemed to many to be good symbolism). Learning that the painting had cost £1,000 Thomson was beset by doubts lest Tony had been too extravagant. In the end he worried so much that he secretly called in an art expert to vet his purchase, only to be assured that within a year the picture would be worth twice as much as Lord Snowdon had paid.

Having privately designed the press lord's office, Lord Snowdon in his more official capacity had it photographed for C.o.I.D. In his private role, he informally made a series of camera portrait studies of the Queen, and one of the photographs was eventually used for Arnold Machin's designs of the new coinage. In his fourth year of marriage, too, Tony was privately preoccupied by his efforts to save the secret hideaway of Rotherhithe Street from the apparently irreversible L.C.C. plans to demolish all the buildings to make way for a riverside walk. Clearly, Princess Margaret could at once be accused of taking advantage of her position if she begged the planners to spare the old houses. At a royal garden party, Tony seized the opportunity of talking to Robert Mellish, the Labour M.P. for the Rotherhithe division of Bermondsey, and it must be said that Mr. Mellish was sporting enough to arrange a meeting with officials at the local town hall. Lord Snowdon spoke persuasively, advancing every possible argument, but nothing came of it. "I'm afraid they were more interested in seeing me than in hearing what I had to say," was his sad comment.

Early in 1964 Tony with his Princess visited the Rotherhithe room for the last time. It had meant so much to them, and soon there would be nothing tangible left except his photographs of it, taken from every angle, pinned to a screen in his workroom. "I don't know how we shall ever get along without this wonderful room and everything it's meant to us," he told Bill Glenton.

Both sets of engagement books, are of course, blank for the Rotherhithe hours. Pleasant blank spaces also occurred in September, 1963, after Stavros Niarchos had hospitably invited the Snowdons to spend a holiday based on his Aegean isle of Spetsoupoula. It was their first experience of Greece, and the Niarchos yachts, helicopters and private planes of course helped in making the most of every jet-set sight-seeing minute. They cruised to Rhodes and later visited Olympia and Athens. Nothing was planned ahead. They had time to pretend to consult the Oracle of Delphi—who may have whispered of further personal happiness in store—and they were a bonus themselves to the sightseers of the Acropolis.

In contrast, a year later, the professional engagement books were to record the crowded itinerary of Princess Margaret and Lord Snowdon's visit to Copenhagen for British Week in Denmark. The idea of royalty taking an active part in a sales drive for British goods in foreign cities was a new experiment. The persuasive force of a special week had been tried out in Dusseldorf and put into royal play by Princess Alexandra in Stockholm. The Snowdons were however the first to dedicate themselves to the high-pressure technique of showing the commercial flag in a British Week. They were the guests of King Frederik and Queen Ingrid in the Fredensborg Palace, and travelled by helicopter day by day to all the different Danish towns where British goods were being specially featured.

Ten thousand shops participated in this sales drive, and the Princess and Lord Snowdon toured the larger department stores, inaugurated touristic "model pubs" and attended British military tattoos and fashion shows. The result of this comparatively simple effort was a £6,000,000 rise in British sales that year to Denmark. In 1965, similarly, the Snowdons made a spectacular arrival aboard the royal yacht *Britannia* for a British Week in Amsterdam. By way of achieving maximum publicity, Lord Snowdon drove a British jeep, the Princess at his side, heading a procession through the heart of the city. Not very long afterwards, Kensington Palace received a report showing that the Week had caused Netherlands imports of the featured British goods to rise by 20 to 75 per cent. It had all been a worthwhile effort, and Parliament was presently to be told of the Snowdons' "immense contribution".

In 1966 it was Hong Kong's turn; and in 1967, when Princess

Margaret had laryngitis at the last moment, Lord Snowdon depu-
tised to inaugurate the British Week in Brussels, evoking a demons-
tration, it was noted, of "his fantastic popularity". Royal travel is no
longer news, and press coverage of an overseas journey often
shrinks to a few inches, so that one hardly realises what has been
involved. Flying out to Hong Kong, which is eight hours fast on
Greenwich time, Princess Margaret and Lord Snowdon found
themselves awakened at what was midnight by their innermost phy-
siological clock, to embark on a twelve-hour round. By this personal time factor, they inaugurated the Week at three a.m., opened a
British engineering exhibition before dawn and smilingly toured
hospitals and a massive housing estate at equally inopportune
inward hours. It was admittedly more comfortable to attend
Cantonese opera in the Hong Kong evening, high noon by Greenwich.

But the dividing line in the two sides of Lord Snowdon's professional and monarchist life were also strikingly illustrated when he
returned to London from Japan with Princess Margaret and flew off
again, four days later, back over the same air-route, for a *Sunday
Times* assignment in India. In Calcutta, in his playing of many parts,
the man of public affairs became the working photographer. Instead
of the sociable group of Princess Margaret, her secretary, Major
Francis Legh and Lady Elizabeth Cavendish, he now travelled
with David Holden, the foreign correspondent.

Besides, the Princess knew how important the spasms of anonymity were to Tony in helping him to unwind after a spell of public
duty when he had been much "on show". His travels exercised the
therapy of Rotherhithe all over again, though India was admittedly
a larger, fuller "cure" than most. The idea was that Snowdon
should move across the huge and dusty face of India with packs
of colour film, making a photographic record of the national image
at that moment in time. He photographed the modern office blocks
of Calcutta with sacred cows in the foreground; and at the Calcutta
race track focused not upon the old-time fashionable throng but at
the unexpected spectacle of the Indians in the crowd who might
wager two weeks' pay on the horses.

His lens captured Mrs. Indira Gandhi working at State papers
in her aeroplane and the contrast of women cleansing irrigation
ditches with their hands. He turned his camera equally upon the
holy men of Benares and a young man of Benares spinning silk with
an improvised bicycle wheel. He tellingly photographed, for the

same page, the suppliant hands of the beggars . . . and the impassive features of J. D. R. Tata, India's greatest private industrialist. For three weeks, through Delhi to Bombay and Chandigarh, the new capital of Punjab State, he distilled his travel impressions into a fabulous colour lay-out. And it was all the more wonderful at last to get home to the daffodils of Kensington and the delectable welcome of his wife and children.

The two sides of the coin, public and private, had their milled edge of innermost family happiness. On May 1st, 1964, Princess Margaret gave birth to a daughter at Kensington Palace, a tiny fair-haired charmer, and once he had reassured himself by seeing mother and child Lord Snowdon drove off to Stafford Terrace to fetch his mother to see the baby. When ten weeks old, little Lady Armstrong-Jones was christened Sarah Frances Elizabeth in the private chapel of Buckingham Palace. The sponsors included the Earl of Westmorland and Anthony Barton, a friend of Lord Snowdon's since his Cambridge days, as well as Mrs. Jocelyn Stevens, whom he had known in Pimlico long ago as Jane Sheffield. And then there were Princess Margaret's own friends, Marigold Bridgeman and Prudence Penn, as smiling godmothers to weave their special spells around the infant. It was a delightful family occasion and the centre of it all, though wide awake, cooed in perfect contentment.

V

It is well known that Princess Margaret had long wanted to visit the United States and in 1965 an invitation that had been constantly extended by her girlhood friend, Sharman Douglas, daughter of the former U.S. Ambassador to Britain, was proffered yet again and gladly accepted. Lord Snowdon was anxious for his wife to share his own impressions of the champagne atmosphere of the New World and now all seemed to be set fair. The proposed private visit to Hollywood under Sharman's auspices and to the Douglas ranch near Tucson, Arizona, immediately escalated however, into a broader official project on British Week lines. A show of British motor-bikes was opening in San Francisco and it needed only a royal round of chosen local factories to acquaint Californians with all the varied British interests in their midst. The big stores would also climb on to the cable car by staging British displays to link with "Meg and Tony" topicality. In New York itself the British Exports Committee had plans for staging a British fashion show aboard the liner *Queen Elizabeth* and Princess Margaret's presence would, in the official jargon, "widen American store participation".

The Foreign Office "latched on". Surprisingly, there had been no royal visit to the United States since the Queen and President Eisenhower opened the St. Lawrence Seaway in 1957 and, on diplomatic grounds alone, Princess Margaret's visit with Lord Snowdon was timely and desirable. When the Snowdons enthusiastically made their plans, no hint arose of the ill-informed complaints that were to follow. It was as if all the gusts of criticism that had blown for so long around Tony spent their strength with a final flurry of storm until, in the seventh year of his marriage, the skies suddenly cleared for a fairer evaluation.

Yet the impending outcry was unforeseen when Princess Margaret and her husband boarded the Super VC.10 at London Airport on November 4th and Lord Snowdon studied the foolscap sheets of his schedule. Sixty official and public engagements were to occupy fourteen of the next twenty days. It seemed at the time a stroke of originality to launch the visit on the West Coast. When they arrived that night and gazed from the top floor of the Mark Hopkins Hotel at all the jewelled lights of San Francisco, they found it "twice as fabulous as we've ever expected". Within an hour, their programme opened with an ecstatic Press Club reception, and when secretary Francis Legh spread open the fresh thick morning papers it was evident that a Californian love affair was in full blaze.

"My husband and I are looking forward to meeting people in all walks of life . . . everybody!" the Princess told the press group, and this was true of architects, publishers, nuclear scientists, Nobel Prize winners, university students, fashion writers, film folk, policemen, parsons, department store saleswomen, art curators, trolley car drivers, down to the last lady to shake hands at the English-Speaking Union. All this made for goodwill. The San Franciscans had never before seen a royal motorcade complete with the newest de luxe silver-grey Rolls Royce. They had only just begun to experience the great renaissance of British fashion in the swinging scene. Until their visitors crossed the Bay by hovercraft to visit the Berkeley campus, the San Franciscans probably had not realised that their local hovercraft were British-made.

For Princess Margaret and Lord Snowdon, sheer exhilaration overcame fatigue as they trekked through department stores (Magnin's superb British fashion show was an outright sales success) and, on a more usual beat, inspected technological institutes where

Lord Snowdon seemed to exercise an uncanny eye for British equipment. "Now we'll show you something really worth photographing," his hosts would say, and on the sight-seeing trips—Telegraph Hill, Pebble Beach, culminating in a wild-boar barbecue at one of the lush homes on Mount Carmel—Tony movie-filmed madly with his Bolex cine-camera.

Then they zoomed to Los Angeles in an Andover of the Queen's Flight, which had been standing by as not the least impressive of the British exhibits. The engagements of the next sixty hours were unbelievably strenuous—from the full tour of the L.A. art museum to the trip to the Owen Valley radio laboratory—but little survived the sub-editorial scissors in the newspapers at home except the late-night dancing with the film-stars—Julie Andrews, Natalie Wood, Elizabeth Taylor, Danny Kaye, Fred Astaire, Gene Kelly, Shirley Maclaine—at the private party that Sharman Douglas gave for them at the Bistro Club and the Charity dinner staged on another night for the World Adoption Fund.

The "rest weekend" at Pontano Farm, the Douglas' home near Tucson, can only satirically have been called a respite. "The only planned event," I had occasion to note at the time, "is a cocktail party for 250 friends of the family!" But this was the cottonwood and jacaranda and adobe America, where Tony went horse-riding in denims strictly for a camera session and water-skied afterwards for sheer relaxation on Arizona's largest man-made lake. The highlight was a low-level cineramic plane flight over the Grand Canyon and Painted Desert, the thrill of sweeping in and around the jutting spires of primeval rock . . . and then, at the Lake Powell Inn, the peace of the night under the flashing desert stars . . .

Next, lavish Washington spread out the carpet. In their suite at the British Embassy, Tony found that the latest issue of *Life* flourished the headline, "This radiant moment in history" and, in London, even the *Observer*, that arch-rival of the *Sunday Times*, chivalrously acknowledged the trip "perhaps the most successful royal tour America had ever had". The oddity perhaps was that, amid the welcome, no one realised that Lord Snowdon was faithfully re-enacting the great American dream. Seven years earlier, when working with Oliver Messel in Philadelphia, he had briefly popped down to Washington as a tourist . . . and a stranger. Now he and his wife stayed at the British Embassy, and the White House staged a dinner and dance in their honour. It was a time for fun, and in proposing a toast President Johnson sagely advised Lord Snowdon,

"I have learned only two things are necessary to keep one's wife happy. First, let her think she is having her own way. Second, let her have it."

And so to New York, where a more personal dream came true. Tony had longed to show Princess Margaret the city as he had first seen it, from the crowded sidewalks, just the two of them, and to his great delight this was precisely the way it was. He and his Princess had arrived at the Waldorf-Astoria with an escort of police cars and motor-cycles, sirens screaming, and they stole out next morning, alone together, just the two of them to make a quick safari around the blocks, quite unrecognised. As for the rest, it was sight-seeing to programme, and a programme to schedule, from the Empire State to the United Nations in session. At the Waldorf 1,100 guests paid a hundred dollars each for the privilege of joining them at a ball to inaugurate the Winston Churchill Memorial Fund. Another day, the whistle-stop tour of a few sample hours took the couple plunging through the roped-off aisles of four department stores where Union Jacks hung by the hundred over special displays of British goods. For let-up, at the Marlborough-Gerson gallery, they opened an exhibition of contemporary English painting and sculpture. And so to lunch with forty bankers on the sixtieth floor of the Chase Manhattan Bank, and then a reception of City Hall and next a tour of the Lincoln Centre for Performing Arts . . . Lord Snowdon had long since stopped nervously twiddling his ring and found he had grown accustomed to the million faces. "Tony has been the star of the royal marathon," summed up the frequently sour but oft-quoted *Women's Wear Daily*. "This city loves star quality and Tony has it."

From the Snowdons' viewpoint, the tour looked like a success to the very last lap, when they stopped off at Bermuda for the Princess to present Colours to the Bermuda Regiment, which some interpreted as maybe a tactful manoeuvre to remind New Yorkers of the accessibility of a Bermuda vacation. But back in London, after the excitement and clamour, the first bundle of press clippings were cruel and hurtful as hailstones on a summer lawn.

From a distance, it turned out, the journey looked less like a royal tour than an extravagant pleasure jaunt, and the *New Statesman* claimed that Princess Margaret had rejected the first schedule of crowded working engagements "saying she wasn't having any". Other journals took up the cry, demonstrating the usual love-and-hate phenomenon, to which Tony had now at last become accustomed. In particular, that inveterate watchdog of public expenditure, Mr. William Hamilton, Labour M.P. for West Fife, was determined to find out how much the expedition had cost, for an outlay as high as £200,000 had been alleged. He enquired of the Board of Trade. He set down questions for the Secretary of State for Foreign Affairs. He challenged the Chancellor of the Exchequer and learned that the cost had been not half or a quarter of the rumoured figure but £30,000, which had included specific government planning. "Far from objecting to any of the suggestions for official engagements," the Minister of State for the Foreign Office assured the House of Commons, "the Princess proposed a number of additional engagements . . . The twin purposes of fostering Anglo-American goodwill and promoting American interests were nobly achieved."

12 *Maturity in Focus*

I

"I am basically a carpenter," the Earl of Snowdon once said, at the time when his workroom in Kensington Palace, with its self-made furnishings, was gleaming new to admire. "I am a working photographer," he claims more often, and in the course of practising his profession the celebrity drops out of view as he visits Venice for the Biennale or flies to New York to discuss new projects with the Columbia Broadcasting System or with *Look*, *Life* or the American *Vogue*. Snowdon is "agile as a dragonfly" and gifted among much else with "an inquisitive and exceptionally tenacious intelligence", in the view of his close colleague, John Russell. And with his energy, his lively and darting curiosity, these qualities complement the pattern as the innumerable threads of Lord Snowdon's interests are drawn together into the definitive texture of maturity.

In the second year of his marriage, when Lord Snowdon resumed his career as a professional photographer, he found stimulus in his personal social context much as he had when his photographs first appeared in print in his early twenties. He looked up his friend, Anthony Fry, who was teaching at the Camberwell School of Art, for instance, and through him met on a personal footing such teaching artists of the new school as R. B. Kitaj and Patrick Procktor. This led the new art adviser of the *Sunday Times* into impatience with his own ignorance of many aspects of the British art scene and self-reproach provided an incentive to energetic discovery.

Bryan Robertson, the imaginative director of the Whitechapel Art Gallery, had discussed a plan for an atlas or panorama of the London art scene with John Russell, taking the form perhaps of an

193

Athenian conversation on influences, schools and personalities. Lord Snowdon's camera could provide both illustration and commentary—his features on art were already appearing in the colour supplement—and for three years part of the spare working time of all the trio was devoted to the remarkable collaboration of *Private View*.

When Lord Snowdon presented a copy to President Lyndon Johnson, he took pride in giving his best. Princess Margaret, too, was immensely proud of the book, repeatedly introducing it into conversation in their progress across America, praising her husband's work as a wife should do. The book had also just come fresh from the presses in the autumn of 1965; the new prestige of British art was jointly its theme and part of the mission of the tour. One takes the volume down from the bookshelf today with a sense of its amplitude and completeness. Within the thick linen covers is the whole of the British art scene and, as if an all-embracing television documentary had been frozen with the written commentary, the images remain superbly comprehensive and accessible. All the activities of London as a centre of art flicker to the eye as the pages turn: the critics, the pundits, the schools, the galleries and the artists, graded from Henry Moore and Ben Nicolson to an array of young painters and sculptors at the gates of their reputation.

The book is metropolitan, and yet charts the pilgrim's progress of Lord Snowdon as he travelled towards his mid-thirties, meeting, talking, photographing and at times making quite new friends. It is possible that the impact of his name (which he nevertheless distrusts) took him into the "places of power and authority normally marked Private", as his collaborators suggested. Old friendships were confirmed with people like John Piper, Sir Kenneth Clark, Lynn Chadwick, Barbara Hepworth and a hundred others. But new and promising links were also forged with Philip Sutton, with the Kitaj family in Dulwich and many more. When the former Tony Armstrong-Jones first appeared in the news as a royal bridegroom, the world was astonished that he could move from his Pimlico basement into Buckingham Palace, that somewhat larger Pimlico residence. But his movements in contemporary London are unremarked as he drives in his Aston Martin DB5 or Mini-Cooper S down to the homes of the new Bohemia in Battersea, Islington, Hammersmith and Clapham. His camera is the magic talisman and the file of bygone features in the colour supplement of the *Sunday*

Times will provide historians with an admirable index to a successful photographer's working life in our time.

Perhaps the day's journey is only to Bloomsbury and on to Highbury to provide a perceptive study of the Drabble sisters, the novelists Margaret Drabble and Antonia Byatt. Or perhaps the paper has arranged an early morning rendezvous to meet a man newly released from Wandsworth gaol, so that the camera may chronicle all the facets of his experience on that first day of freedom. In his creative essays, Lord Snowdon has journeyed to Venice with Francis Wyndham to record a city in decay, and to Tokyo with Brian Moynahan to depict a city in semi-hysteria.

In Japan, in 1967, he photographed the Honda brothers, the pinball parlours, the Hirokawa Marriage Centre, the oldest Geisha, the university scientists working on a communications satellite, the hostesses, the Kyoto temple, prodigal with hundreds of negatives for thirty-five published pictures.

For anonymity's sake Lord Snowdon grew a beard and was content when the hotel room clerk misread his signature as an unknown "Mr. Shoten". In fact, there was no secret. Interviewed for television, he carried cameras slung round his neck to help viewers' identification and pleased his audience with a few words of thanks in Japanese. He wrote to his wife daily and pored over picture postcard stands, choosing cards to airmail to the children. But this led to a situation of Feydeau farce when he arrived in New York to find crowds of frenzied reporters frantic to question him on the break-up of his marriage. "It's news to me," said the supposed fugitive, "and I'd be the first to know." It turned out that the rumours of matrimonial disaster had originated in Paris. The invincible logic of French journalists had drawn the wrong and the worst conclusions from the absence of a husband while his wife was having a routine check-up in hospital.

Lord Snowdon and his Princess had planned to link up for a holiday in the Bahamas but Lord Snowdon first had business matters to settle in New York with Alexander Liberman of *Vogue* and producer Don Hewitt of the C.B.S. He had meanwhile renewed his contract with Thomson on modified terms. One of the charms of working in journalism was that one never knew where any particular photo-feature would end. Pleasant sequels were forever apt to open out, like the silken folds in one of Grandmama Messel's treasured antique fans.

II

A Snowdon photo-feature on loneliness and its partner in solitude, old age, had chanced to catch Don Hewitt's eye in 1965. Hewitt was then producing a series of television documentary films on the arts for the American C.B.S. network, and he wondered whether Lord Snowdon might participate in a future film-making effort. The optimism and the obvious obstacles, the pitfalls and persuasions, can be left to the imagination but it must have seemed significant at Kensington Palace that this new and inviting prospect should open so soon after the launching of *Private View*.

Inside every still photographer, it has been said, there is invariably a film cameraman struggling to get out. Lord Snowdon had often made his own "amateur" cine-films—in Ireland and the West Indies, in India and Japan—films intended, as he once cautioned an interviewer, "for private entertainment only". For some years, indeed, a "Snowdon Production" could be relied on to strengthen the short features in a Balmoral movie programme, and one remembers a particularly effective film of the Chatsworth trees and fountains set to music from Beethoven's Emperor concerto. When the C.B.S. London man, Bill McClure, first approached Lord Snowdon, his quarry, however, gave little sign of enthusiasm. Hewitt flew over to attempt to entice him with four of the documentary films which he had built around Henry Moore, Igor Stravinsky, Pablo Casals and Frank Sinatra, and was gratified to be invited to run them through the projectors at Kensington Palace. His host was impressed but apparently still dubious.

Lord Snowdon suggested he should first make a ten-minute test film at the Royal Ballet School, and Princess Margaret greeted the sparkling result with great enthusiasm. Negotiations progressed smoothly from that moment, even though Lord Snowdon insisted on an unprecedented clause in the C.B.S. contract that, at the rough cut stage, he could destroy the whole of any film he made if he wished.

Fortunately, the months of work that followed—scripting, discussing and photographing—were not wasted. The sequel was, of course, the TV film, *Don't Count the Candles*, which Lord Snowdon both directed and photographed. Intended as an essay on growing old, seen through the eyes of rich and poor, the famous and the obscure, the director youthfully found no problem in interviewing such "elderly" friends as Noel Coward, Cecil Beaton and Barbara Hepworth, as well as the octogenarian Field Marshal Montgomery,

Compton Mackenzie and Lady Patricia Ramsay. (The latter was a dramatic choice to those who recollected that, as Princess Pat, she had been the first of Queen Victoria's descendants to marry a commoner, although Tony did not force the moral.) Mr. Hewitt anticipated difficulty in selecting a commentator but Lord Snowdon "knew the very man". The events in his life were close-knit as ever, for he had only recently appeared in a TV film about his Regent's Park aviary, in which he was interviewed by Derek Hart. Derek had left the B.B.C. to branch out on his own, and there could be no better narrator. "We are a team. Derek and the editor, Jules Laventhol, are as much a part of it as I am," the director-cameraman always insisted, a generous point of view which the C.B.S. publicists played down.

Lord Snowdon's shortest commodity was time, but while the Royal Family were at Balmoral in the summer of 1967, he and his team were busy filming old ladies in retirement at Bournemouth, water drinkers at Vichy and the sickening sacrifice of an embryo lamb for the manufacture of an elixir of youth in a Swiss laboratory. The fifty minutes of film probed both the problems and the panaceas of old age; it was astringent and controversial, and compassionate in causing the viewer to consider the too readily accepted treatment of old people. Shown for the first time in New York in March, 1968, a typical review judged it "chilling but brilliant". Shown by the B.B.C. a week later, the majority of the critics thought it depressing in theme, but distinguished in handling and brilliantly visual.

But Lord Snowdon was more concerned with the hundreds of letters from ordinary viewers, in the main appreciative, that poured in by every post. He answered each one personally, a painstaking task. Perhaps no one in a palace had ever before forged so swift and strong a link with the people. He had used his camera to express sentiments of ruthless force and candour and, as he signed the letters, he knew that he would make more films. The grinding absurdity was that the American C.B.S. should have commissioned the picture, and not the British Broadcasting Corporation. It is clearly no longer always to the advantage of the Establishment to cast Lord Snowdon's private and official roles in separate and opaque compartments.

III

In the hall of fame it is sufficient that Edward Steichen, Cartier-Bresson and Hoyningen-Huene should be good photographers. No wider passport is demanded than their talents. Other than their work, no social contribution is expected of the many gifted young men—artists, musicians, writers—who are rising to celebrity in Lord Snowdon's generation. Apart from their art, their social conscience may be dormant, their philanthropy negligible, their interest in national concerns nil, and their fellows will think no worse of them. But as a member of the Royal Family Lord Snowdon must follow the monarchial pattern of being constantly seen to do good, and this under the handicap that very little of his individual good-doing can be adequately publicised. The Duke of Edinburgh's national activities are made known in the Court Circular but Lord Snowdon appears in that quaint bulletin only when accompanying his wife. He would not wish it otherwise and yet, as also with Mr. Angus Ogilvy, there is a case to be argued for his example of individual services to the public to be made better known.

The publicists of the Council of Industrial Design nail the popular appeal of Lord Snowdon's name to their masthead whenever possible, although his position there is ambiguous and much of his work anonymous. Few people realise, for instance, that he studies every issue of *Design Magazine* at an early editorial stage, suggesting improvements and frequently contributing future feature ideas and photographs. There is seldom publicity on a national scale for his persuasive visits to textile mills, glassworks, factories, art schools or local exhibitions. Yet if the promotion of good design is part of the trade-winning strategy of commerce, with the Design Centre in London as its battle G.H.Q., Lord Snowdon has more than played his part by undertaking—on the estimate of Sir Paul Reilly, director of the C.o.I.D.—"not fewer than two hundred and fifty missions in seven years".

This may entail nothing more than a visit to a trade fair, drawing attention to the design of praiseworthy products as he tours the stands. The reporters surround him as he admires caravan door handles at a trailer exhibition or inspects new equipment at a boat show. The tasks have also ranged, however, from the crowded schedules of industrial tours to his visit to Czechoslovakia in 1965, when he opened the British Design Exhibition in Prague with the biggest press and TV coverage of such an occasion that British Embassy officials had ever known. Lord Snowdon had freighted out his Aston Martin DB5 convertible as a feature attraction, incidentally at his own expense, winning such attention as he drove it around that it inevitably also drew notice to the "inter-governmental programme of exchanges in the cultural, educational, scientific and technological fields" that were going on. The point was not missed that, as the first member of the Royal Family to visit an Iron Curtain country, he was probably trail-blazing for Prince Philip and even, possibly, the Queen. As part of the exchange however it was also his job to advise his Czech opposites on which of their products would most interest the British, and much of his choice was subsequently seen at a Czech display in the Design Centre in 1967.

In a more limited sense, the success of this visit was repeated in Yugoslavia, when he flew into Belgrade for the opening of a similar exhibition, "an act of friendship between our two nations", as he said, "since it is right that designers and craftsmen should see each other's work and compete in friendly rivalry".

Energetically talking, visiting, touring, Lord Snowdon is content to describe all this effort as merely an association with the C.o.I.D. "on a consultative basis". An equal modesty tends to obscure some of his work as a council member of the Polio Research Fund. Visiting Uganda with Princess Margaret, he had a wonderful time, enjoying his own version of big-game hunting by shooting the tropical birds with his colour camera. The couple cruised up the Nile to Murchison Falls, were tremendously appreciative of every display of tribal dancing, and gave their hosts certainly as much enjoyment as they gained themselves. But, back-stage, Lord Snowdon talked to President Obote about the polio problem and discovered that more work was being done in Uganda in rehabilitation than prevention. Immunisation, in particular, was too expensive.

Lord Snowdon suggested that he might help with the money, and as the direct outcome of his practical interest and influence, preliminary finance was found, gifts of vaccine organised and a pilot immunisation scheme set in motion. An insight into the idealism of the Snowdons' marriage is to be gained by observing the cogwheels in these events. Just before Christmas in 1967 Tony flew to New York to open a display of British creative and graphic art. In his absence, it was not a coincidence that his wife attended a fashion pageant at Marlborough House to raise funds for the Commonwealth Appeal for Action for the Crippled Child.

After visiting Jamaica with his Princess, Lord Snowdon similarly turned over the total proceeds of his local photographs to Jamaican polio victims. Working mysteriously late at his metal bench one night, he showed his wife next morning the model "chair on wheels" he had just made and then glumly pointed out to her all the things he found wrong with it. The ultimate sequel was that designers and research men met at a buffet lunch at Kensington Palace one day simply to discuss wheelchairs and the possibility of evolving one perfect and universally useful design for the disabled. Lord Snowdon has made other models—including a motorised glassfibre platform to fit under any ordinary chair—and, as I write, his wheelchair project remains in progress.

"When I ask questions," he once said, apropos the technique of making conversation while touring exhibitions, "it's because I want to know the answer. That's the criterion." As president of the British Theatre Museum, he has devoted the same measure of enthusiasm to making appeals, organising exhibitions and even staging auctions to help maintain working funds for an admirable but needy Valhalla of theatrical art. Among other interests, Lord Snowdon is Patron of the National Youth Theatre and of the Metropolitan Union of Y.M.C.A.s, and President of the Contemporary Art Society for Wales, the Welsh Theatre Company and the Civic Trust for Wales, and all these organisations can provide many illustrations of his practical help. The Dyestuff Division of I.C.I. one year circulated a calendar of Lord Snowdon's Uganda bird and animal photographs, and the proceeds went, of course, to Uganda polio. More recently, the Earl of Snowdon undertook a photographic mission to Wales for another I.C.I. calendar, bearing in mind its implicit usefulness to the Civic Trust.

One recalls the home-made time-bomb that exploded, sadly damaging the façade of the so-called Temple of Peace, a few hours before Lord Snowdon attended the first conference in Cardiff for plans on the Investiture in 1969 of the Prince of Wales. He had anticipated a calm day discussing a programme to attract tourists to the Principality through the three summer months. He came instead into a melee of banner-waving nationalists who were shouting "Republic not royalty!" and who inevitably looked a little foolish as he insisted on walking rather quizzically through their ranks. In the ceremonies of 1911, Mr. Lloyd George had played a leading role as Constable of Caernarvon Castle. It has seemed appropriate to many that his mantle should fall upon Lord Snowdon, who has indeed found an express dedication in all his associations with Wales.

The ceremonial ritual of the Investiture remains the responsibility of the Earl Marshal. The human element of the pageantry has been chiefly the consideration of Garter King of Arms, including as it does the assemblage of Cabinet Ministers and Privy Councillors, Bishops and other Divines, Druids and Bards, the Gentlemen-at-Arms, the Yeomen of the Guard, Heralds and State trumpeters. Lord Snowdon's closer interest, in liaison with the Ministry of Works, has been in preparing, within the grey towers and serried battlements of Caernarvon Castle an ampitheatre for some seven thousand people and in ensuring that the ultimate result will perfectly blend medieval pageantry with a sense of contemporary history.

He has been keenly concerned with the design of the dais and canopy and the stands that will rise tier upon tier against the grey walls. The arms of the Fifteen Tribes of Wales are traditional but must bear the best stamp of the twentieth century and Lord Snowdon, though designing nothing himself, has worked directly with the Ministry in ensuring the skill and artistry of the finished effect. In 1911 a gleaming figure of St. David surmounted the green and white canopy of the royal dais. Should the effect be repeated in 1969? Such questions have been threshed out in early morning discussions at the College of Heralds and in St. James's, with innumerable visits to the castle itself. Since 1911, moreover, a new dimension has been added by the effect of television. The spectacle will probably be watched throughout the world by at least 400 million people, and it has been part of Lord Snowdon's role to ensure that Caernarvon Castle—bis castle—appears to the best advantage before the cameras. Not least, Lord Snowdon is also chairman of the judging panel to award certificates to the manufacturers of well-designed souvenirs of the occasion. The meretricious and the shoddy will have no place in the occasion if he can help it.

IV

One must trespass at last to the heart of the man, constant in his quest for perfection in everything he undertakes, tirelessly driving himself and others when the need arises, glossed with an impression of superficiality in the veneer that hides his inward personality, and beneath it kindly, affectionate, with deep veins of sentiment, domestic tenderness and inward religious feeling unknown to the world.

The Queen herself, with her trained concern for tradition, already possessed an insight into a part-submerged sector of his personality when she appointed him Constable of Caernarvon Castle. Those close to Lord Snowdon consider that he has evinced deeper interest in Wales since his father died, as if latent Celtic qualities were rising into their own in the stream of time. Ronald Armstrong-Jones died at Plas Dinas in January, 1966, in his sixty-seventh year, and Princess Margaret and Lord Snowdon joined the local farmers, neighbours and tenants at the funeral service in the ancient parish church of Llanwnda. By a strange chance, Carol Coombe was killed in a car crash with her Italian husband, Guiseppe Lopez, only a few months later. She had been gaily talking of returning to make her home in London, and now her stepson sadly attended her funeral in the English cemetery in Rome.

Nor was that all. It is always a sign of "unwinding", of recuperation, when Lord Snowdon goes to his workroom in the Palace basement to occupy himself for an hour or two late at night, "a kind of therapy", as he calls it. He was there late on the October night when the extent of the Aberfan disaster became fully known. He went to explain to his wife and then got out the car and drove down to Wales through the night, swept with emotion, while the bulletins continued to come over the radio. The coaltip that had engulfed the village school was still moving, delaying the rescue workers. Lord Snowdon reached the stricken village at four a.m., the first member of the Royal Family to arrive on the scene and thus to personify the sympathy of the whole nation to the stunned mourners. He was the first, I believe, to telephone the Duke of Edinburgh and the Queen. But it is sufficient that he was there, sadly trying to restrain his sense of tragedy so that he could give comfort, returning to the disaster scene later that morning and then going to see the survivors in hospital, quite unable at times to steady his voice, he who had two children of his own.

Perhaps 1966 was the year of maturity for the boy who had divided his childhood between Stream House and Birr Castle, the youth who had been stricken with polio, the young man who had longed to be a good photographer, the man who had hurried that night to Aberfan. Maturity did not ensue automatically on his Albany coming-of-age or even upon his marriage to the sister of the Queen in Westminster Abbey. His precedence as the third gentleman of the realm must diminish as the Queen's younger sons grow older but his position in public esteem improves year by year and it can be readily seen that the expression of his natural talents, of his own personality, assumes new sureness and authority.

It is occasionally held as a rebuke that Lord Snowdon is not another Prince Philip, as though royal consorts should resemble one another as peas in a pod. Lord Snowdon was grounded in a sense of duty at Eton, not at Gordonstoun. His sense of discipline is largely self-taught and partly self-imposed. His willingness to shoulder the responsibility of appropriate public duty is now however well known and he is often forced, like Prince Philip, to observe a stringent and often oppressive allocation of his time. He has never lacked self-confidence and great determination, but he shares both his mother's impulsiveness and his father's caution and has learned to distrust impetuosity in himself. On any salient decision, as someone close to him says, "he likes to keep quiet for a few days and then make up his mind".

Perhaps for this reason his speeches are seldom impromptu and lack his rapid private wit. His sense of fun, still impish and uppermost, contains no cruelty. He is totally without self-importance, a potential handicap in British public life that he masks with gaiety and acting ability. Like Prince Philip, he does not suffer fools gladly but neither does he suffer intense intellectuals: metaphysical argument he meets with a shrug. He possesses guile but not gullibility. He is fastidious yet not effete. He is rarely irascible: his staff and his colleagues know that his moods of frustration or irritability are as swiftly over as a summer storm. One of his intimates said long ago, "I know Tony is in real trouble when he shrinks into his shell". But this is not to be confused with his silence when he retires into a mood of contemplation. One of the least-expected books on his bookshelves is a king-sized volume entitled *The World's Great Religions*, which tells us a good deal of the owner. A better-known facet is his capacity for becoming completely absorbed, to the point of being oblivious of passing time, in whatever occupies him at the moment.

A man is a citadel, many-sided, and Lord Snowdon is still too often judged by the flat stereotyped public image created by the thumbnail impressions published when he first became known. He is supposed to be an astute self-publicist but when he spent a morning photographing spastic children, deeply stirred by tenderness and pity, creating an appeal poster for the Spastics Society, he asked that there should be no credit to himself on the 12,500 placards. On the other hand, when he and Princess Margaret held a party at Kensington Palace for the launching of his book *Private View*, each of the 120 guests received a tankard engraved with the autographs of the authors, Bryan Robertson and John Russell, and himself. The gesture personally cost him a lavish slice of his profits, but did not diminish the royalties paid into a small charitable trust.

He is neither a yachtsman nor polo-player and would be the first to say he could not afford it. Seldom seen riding, he is not interested in horse-racing and yet shares with the Queen and his own sister a deeper affection for horses—and all aspects of country life—than is commonly known. The verve and concentration of fast driving deeply appeals to him as a personal accomplishment, though he rarely spends time watching motor racing. Visiting the Isle of Man with Princess Margaret, he could not resist borrowing a motor-bike to try out the TT course. Though disappointed that he took double the Grand Prix time of twenty-two minutes to do the lap circuit and never touched more than ninety miles an hour, an action photograph of him speeding on the course held its own for some time, proudly pinned up on a photo-screen in his study. "Photographs should have a transient look," he says, "I take one down and pin up another." But a favourite photograph of Princess Margaret on the board is never disturbed.

His favourite athletic recreation is, of course, water-skiing, a sport he first took up in 1961. In 1967, he competed in the England-France water-ski race, his team—with Jocelyn Stevens and Anthony Richardson—finishing fourth in the forty-two mile crossing to Cap Gris Nez in a stormy sea. In the same year, he first tried water-ski kiting, rising with his kite to seventy feet and airborne for ten minutes. "That's living it up," he said, thrilled and enthusiastic. He has similarly helped to train his Princess to water-ski, and she whole-heartedly shares his enjoyment, but what is more remarkable is that he also taught his son to keep his balance on skis behind a launch . . . at five years old.

The schoolboy is still vivid in Lord Snowdon, although he faces the foothills of his forties. Much has been said of his love of gadgetry, but he experiences a deeper, more primitive contentment as he works at his carpentry bench, making a wooden model steamboat for his son, David Linley, or a doll's house for his daughter, Sarah, and touchingly pleased when they show their pleasure. Volatile, emotional though not naive, he remains endearingly sensitive, even in this, to the approval of his family, his friends, his colleagues and his wife.

Many would-be pundits have written about Lord Snowdon's influence on Princess Margaret. The favourite picture is of the wilful younger sister whom he freed from protocol and for whom he inaugurated a modern and unconventional private life. The sequence of photographs since her marriage disclose to any observer her improving—indeed, perhaps perfect—dress sense and sophistication. One remembers the Armstrong-Jones of the photographic studio who would pluck necklaces or ear-rings from a sitter and murmur, "Little girl, you're wearing too much loot!" As a husband, the young man who passionately designed ski-clothes to save English-women from becoming frumps would not be immune from feminine interests. Some chroniclers have set too much stress on the Petruchio and Katharine element, as if any young marriage could coalesce without the occasional tears and fret in the early years that lead to firmer love and understanding. Princess Margaret has found calm and happiness, an emotional stability in her marriage; and all her partner's absences serve only to enhance the idyllic joy of being together again. In all the millions of words that have been written around Lord Snowdon as Princess Margaret's husband, the deeper truth lies rather in the reverse image, implicit in the masculine viewpoint that *Princess Margaret is his wife*.

V

The innermost man is the family man. There are the gaily superficial outer shells, the jet-setter who loves to sweep off with his wife to holiday in Sardinia with Karim Khan rather than loiter too long at Balmoral, the courageous humorist who finds it permissive to clown in public . . . as when he turned up at London airport in an outrageous broad-striped suit with matching overcoat, trendy stuff to make clubmen choke over their tiffin, wonderful stuff for the cameras. But the Snowdons were off on holiday to Oliver Messel in Barbados, and Tony knew how his Uncle Oliver would enjoy laughing at the outfit and find it a tremendous lark. When he wore an eye-catching striped straw hat, it was similarly because the Queen Mother had bought it for him in the West Indies and he flourished it for her amusement with tremendous dash.

The family man is unknown to the world. New visitors to 1A Kensington Palace anticipate a regal atmosphere and find it an elegant but domestic amalgam of Princess Margaret's classic taste and Lord Snowdon's flights of fancy. There are pictures of the children everywhere, at all ages, from a recent snapshot of Sarah on a pony to the framed colour photograph on Lord Snowdon's dressing-shelf of David as a baby in his bath. It is essentially a home Lord

Snowdon has created for his wife and children and around himself, full of his own private family interests.

Susan's children go to school in England and at mid-term they invade Kensington Palace, knowing it now fully as well as Abbey Leix or Birr Castle, and these three teen-agers, Tom, Catherine and Emma, adore their aunt and uncle. It is a special day, too, when a letter comes from Australia, where Tony's younger half-brother, Martin Parsons, now lives in Melbourne, working on the "admin" side of Qantas airlines. Martin's wife, Aline, often writes a family letter, and snapshots of their baby son, Rupert, are passed from hand to hand. Tony's elder half-brother, Lord Oxmantown— William—met his own wife when they were undergrads at Oxford. Both worked for the United Nations—William in Ghana and Dahomey, Alison in Rome—and at their wedding, in a village church near Barnard Castle, David Linley, then aged four, was a pageboy in white and cherry-red, while Princess Margaret and Lord Snowdon looked on with just the right mixture of parental pride and watchfulness. The intermesh of fate's small world, too, was still evident, for from this region came young Viscount Linley's Armstrong and Bowes-Lyon forebears alike, a circumstance that would have delighted Lord Snowdon had he known it at the time.

For perhaps the noontide of maturity is attained when the past calls with a more resonant note, sweet as the Kensington Palace clock that chimes the hours above Clock Court, and suddenly one wishes the happiness of days past to be renewed for one's own children.

When Lord Snowdon was a little boy his grandparents would sometimes take him and Susan for picnics to a cottage deep in the Nymans woods; and Tony always remembered those pre-war summer afternoons, the enchanted moment when the key was inserted in the nail-studded oaken door and he could suddenly rush into a coolness scented with beeswax and ancient timber.

His grandmother would go round the house, pulling curtains wide and opening windows, from the old kitchen to the sitting-room. Colonel Messel kept some of his collection of Tudor and Jacobean furniture here—rich old chests, polished gateleg tables—so that, as the sunshine leapt in, the rooms were full of solidity and strength. On a beam over the old kitchen hearth were the figures 1652, and grandpapa Messel would gravely explain that this was in the reign of good King Charles, perhaps the year when the house had first been built. Tony would always associate his gentle voice with the glint of pewter, the hum of bees, the scent of flowers.

Colonel Messel ultimately left a tenancy of the Old House, as it was known, to Oliver Messel for life; and when the Snowdons' daughter, Sarah, was born in 1964 their Uncle Oliver hinted that it might be just the place for the children. Lord Snowdon needed no second bidding. The place might need refurbishing; it had become a little dark and overgrown, too closely shadowed by trees. Oliver Messel proposed that his nephew should have a free hand in any renovation, and Lord Snowdon was delighted.

He had just completed his art book, and from the time-consuming interest of *Private View*, Lord Snowdon and his Princess escaped together into their new private world, so different and enchanting to Princess Margaret, so steeped in old happiness for her husband. The woods were not the deep forest of his childhood imagination but merely a hazel coppice; the only approach track was as long but far muddier than he remembered. The house had once been three tiny cottages; and a little Georgian house, not unlike the "doll's house" of 10 Kensington Palace, had at some time been built against the tile-hung seventeenth-century kitchen, creating a maze of larders and sculleries which Tony had half-forgotten.

No married couple were ever happier than husband and wife as they measured the rooms, here envisaging a glazed garden door to let in light or here the possibility of flinging out a bay to give more space. The Old House was to be as it always had been, but newly incarnated, and so it has proved. In the fun of self help about the house and garden Lord Snowdon has laid flagstones and built a low balustrade wall and instructed his son a little in the mysteries of sand and cement and paint, and found a true and tangible fulfilment. When Lord Snowdon and Princess Margaret disappear from the news, when they drop out of sight, it is usually to rest unfettered and secure within their own sanctuary. Only the churlish or the foolish would wish to intrude, and against these and the inquisitive the glades and paths are necessarily guarded with vigilance and strength.

If it is asserted that Princess Margaret plays at being a housewife, it is a role of deep happiness and self-realisation. A small boy and his sister played here long ago, and now David and Sarah skip around their parents. The old people are gone, and yet Lord Snowdon and his Princess wife recapture the essence of true contentment.

As Sir Harold Nicolson said, the sovereign and the royal family are expected in their private lives to be patterns of perfect domesticity. The Queen must seek to symbolise and enhance the finest elements in the national character; and in that royal quest today we may know that her younger sister and brother-in-law are staunchly representative contemporary allies at her side.